Artificial Neural Networks and Their Applications

Edited by Abdelhamid Mellouk

Published in London, United Kingdom

Artificial Neural Networks and Their Applications
http://dx.doi.org/10.5772/intechopen.1008040
Edited by Abdelhamid Mellouk

Contributors
Abdul Malik Maheen, Badr Mouazen, C.S. Sree Thayanandeswari, Chama Mabrouk, Houcine Barhoumi, Jassem Wannassi, Jian Weng, Jiasi Weng, Jiayang Xiao, Jiewei Chen, Jiexiong Li, Jing Wang, Jinlong Wei, Junyi Li, Ming Li, Nicole Jaffrezic-Renault, Niyas Ahamed Sirajudeen, Pravin Kumar Raja Mahendran, Shreyas Subramanian, Shuliang Zhou, Tao Zheng, Tianyue Wang, Xinyi Wu, Yuhao Liang, Zainab El Bouyed, Zhaopeng Xu, Zhiyu Zhang

First published in London, United Kingdom, 2026 by IntechOpen
IntechOpen is the global imprint of INTECHOPEN LIMITED, registered in England and Wales, registration number: 11086078, 167-169 Great Portland Street, London, W1W 5PF, United Kingdom

For EU product safety concerns: IN TECH d.o.o., Prolaz Marije Krucifikse Kozulić 3, 51000 Rijeka, Croatia, info@intechopen.com or visit our website at intechopen.com.

British Library Cataloguing-in-Publication Data
A catalogue record for this book is available from the British Library

Artificial Neural Networks and Their Applications
Edited by Abdelhamid Mellouk
p. cm.

This title is part of the Artificial Intelligence Book Series, Volume 43
Topic: Computational Neuroscience
Series Editor: Andries Engelbrecht
Topic Editor: Magnus Johnsson

Print ISBN 978-0-85014-715-5
Online ISBN 978-0-85014-714-8
eBook (PDF) ISBN 978-0-85014-716-2
ISSN 2633-1403

IntechOpen Book Series
Artificial Intelligence
Volume 43

Aims and Scope of the Series

Artificial Intelligence (AI) is a rapidly developing multidisciplinary research area that aims to solve increasingly complex problems. In today's highly integrated world, AI promises to become a robust and powerful means for obtaining solutions to previously unsolvable problems. This Series is intended for researchers and students alike interested in this fascinating field and its many applications.

Meet the Series Editor

Andries Engelbrecht received the Masters and Ph.D. degrees in Computer Science from the University of Stellenbosch, South Africa, in 1994 and 1999 respectively. He is currently appointed as the Voigt Chair in Data Science in the Department of Industrial Engineering, with a joint appointment as Professor in the Computer Science Division, Stellenbosch University. Prior to his appointment at Stellenbosch University, he has been at the University of Pretoria, Department of Computer Science (1998-2018), where he was appointed as South Africa Research Chair in Artifical Intelligence (2007-2018), the head of the Department of Computer Science (2008-2017), and Director of the Institute for Big Data and Data Science (2017-2018). In addition to a number of research articles, he has written two books, Computational Intelligence: An Introduction and Fundamentals of Computational Swarm Intelligence.

Meet the Volume Editor

Abdelhamid Mellouk is a Full-time Professor at the University of Paris-Est (UPEC), an active member of the IEEE Communications Society, and has held several offices, including leadership positions in IEEE Communications Society Technical Committees. He has published/coordinated 17 books in IT areas and more than 250 refereed international publications in journals, conferences, and books, in addition to numerous keynotes and plenary talks at flagship venues. He serves on the Editorial Boards or as Associate Editor for several journals (including IEEE CST and IEEE TVT), and he is chairing or has chaired (or co-chaired) some of the top international conferences and symposia (including IEEE ICC and IEEE GlobeCom). He is also the founder of Network Control Research and Curricula activities at UPEC and President of several other scientific, national, and international institutions.

Contents

Preface

Artificial Neural Networks (ANNs) are often referred to as a branch of artificial intelligence and have been a central topic in a broad range of scientific fields for the last two decades. Understanding of ANNs is expected to provide a systematic understanding of adaptive behaviors, including simple classical and operant conditioning in animals, as well as complex social and economic human behaviors designed to maximize benefits, and is also useful in machine learning and robotics. ANNs aim to find an appropriate mapping from situations to actions. It can be defined as a class of problem-solving approaches closely related to various scientific domains, such as Optimization, Vision, Finance, Neurobiology, Automatic Control, Theoretical Computer Science, and Supply Chain.

This book brings together many aspects of current research across several fields associated with ANNs. It covers a wide range of topics in ANN and their applications in autonomous systems. A set of chapters in this book provides a general overview of ANNs, while other chapters focus mostly on the applications of ANNs paradigms.

Chapter 1 provides a comprehensive review of ANN models, ranging from their theoretical foundations, such as neuron models, activation functions, and backpropagation, to application-specific models such as conventional neural networks (CNNs), recurrent neural networks (RNNs), long short-term memories (LSTMs), Gated Recurrent Units (GRUs), and attention models. From a mathematical description of their dynamics and learning paradigms to their behavior, the chapter builds a rigorous framework of ANN behavior. Special focus is given to cross-industry applications across manufacturing, cybersecurity, healthcare, finance, retail, transportation, agriculture, and smart cities.

Chapter 2 examines the computational mechanics underlying artificial neural network training and inference, analysing the fundamental algorithms, optimization strategies, and resource allocation patterns that govern these two distinct phases of neural network operation. We explore the evolution from basic stochastic gradient descent to modern optimizers like AdamW, investigating how hyperparameters such as learning rates, batch sizes, and scheduling strategies influence convergence behavior and computational efficiency. The discussion covers the transition from training's memory-intensive backpropagation, which requires simultaneous storage of activations and gradients, to inference's streamlined forward-pass computation, highlighting how this shift fundamentally alters optimization objectives from loss minimization to throughput and latency optimization. The chapter analyses the unique challenges posed by large language models, where autoregressive generation transforms inference from fixed-cost operations into iterative, variable-cost processes that scale without imposing length constraints and introduces complex memory bandwidth constraints through attention mechanisms and key-value caching.

Chapter 3 provides neurobiology-inspired design principles and practical guidance for developing next-generation visual technologies. It explores the visual systems of insects and their transformative potential for advanced visual sensors. Specifically, it focuses on the neural mechanisms of insect vision, particularly the adaptive signal processing by graded neurons and direction-selective circuits. The chapter examines how these biological systems achieve unparalleled efficiency in motion detection, object tracking, and optic flow analysis, and bridges biological principles with engineering applications, detailing the design and implementation of bioinspired vision sensors that replicate these capabilities. The discussion extends to industrial applications such as high-speed defect detection and unmanned aerial vehicle obstacle avoidance, and concludes with the future directions and challenges in this interdisciplinary field.

Chapter 4 analyses ethical and transparency issues in EEG-based BCIs, examining their implications for privacy, autonomy, equity, and human dignity across three dimensions: technological foundations, emerging ethical risks, and practical solutions. Key challenges include "neuro-privacy" concerns, threats to mental autonomy, algorithmic bias, informed consent complexities, and security vulnerabilities. Neural data's inferential potential through AI creates new categories of personal information exposure. We propose a framework integrating explainable AI, ethics-by-design principles, adaptive governance, and legal recognition of "neuro-rights". Technical transparency and ethical integration are the essential conditions for responsible BCI development. While EEG-BCIs offer therapeutic potential, preserving human dignity requires ethics-centred innovation. This work provides theoretical frameworks and practical guidelines for navigating the ethics of brain-machine interfaces.

Chapter 5 focuses on recent advances in hardware-friendly Artificial Neural Networks (ANNs) designs for intensity-modulated direct-detection (IM/DD) equalization, highlighting effective complexity-reduction strategies such as network pruning, low-precision quantization, and multi-task learning. We examine a range of ANN architectures and evaluate their adaptability to low-power, low-latency implementations. Furthermore, this chapter discusses practical trade-offs between accuracy and computational cost, with insights into deployment in real-time systems. It outlines future directions for scalable, resource-efficient NN equalization, paving the way for intelligent digital signal processing in next-generation optical communication links.

Chapter 6 examines the groundbreaking fusion of artificial intelligence and robotic process automation (RPA), emphasizing the vital role of neural networks in developing advanced automation systems. The implementation of neural network models enables the creation of automated systems that exhibit greater adaptability and intelligence. Conventional RPA systems faced constraints in managing unstructured data and in situations that require adaptive decision-making. The chapter aims to explore how deep learning architectures can enhance process cognition, natural language interpretation, and predictive decision-making. It examines the latest advancements in robotic process automation driven by artificial intelligence.

Chapter 7 examines the applications of ANNs in three key areas: warehouse management, demand forecasting, and supply chain route optimization. In warehouses, ANNs support inventory control, space utilization, and automation. For demand forecasting, it analyzes historical data and market trends to accurately predict fluctuations, minimizing stock-related risks. In route optimization, ANNs dynamically adjust transportation paths using real-time data such as traffic and weather conditions. Compared to traditional methods, ANNs deliver greater adaptability and predictive accuracy. Despite challenges such as data complexity, ongoing AI advancements are continually improving the role of ANNs in logistics, driving smarter, more efficient operations.

The last chapter delves into watermark-based methods for AI-generated text, including statistical and cryptographic approaches, outlining their underlying principles, technical architectures, existing challenges, and potential future directions. It aims to serve as a foundational guide for newcomers and a useful reference for researchers exploring this rapidly evolving field. In fact, artificial intelligence (AI)-generated text has advanced to the point where it is nearly indistinguishable from human-written content, bringing significant gains in efficiency and productivity. However, this progress has also caused a range of ethical concerns, including the spread of misinformation and the risk of content plagiarism. As a result, distinguishing AI-generated text from human-authored content has become a pressing issue for ensuring the responsible use and regulation of generative AI technologies. While one solution is to train detection models to identify AI-generated text, existing approaches often lack accuracy and are prone to false positives, leading to confusion and unintended consequences.

This book shows that ANNs are a dynamic field in both theory and application. The field of ANNs has been growing rapidly, producing a wide variety of learning algorithms for different applications.

There is also a very extensive literature on ANNs, and providing a complete bibliography and a historical account of the research that led to the present form would have been impossible. It is thus inevitable that some topics have been treated in less detail than others.

I would like to thank all contributors to this book for their research and effort. I hope you enjoy reading this book and get many helpful ideas and overviews for your own study.

Abdelhamid Mellouk
IT4Health Department, EPISEN,
Network and Telecom Department, IUT CV,
TincNET Research Team (CIR.LISSI.UPEC),
University Paris-Est Creteil (UPEC),
Créteil, France

Chapter 1

Artificial Neural Networks for Decision-Making Industry-Wide Applications and Innovations

Niyas Ahamed Sirajudeen, C.S. Sree Thayanandeswari and Abdul Malik Maheen

Abstract

Artificial Neural Networks (ANNs) are now indispensable tools for intelligent decision-making in most industries. Inspired by the topology of biological neurons, ANNs are especially well suited to handle high-dimensional, nonlinear data and are the building blocks of modern Deep Learning Architectures. The chapter provides a comprehensive review of ANN models, ranging from their theoretical foundations such as neuron models, activation functions, and backpropagation to application-specific models such as conventional neural networks (CNNs), recurrent neural networks (RNNs), long short-term memories (LSTMs), Gated Recurrent Units (GRUs), and attention models. From a mathematical description of their dynamics and learning paradigms to their behavior, the chapter builds a rigorous framework of ANN behavior. Special focus is given to cross-industry applications across manufacturing, cybersecurity, healthcare, finance, retail, transportation, agriculture, and smart cities. A special section is devoted to real-world case studies at Siemens, DeepMind, JPMorgan, and Tesla, showcasing the scalability and robustness of ANN-based solutions in predictive maintenance, medical diagnosis, fraud detection, and autonomous systems. Apart from that, the chapter critically assesses technical as well as ethical concerns, such as interpretability, dataset bias, privacy, energy efficiency, and regulatory accountability. New frontiers, such as federated learning, lightweight models for edge computing, Spiking Neural Networks (SNNs), and Green Artificial Intelligence (AI), are identified as leading future directions. By integrating deep technical insights with practical examples and visions to the future, the chapter is an invaluable guide for scholars, engineers, and policymakers charting the transformative potential of ANNs in industrial and societal decision-making systems.

Keywords: artificial neural networks, deep learning, decision-making systems, industry 4.0, convolutional neural networks, LSTM, predictive analytics, intelligent automation, cross-industry AI applications, machine learning models

1. Introduction

The development of AI in recent decades has been characterized by an extraordinary paradigm shift, one driven by the emergence of ANNs. ANNs were initially motivated by the neurobiology of the human brain and have since evolved into robust computational tools that can solve hard, nonlinear, and high-dimensional problems that conventional algorithms find difficult to tackle. Their adaptive learning capacity, scalability, and data-driven modeling capabilities have allowed them to revolutionize decision-making operations in a broad range of industries from real-time financial predictions and medical diagnosis to automated quality control and cyberattack defense [1, 2]. Fundamental to contemporary ANN architectures is their capability of learning hierarchical representation from raw input data, thus allowing machines to make sensible decisions, discover faint patterns, and generalize for unseen settings. Recent breakthroughs in deep learning, especially CNNs for spatial data and RNNs for sequential data, have further strengthened the capacity of ANNs to interpret sophisticated datasets autonomously and carry out real-time intelligent decisions [3, 4]. These breakthroughs have accelerated the rollout of ANN-driven systems in fields where accuracy, dependability, and expediency are crucial.

In the industrial setting, ANN-based decision-making is no longer in the experimental stage but in use. In production, ANNs maximize predictive maintenance and improve the quality of production [5]. In finance, they evaluate credit risk and identify fraud with remarkable accuracy [6]. In medicine, they provide decision support in disease prediction and patient surveillance through medical imaging and time-series clinical data [7]. In cybersecurity, deep neural architectures constantly monitor for anomalies to protect systems from advanced attacks. These applications not only highlight the adaptability of ANN models but also illustrate their pivotal role in data-driven automation, risk management, and strategic operations. Despite increasing ubiquity, several core challenges remain. Challenges like interpretability of the model, ethical implications of biased results, computational expense, and requiring enormous annotated datasets are still at the forefront of ANN research [8]. In addition, incorporating ANN systems into real-time decision-making environments brings into question responsibility, credibility, and the performance versus transparency trade-off. These challenges need to be continually addressed through academic and industrial collaboration to bring about responsible innovation.

This chapter delivers a comprehensive analysis of Artificial Neural Networks for decision-making, emphasizing theoretical foundations, deep learning developments, and industry-oriented applications. It includes modern case studies that emphasize ANN-driven innovation and scrutinizes contemporary research challenges, such as interpretability, scalability, and ethical concerns. In this step-by-step breakdown, the chapter not only exposes how ANNs are reshaping decision-making in key sectors but also outlines future trajectories for sustainable and intelligent ANN progress. **Table 1** illustrates the overview of ANN applications across major industries, highlighting commonly used models, target use cases, and representative systems or organizations.

2. Theoretical foundations of artificial neural networks

ANNs constitute a category of computational models based on the structure and function of the human brain. ANNs have the ability to map complex functions, learn from examples, and make decisions. ANNs constitute the basic backbone of several deep learning systems and are extensively used in areas ranging from image recognition, financial prediction, industrial automation, to natural language processing. This part offers the basic theoretical components of ANNs, such as their elements, designs, training algorithms, learning paradigms, and mathematical expressions.

Industry	ANN models used	Application areas	Example organization / system
Manufacturing	CNN, LSTM	Fault detection, predictive maintenance, quality control	Siemens – Turbine monitoring
Healthcare	CNN, RNN, 3D-CNN	Disease diagnosis, medical imaging, patient risk analysis	DeepMind – Retinal disease detection
Finance	DNN, Autoencoder, MLP-RNN	Fraud detection, credit scoring, portfolio optimization	JPMorgan – Real-time fraud detection
Transportation	Multi-stream CNNs, LSTM	Object detection, scene understanding, navigation	Tesla – Autopilot vision system
Cybersecurity	DNN, Autoencoder, GRU	Intrusion detection, malware classification	Various IDS frameworks (e.g., KDD99 datasets)
Retail / e-commerce	CNN, DNN	Customer behavior prediction, recommendation systems	Amazon, Alibaba – Recommender systems
Agriculture	CNN, LSTM	Crop disease detection, yield forecasting	SmartFarm platforms

Table 1.
Summary of ANN applications across industries.

2.1 The artificial neuron model

At the core of an ANN is the artificial neuron, a reduced abstraction of a biological neuron. Every neuron takes input signals, performs a transformation through related weights and a bias, and generates an output based on an activation function. Algebraically, the output of one neuron can be represented as,

$$z = f\left(\sum_{i=1}^{m} v_i y_i + a\right) = f\left(V^T Y + a\right) \tag{1}$$

Where $Y = [y_1, y_2, \ldots .. y_m]^T$ is the input vector, $V = [v_1, v_2, \ldots .. v_m]^T$ is the weight vector, the bias term is denoted as a, the activation function is denoted as $f(\cdot)$, and the neuron output is denoted as z. This mapping allows the neuron to make decisions as a function of a weighted sum of inputs.

2.2 Activation functions

Activation functions introduce nonlinearity into neural networks to enable them to represent complex relationships between inputs and outputs. Some typical activation functions are:

Sigmoid function: Smooth and bounded between 0 and 1; historically used in binary classification.

$$f(x) = \frac{1}{1 + e^{-x}} \tag{2}$$

ReLU (Rectified Linear Unit): Widely used in deep networks for its computational simplicity and ability to mitigate the vanishing gradient problem

$$f(x) = \max(0, x) \quad (3)$$

Softmax function: Converts logits into a probability distribution; typically used in multi-class classification problems.

$$f_q(x) = \frac{e^{x_q}}{\sum_j e^{x_j}} \quad (4)$$

Each activation function has its pros based on the task and network architecture. For example, ReLU is utilized in convolutional layers, whereas softmax is applied in output layers for classification [9].

2.3 Feed-forward neural networks (FNNs) and multi-layer perceptrons (MLPs)

Feed-Forward Neural Networks (FNNs) are the simplest types of ANNs. In an FNN, data move from the input layer to the output layer without any loops or cycles via one or more hidden layers. A MLP is an FNN where one neuron in a given layer connects with every neuron in the next layer. Each layer applies the following operation:

$$g^{(r)} = f\left(V^{(r)} g^{(r-1)} + a^{(r)}\right) \quad (5)$$

Where $g^{(r)}$ denotes the activation vector of layer r, $V^{(r)}$ denotes the weight matrix, $a^{(r)}$ denotes the bias vector, and the activation function is denoted as f. MLPs are universal function approximators and can learn to represent any continuous function provided enough neurons and layers. **Figure 1** illustrates the structure of a MLP showing fully connected layers. Inputs X_1, X_2, X_3, and X_4 are processed through

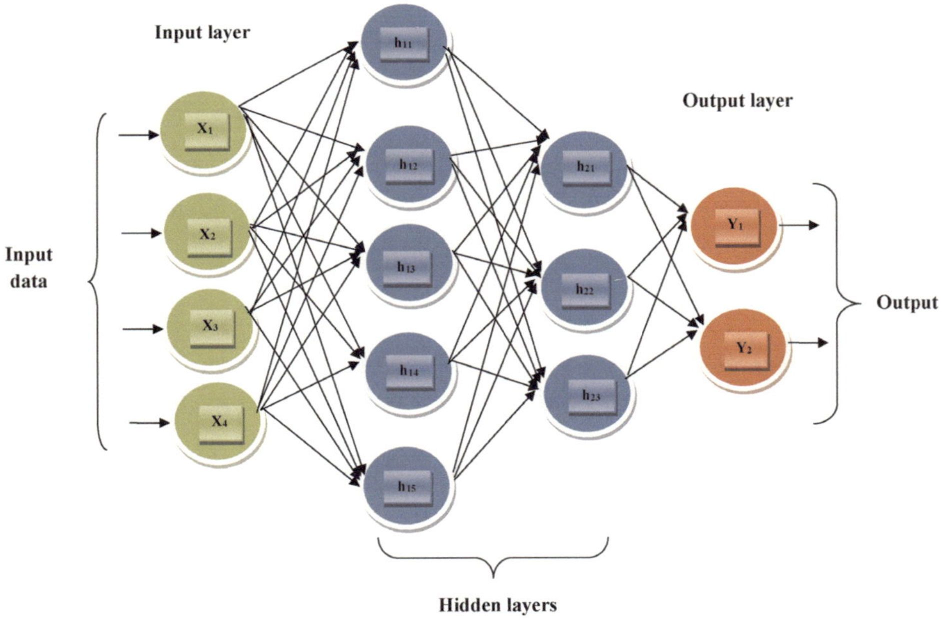

Figure 1.
Structure of a MLP showing fully connected layers between inputs, hidden neurons, and output.

hidden neurons using weighted connections and activation functions to produce the output Y_1, Y_2.

2.4 Learning via backpropagation and gradient descent

Training a neural network involves adjusting weights and biases to minimize a predefined loss function $R(\theta)$, which quantifies the difference between the predicted and actual outputs. This is done using gradient descent and the backpropagation algorithm. The flowchart of gradient descent training cycle illustrating initialization, forward pass, loss computation, gradient backpropagation, and parameter update until convergence. Gradient Descent Update Rule:

$$\theta^{(s+1)} = \theta^{(s)} - \eta \nabla_\theta R\left(\theta^{(s)}\right) \tag{6}$$

Where, θ represents network parameters (weights and biases), the learning rate is denoted as η, and the gradient of the loss with respect to the parameters is denoted as $\nabla_\theta R$.

Backpropagation is an efficient method to compute gradients using the chain rule of calculus. The weight update for a specific layer l in the network can be written as,

$$\Delta V^{(r)} = -\eta \delta^{(r)} \left(g^{(r-1)}\right)^T \tag{7}$$

$$\delta^{(r)} = \left(V^{(r+1)}\right)^T \delta^{(r+1)} \Theta f'\left(x^{(r)}\right) \tag{8}$$

Where, $\delta^{(r)}$ is the error term for layer r, f' is the deviation of activation function, and Θ denotes elementwise multiplication. These updates continue until the network converges to an optimal set of parameters minimizing the loss function (**Figure 2**) [10].

2.5 Learning paradigms in neural networks

There are various learning paradigms by which neural networks can be trained based on the availability and nature of data:

2.5.1 Supervised learning

Supervised learning involves learning from labeled data. The network is trained on input-output pairs to learn the mapping $f : x \rightarrow y$. This is the most common paradigm used in classification, regression, and forecasting tasks.

2.5.2 Unsupervised learning

There are no labeled outputs. The network finds patterns or structure in the input information. Typical applications include clustering, dimensionality reduction (e.g., principal component analysis (PCA), autoencoders), and anomaly detection.

2.5.3 Reinforcement learning

Reinforcement learning involves learning through exploration of an environment. The agent is rewarded or punished based on the action taken and try to maximize the

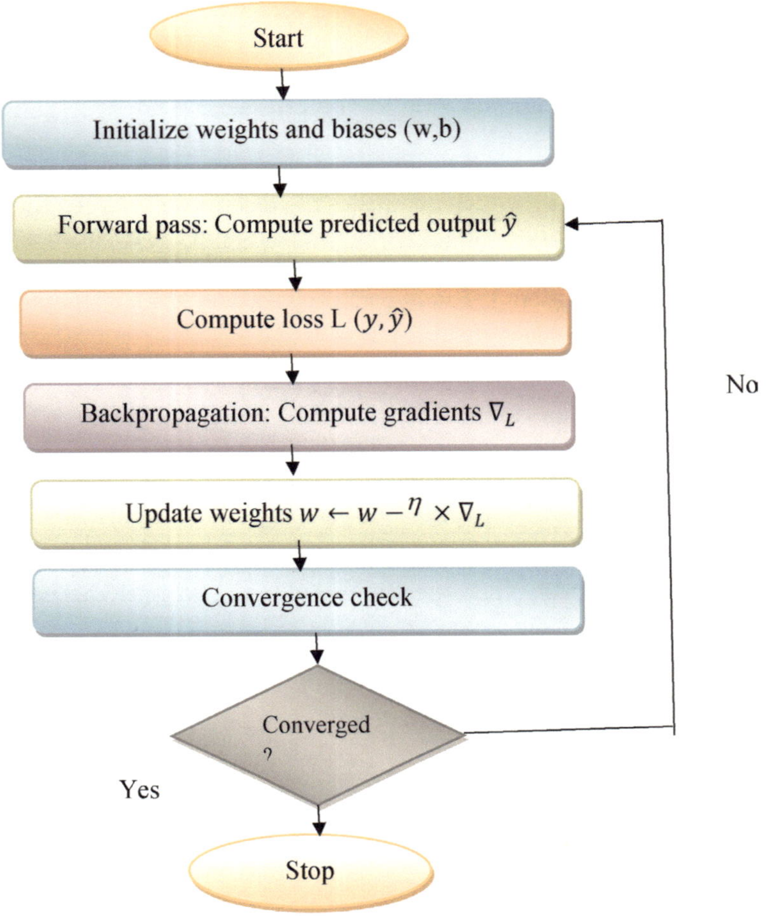

Figure 2.
Flowchart of gradient descent optimization in neural network training.

sum of reward over time. Deep neural networks (DNNs) are used as approximators of value or policy functions in algorithms like Q-learning and Policy Gradients [11].

2.6 Loss functions

Loss functions quantify difference between predicted output and actual output. Popular loss functions are:

Mean Squared Error (MSE): Utilized in regression problems.

$$R = \frac{1}{M}\sum_{i=1}^{M}\left(z_i - \hat{z}_i\right)^2 \tag{9}$$

Cross-Entropy Loss: Utilized in classification problems with softmax outputs.

$$R = -\sum_{i} z_i \log\left(\hat{z}_i\right) \tag{10}$$

Selecting an adequate loss function is important for successful learning and is based on the type of problem and output type. The present section has described the fundamental theoretical principles that constitute the building blocks of Artificial Neural Networks. By knowing the neuron model, activation functions, architectures such as MLPs, training algorithms including backpropagation, and learning paradigms, researchers and practitioners are more capable of designing and building neural networks for intricate decision-making problems. These concepts are also further elucidated in the following sections, which discuss their industrial applications and breakthroughs.

3. Deep neural architectures and decision-making

The rising sophistication of real-world data and decision-making contexts has given rise to deeper and more specialized neural architectures. These models improve decision-support systems by learning high-level features automatically, capturing temporal dependencies, and learning sequential or spatial patterns. This section explores key deep neural architectures such as CNNs, RNNs, LSTM networks, Gated Recurrent Units (GRUs), and hybrid architectures and examines their suitability and performance in diverse decision-making contexts.

3.1 CNN for visual decision support

CNNs are well known to learn spatial hierarchies in data and are commonly deployed in visual decision-making problems, including medical imaging, industrial defect inspection, and satellite observation. They consist of convolutional layers for feature extraction, pooling layers for reducing dimensions, and fully connected layers for classification or regression applications. CNNs have reported encouraging outcomes in industrial visual inspection systems, as reviewed by Patra et al. [12], where they were employed for identifying flaws in surface textures at high precision. Tayal et al. [13] also employed CNNs in the healthcare context for classifying retinal disease. CNNs are strongly adept at teaching spatial hierarchies, providing translation invariance and a scalable, module architecture that is conducive to deep architecture development. These capabilities render them extremely efficient in recognition of patterns and images. Nevertheless, CNNs are not appropriate for time-dependent or sequential data, and they also need large quantities of labeled training data to function best.

3.2 Recurrent neural networks (RNNs), LSTMs, and GRUs for time-series decisions

RNNs and their sophisticated counterparts such as LSTMs and Gated Recurrent Units (GRUs) are excellent at modeling sequential data and find extensive applications in time-series forecasting, speech recognition, and natural language processing. The classical RNNs are plagued by the vanishing gradient issue, which prevents them from learning long-term dependencies. LSTM networks address this limitation by having memory cells and gate mechanisms that allow the preservation of information for more sequences, for which reason they are well suited for predictive maintenance, finance modeling, and weather forecasting. Another breakthrough by Kong et al. [14] presented the Patch-Shift LSTM (P-sLSTM), which improves long-term forecast precision by combining patching and shifting methods in cutting time-series data. GRUs, however, provide a simplified version of LSTMs by merging forget and input gates into an update gate. The performance remains similar but with reduced parameters, hence ideal for real-time processing where resources are constrained. Xu and Wang [15] introduced the Extreme Event Adaptive GRU (eGRU), which is highly effective in complicated hybrid forecasting where both standard and extreme events are present. While these architectures are strong in encoding temporal dynamics and preserving memory over time, they may suffer from overfitting and need to be carefully tuned and regularized to work best on a wide range of tasks.

3.3 Hybrid neural architectures: CNN-LSTM and attention-based models

Hybrid neural architectures like CNN-LSTM and attention-based models have proved to be strong contenders in dealing with multimodal data and improving learning efficiency in decision-making systems. CNN-LSTM architectures combine the benefits of CNNs for spatial feature learning with LSTM networks for modeling temporal sequences, making them very effective in applications, such as video analytics, human activity recognition, and emotion detection. In a recent work by Geethanjali and Valarmathi [16], a real-time CNN-LSTM framework was proposed for emotion detection in video streams with great accuracy in dynamic real-world settings. Concurrently, transformers and attention-based models have emerged as popular alternatives because they can pay close attention to the most pertinent aspects of the input data, thus enhancing model performance for applications like natural language translation, anomaly detection, and time-series prediction. In contrast to RNNs, transformers rely on self-attention mechanisms that allow for parallel processing and are effective in capturing long-range dependencies. Sakib et al. [17] showed that transformer models surpass LSTMs in multi-step forecasting tasks, providing better scalability and explainability via attention weight visualization. Although they have strengths, attention-based models consume large amounts of computational resources and are hyperparameter-sensitive, making them difficult to tune and deploy, particularly in low-resource settings. **Figure 3** shows the hybrid CNN-LSTM architecture for sequential data modeling. CNN extracts spatial features, while LSTM captures temporal dependencies.

3.4 Deep Q-networks and reinforcement learning

Deep Q-Networks (DQNs) combine Q-learning and deep neural networks to allow agents to make decisions that are optimal in nature through interaction with uncertain and dynamic environments. DQNs have played a significant role in further development of reinforcement learning (RL) and are widely applied in areas, including robotics, self-driving vehicles, smart grid control, and adaptive control systems. First

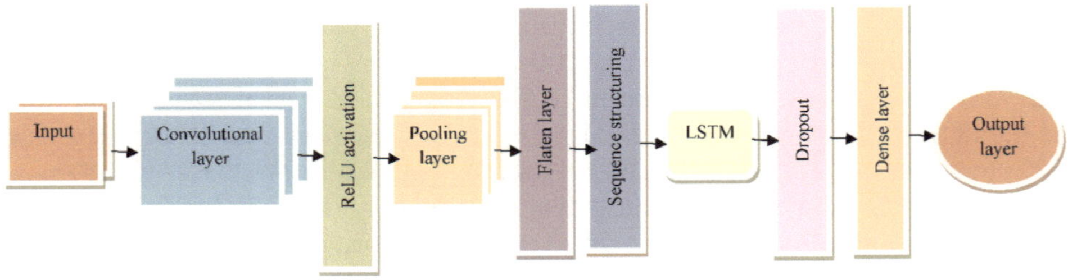

Figure 3.
CNN-LSTM hybrid model architecture.

Architecture	Best use case	Strengths	Limitations
CNN	Image-based decision systems	Excellent spatial feature extraction	Cannot model sequences
RNN	Basic sequential tasks	Simple, good for short sequences	Vanishing gradient, short memory span
LSTM	Long-sequence forecasting	Retains long-term memory	High complexity, computationally expensive
GRU	Lightweight sequential modeling	Faster than LSTM, fewer parameters	Less flexible for very long dependencies
CNN-LSTM	Spatiotemporal decision tasks	Integrates image and sequence learning	High training cost
Attention/ transformer	Language, finance, time series	Long-range dependencies, scalable	Demands large data and compute power
DQN	Reinforcement learning applications	Learns optimal policy in dynamic systems	Unstable and data-inefficient without enhancements

Table 2.
Comparative analysis of Deep Learning Architectures for decision-making applications.

introduced by Mnih et al. [18] as a means of learning control policies in Atari game environments, DQNs proved the value of deep learning to represent action-value functions in high-dimensional state spaces. From here, the advances came in the form of Double DQN and Dueling DQN, which tackled the limitations of overestimation and value function decomposition, respectively. Later, Igl et al. [19] introduced a Noisy DQN variant that adds stochastic noise to the network weights to enhance exploration and prevent overestimation in sparse-reward or complex environments. This helps greatly in enhancing learning stability and decision quality for real-world problems where exploration-exploitation balance is paramount. DQNs have a number of benefits: they do not need to be trained on labeled data because they learn from rewards in the environment, can work with sparse and delayed rewards, and learn well in dynamic environments. They do come with limitations like sample inefficiency that demands a lot of interaction data and training instability that requires the use of methods, such as experience replay and target networks for stabilization. It is despite these difficulties that DQNs are still a foundation of Deep Reinforcement Learning and continue to find new innovations in decision-making systems. **Table 2** shows the comparative analysis of Deep Learning Architectures for decision-making applications.

This **Figure 4** compares the computational efficiency of different deep learning models by plotting training time against achieved accuracy, highlighting the trade-offs between complexity and performance.

4. Cross-industry applications of ANNs

ANNs have shown revolutionary potential in a variety of domains. Their potential to learn intricate patterns from structured and unstructured data, extract features, and facilitate autonomous decision-making has made them essential components in contemporary intelligent systems. This section is an extensive overview of ANN applications in manufacturing, cybersecurity, healthcare, finance, and other new

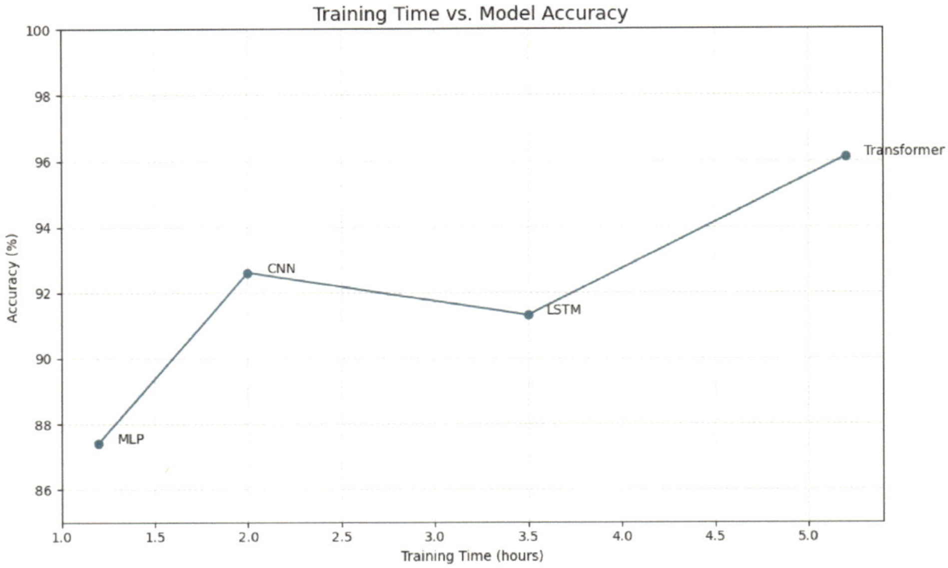

Figure 4.
Training time versus accuracy for ANN architectures.

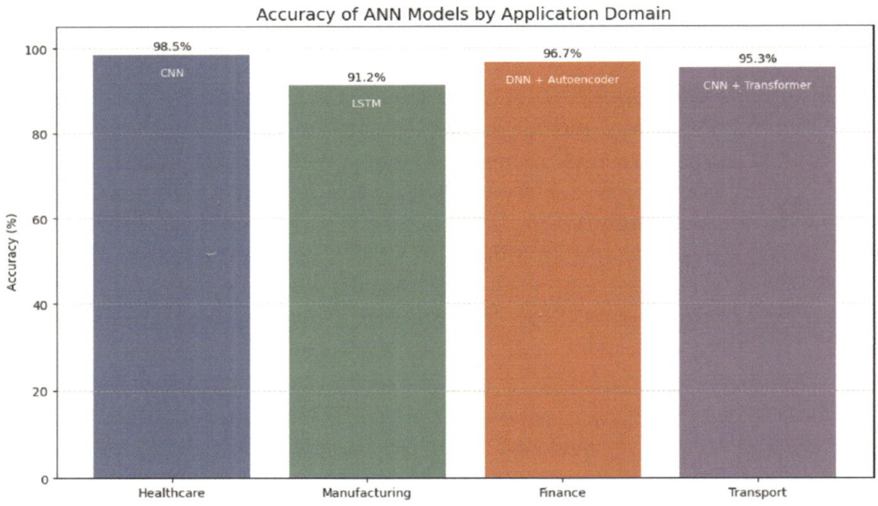

Figure 5.
Accuracy of ANN models across industry sectors.

areas. **Figure 5** flowchart compares the performance of ANN architectures used in different domains, illustrating model selection trends based on application-specific accuracy.

4.1 Manufacturing

With the Industry 4.0 era, the incorporation of ANN into production systems has brought about substantial improvements in automation, predictive maintenance, and quality control.

4.1.1 Quality control using image classification

Visual inspection driven by CNNs is revolutionizing quality control in production lines through real-time detection of abnormalities like cracks, scratches, or discoloration. CNNs are generally trained on thousands of labeled images with both defect and non-defect samples so that these flaws can be correctly recognized. For instance, Zhang et al. [20] introduced a state-of-the-art CNN-based algorithm integrating residual networks and attention mechanisms, greatly improving the efficiency and accuracy of surface defect detection for industrial production systems. Technically, CNNs pull multi-scale spatial features via several convolutional layers, and softmax classifiers provide probabilities that differentiate defect and non-defect classes. Moreover, transfer learning methods, based on pre-trained models such as Residual Network (ResNet) or Visual Geometry Group (VGG), enable a quick deployment of these systems, even in the absence of large training datasets.

4.1.2 Fault detection using time-series sensor data

Time-series sensor readings from machines like consecutive readings of vibration, temperature, or pressure are tracked with the help of RNNs or LSTM networks to identify initial symptoms of machine degradation. These models are usually made up of two or three stacked LSTM layers, followed by a dense layer for binary classification that gives the probability of a fault developing within a specified time window. Wang et al. [21] proposed a hybrid CNN-LSTM model, Bidirectional Principal Component Analysis-Selective Multimodal Long Short-Term Memory (BDPCA-SMLSTM), for motor drive control system fault diagnosis, which showed high detection efficiency and capability to deal with complicated industrial procedures.

4.2 Cybersecurity

As threats in cyberspace become more complex, ANN-based systems offer adaptive, real-time defense through the detection of threats within network traffic, system logs, and malware binaries.

4.2.1 Intrusion detection systems (IDS)

Deep learning-based Intrusion Detection Systems (IDS) leverage Feed-Forward Neural Networks and Deep Belief Networks (DBNs) to detect anomalies in network activity. The models are trained to perform both binary classification, identifying normal traffic and attacks, and multi-class classification, classifying different attack types including Denial of Service (DoS), Probe, Remote to Local (R2L), and User to Root (U2R) attacks. Javaid et al. [22] provided a thorough review of the application of deep learning methods to network intrusion detection, emphasizing their better performance on high-dimensional cybersecurity data when compared to conventional machine learning approaches.

4.2.2 Malware classification using autoencoders

Deep autoencoders are utilized in malware classification by compressing high-dimensional binary features, i.e., opcode sequences and byte strings, into a low-dimensional latent space. The method entails training the autoencoder on clean software samples in such a way that it learns to reconstruct benign data accurately. At detection, samples with a high reconstruction error are identified as anomalies, pointing toward possible malware. The technique provides the benefit of strongly detecting obfuscated malware variants by successfully encoding intricate nonlinear relationships within high-dimensional feature spaces.

4.3 Healthcare systems

Healthcare systems are in the midst of a paradigm shift, with deep learning models being used to augment diagnostics, prognosis, and patient risk prediction.

4.3.1 Cancer classification from radiology scans

CNNs have been shown to outperform radiologists in processes like skin cancer classification, detection of breast cancer, and segmentation of tumors. The conventional processing pipeline is to feed preprocessed and augmented image slices into a CNN with 3 to 10 layers for feature abstraction, followed by a softmax or sigmoid classifier for binary or multi-class classification. Nawaz et al. [23] presented a dedicated deep CNN architecture named Fully Connected Dense Sampling Convolutional Neural Network (FCDS-CNN), specifically designed to deal with class-imbalanced skin lesion datasets, and dramatically improved detection accuracy in skin cancer classification problems.

4.3.2 Patient risk prediction using RNNs

RNNs and LSTM networks find extensive applications in analyzing longitudinal patient histories for predicting essential outcomes like hospital readmission risk, intensive care unit (ICU) mortality, and chronic disease aggravation. These models deal with time-stamped data such as laboratory values, diagnoses, and medication history and cope with missing values by masking or imputing using data imputation techniques. Hama et al. [24] presented the improved predictive ability of deep RNN models on electronic health records, exhibiting higher accuracy than conventional logistic regression methods in patient risk prediction tasks.

4.4 Finance

In finance technology (FinTech), ANNs improve fraud detection, credit scoring, and dynamic investment strategies.

4.4.1 Fraud detection and credit scoring

ANNs are very effective in identifying fraudulent transactions by detecting intricate, nonlinear patterns within financial data. The primary input features are transaction value, timestamp, merchant location, device ID, and user behavior metrics. Different model architectures are used based on the data type: Multi-layer Perceptrons (MLPs) process tabular transaction data, CNNs process spatial relationships like card usage locations, and RNNs process sequential patterns of transactions. Nama et al. [25] introduced a framework for fraud detection based on deep learning in mobile payment systems with impressive accuracy of 99.87% and F1-Score of 0.99, emphasizing the reliability and efficacy of ANN models in detecting financial frauds.

4.4.2 Deep reinforcement learning for portfolio optimization

Deep Reinforcement Learning methods like Deep Q-Networks (DQNs) and Actor-Critic models are used more and more for portfolio optimization by acquiring dynamic trading approaches that update themselves according to market states. Here, the state is constituted by the market indicators and asset prices, and the available actions are buying, selling, or holding assets. The reward function is normally derived from performance measures like the portfolio Sharpe ratio or log returns to steer the learning process toward optimizing risk-adjusted returns. Such reinforcement learning models have reported better performance than static investment rules in backtested simulations through constantly optimizing asset allocation over time.

4.5 Other sectors

Deep learning has penetrated deeply into other industries by powering intelligent automation and predictive power. In consumer retail, RNNs are applied extensively in recommendation systems for personalized recommendation to improve customer interaction, and LSTM networks aid in precise demand forecasting. In the transportation sector, hybrid CNN-LSTM models enhance traffic flow prediction and CNNs are responsible for object detection and path planning in autonomous vehicles. Smart cities owe a lot to ANNs for predicting energy demand and optimizing resources, such as waste management and intelligent grid operations. In farming, CNNs are used to identify plant diseases from leaf images, while deep regression models use satellite images to estimate actual crop yield for precision farming and food safety. Artificial Neural Networks have evolved into domain-specific decision-making tools. The advent of deep learning has seen these models migrate across different modalities of data and patterns in time, facilitating some of the most important breakthroughs in automation, diagnostics, risk analysis, and prediction. Challenges still persist in interpretability, quality of data, and generalizability, but their value, crossing industries as it does, is exponentially increasing.

5. Case studies

To add to the real-world applicability and usefulness of ANNs, this section describes four actual implementations by Siemens, DeepMind, JPMorgan Chase, and Tesla. These case studies cover manufacturing, healthcare, finance, and autonomous systems industries, providing detailed information about how ANN architectures are used for sophisticated decision-making and automation.

5.1 Siemens: Predictive maintenance in gas turbines

Siemens solved the problem of untimely equipment breakdowns in gas turbines prevalent in heavy industry operations using a predictive maintenance solution driven by LSTM networks. These state-of-the-art RNNs are specifically well suited to model time-series data and long-term temporal relationships, ideal for fault prediction using multivariate sensor inputs. Siemens gathered telemetry information from more than

100 industrial gas turbines, including key sensor measurements like vibration, temperature, and pressure. The model architecture used had two LSTM layers of 128 units each, regularized by dropout layers to prevent overfitting, and topped with a sigmoid-activated dense output layer to categorize the presence or absence of faults. Integrated within Siemens' MindSphere Internet of Things (IoT) platform, the model recorded a staggering 92.5% prediction accuracy and F1-Score of 0.91. The model effectively produced failure alarms more than 20 hours, prior to a real event. Not only did this deployment minimize unplanned downtime but it also enhanced operational reliability and provided a reference standard for AI-based asset maintenance approaches in Industry 4.0 environments [26, 27].

5.2 DeepMind and moorfields eye hospital: Retinal disease diagnosis

As part of a groundbreaking partnership, DeepMind and Moorfields Eye Hospital created an advanced AI system to enable the automated diagnosis of retinal conditions from Optical Coherence Tomography (OCT) scans. These conditions, such as diabetic retinopathy and age-related macular degeneration, are leading causes of blindness and traditionally need to be carefully reviewed in detail by specialist ophthalmologists. The original solution employed a Three-dimensional Convolutional Neural Network (3D-CNN) for handling volumetric scan data. The model was trained using more than 15,000 anonymized OCT scans that had been labeled by expert clinicians. It had five 3D convolutional layers, followed by global average pooling and dense layers to provide disease classification and referral advice. The system recorded an area under the curve (AUC) of over 0.99, with a sensitivity of 94.5% and a specificity of 93.7%, comparable to an expert performance. Recently, DeepMind introduced RETFound, a transformer vision foundation model pre-trained on more than 1.6 million unlabeled retinal images employing self-supervised learning. RETFound showcased good generalization to several ocular diseases while substantially minimizing the requirement for labeled data. These developments are a benchmark in clinical AI, offering scalable and clinically relevant solutions for worldwide eye care [28, 29].

5.3 JPMorgan chase: Real-time fraud detection system

JPMorgan Chase improved its fraud prevention feature by adopting an Artificial Neural Network-based system to identify fraud in real time. Conventional fraud detection models did not respond quickly enough to dynamic fraud patterns and tended to produce high false positives, which created customer discontent. In order to overcome these shortfalls, JPMorgan Chase developed a hybrid architecture that merged Multi-Layer Perceptrons (MLPs) with RNNs. The MLP module operated on static transaction attributes like merchant ID, transaction value, and card type, while RNN captured sequential behavior patterns like frequency of purchases and timing. The training data comprised millions of fraudulent and genuine transactions with labels. The produced model had an accuracy level of 98.3%, AUC = 0.989, and decreased false positives by 40%, thus minimizing unwanted alerts and enhancing user experience. Critically, the system was able to alert suspicious transactions in milliseconds, allowing real-time intervention. Such implementation not only bolstered JPMorgan's cybersecurity framework but also touched other areas of the FinTech industry, where ANN-based fraud detection is now a commonplace practice [30, 31].

5.4 Tesla: Autopilot vision system

Tesla's Autopilot vision system is a prime example of the application of complex neural networks in the high-risk arena of autonomous driving. In order to allow cars to drive through intricate real-world settings safely, Tesla designed a multi-stream CNN architecture with added temporal modules based on transformers. The data for training consisted of millions of labeled video frames obtained from on-board cameras under different conditions of environment, such as fog, rain, and night-time illumination. Every stream within the architecture was allocated for object detection from one particular camera viewpoint, and outputs were combined with other data from radar and ultrasonic sensors. In order to make the system temporally consistent in understanding the scene, Tesla included recurrent layers and transformer-based attention mechanisms that enabled the system to model object and environment changes over time. The framework had an Intersection-over-Union (IoU) of more than 0.75 on object detection and held the inference latency below 50 milliseconds per frame as required for real-time processing in autonomous driving. Tesla's vision architecture is a foundation of self-driving technology and has motivated deep research into edge-deployable real-time neural networks for robotics and intelligent mobility [32].

6. Challenges, interpretability, and ethical considerations

Despite their impressive predictive capabilities, ANNs face significant challenges, particularly when deployed in high-stakes domains, such as healthcare, finance, and public policy. These challenges include interpretability, fairness, data privacy, environmental sustainability, and ethical accountability. Interpretability remains a central concern, as most deep learning models function as opaque "black boxes," making it difficult to understand how inputs are transformed into outputs. This is especially problematic in healthcare and finance, where decisions can have life-altering

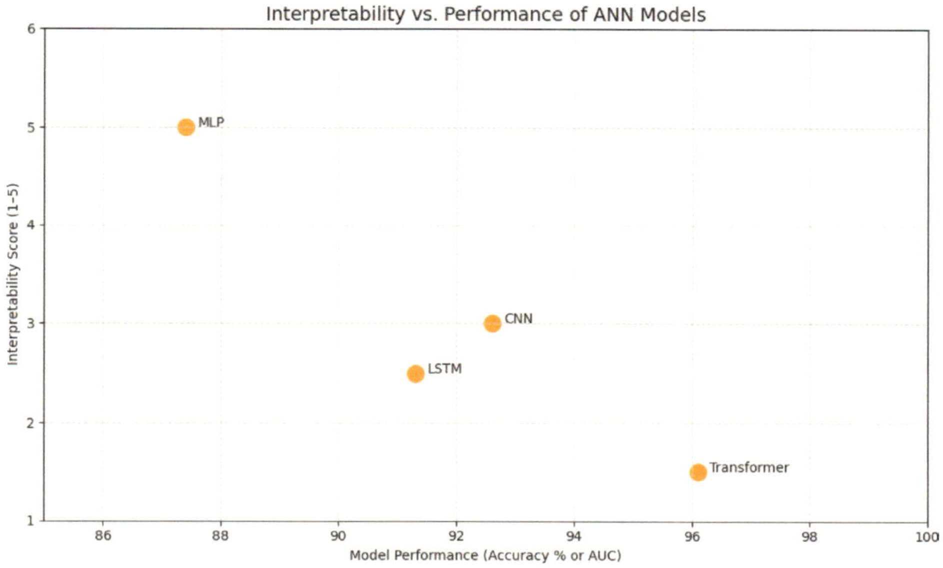

Figure 6.
Interpretability versus performance of common ANN models.

consequences. Tools such as SHAP (SHapley Additive exPlanations) and LIME (Local Interpretable Model-Agnostic Explanations) have been developed to improve model transparency, yet they often lack consistency across datasets and models [33, 34]. This **Figure 6** scatterplot illustrates the trade-off between interpretability and model performance, showing that more complex models often offer higher accuracy at the cost of reduced transparency.

Bias and fairness in ANN systems are also growing concerns. These models are only as fair as the data they are trained on. In healthcare, for example, a widely used commercial algorithm systematically underestimated the health needs of Black patients, as shown in a 2019 study published in Science [35]. Similarly, in finance, neural network-based credit scoring models have shown discriminatory behavior due to biased historical data, disproportionately rejecting minority applicants [36]. Transparency in algorithmic decision-making has also been challenged in judicial systems. A well-known example is ProPublica's investigation into the COMPAS (Correctional Offender Management Profiling for Alternative Sanctions) algorithm, which showed significant racial bias in predicting recidivism [37]. The model was proprietary and lacked explainability, highlighting a critical need for algorithmic accountability.

Data privacy is another concern, as ANN models typically require large datasets for training. Approaches like federated learning and differential privacy have emerged to mitigate this by enabling decentralized training and noise injection to protect individual records [38]. The environmental impact of large-scale ANN models is also under scrutiny. Training modern deep learning models like Generative Pre-trained Transformer 3 (GPT-3) and large CNNs consumes massive computational energy, prompting a shift toward Green AI, an initiative focused on reducing the carbon footprint of AI systems through model compression, quantization, and pruning techniques [39]. Lastly, ethical responsibility is a growing regulatory and societal concern. As AI systems increasingly participate in decision-making processes, assigning accountability becomes complex. Global initiatives such as the European Union's (EU's) Artificial Intelligence Act and The Institute of Electrical and Electronics Engineers' (IEEE's) Ethically Aligned Design aim to enforce human oversight, fairness, and transparency in ANN-driven systems [40]. **Figure 7** flowchart

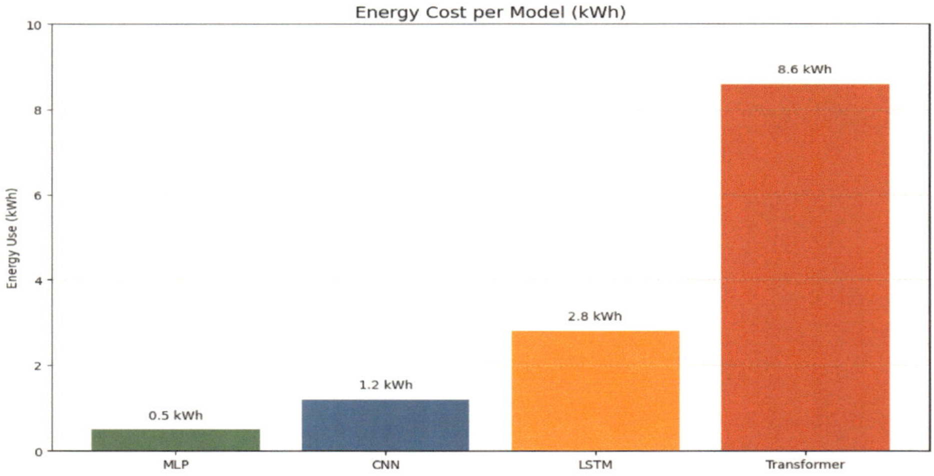

Figure 7.
Energy cost per model (kWh).

visualizes the relative energy consumption of different ANN models during training, highlighting the importance of energy-efficient AI practices for sustainable model deployment.

7. Future research directions

The ongoing evolution of ANNs has given rise to several promising research directions aimed at overcoming current limitations and broadening their application across diverse domains. One critical area is the development of lightweight and edge-optimized models that can operate efficiently on resource-constrained devices, such as smartphones, drones, and IoT sensors. Techniques like model pruning, quantization, and knowledge distillation are gaining traction to minimize computational overhead while maintaining predictive accuracy [38]. Spiking Neural Networks (SNNs) and neuromorphic computing represent another fast-growing frontier. These biologically inspired models mimic the firing behavior of neurons and enable ultra-low power consumption, making them ideal for real-time embedded intelligence and edge computing scenarios [39].

In data-scarce domains, few-shot learning and transfer learning are becoming essential. These methods allow models to generalize from limited labeled examples, which is particularly useful in specialized fields, such as personalized medicine, rare disease detection, and natural language understanding in low-resource languages [40]. Federated learning is also gaining ground as a privacy-preserving approach that enables decentralized training without exposing raw user data. However, it introduces new challenges such as data heterogeneity, communication bottlenecks, and susceptibility to adversarial attacks making it a rich area for ongoing research [41]. As sustainability becomes an urgent priority, Green AI has emerged as a movement focused on reducing the environmental impact of AI development. Current efforts involve minimizing parameter counts, applying neural architecture search (NAS) for energy-efficient model design, and implementing carbon-tracking frameworks during model training and deployment [42].

Another promising advancement is Graph Neural Networks (GNNs), which model data with inherent relational structures, such as social networks, molecular compounds, transportation grids, and financial transaction graphs. Unlike traditional CNNs or RNNs that operate on grid-structured data, GNNs allow for relational reasoning and can infer complex dependencies in graph-based domains. These models show great potential for decision-making tasks involving community detection, drug discovery, fraud detection, and recommendation systems, marking a significant expansion in the ANN paradigm [43]. Looking forward, the integration of ANNs with emerging technologies such as quantum computing, biologically inspired intelligence, and explainable AI systems could reshape the boundaries of artificial intelligence. However, these advances must be guided by principles of fairness, transparency, and human-centered design. Future research must therefore prioritize not only performance and scalability but also ethical alignment with societal values.

8. Conclusion

ANNs have transformed decision-making based on data by allowing machines to learn from complicated, changing data in a manner more effective than conventional computational algorithms. This chapter has detailed how building-block models such as MLPs, CNNs, LSTMs, and attention networks enable smart systems across industries such as manufacturing, healthcare, finance, cybersecurity, and autonomous mobility. Through the fusion of theoretical power and deployment strategies, we show that ANNs are not only theoretically powerful but also industrially revolutionary. Real-world applications further validate their worth. Such as how Siemens cut equipment downtime, DeepMind enabled supercharged diagnostic capabilities, JPMorgan optimized fraud detection effectiveness, and Tesla took real-time AI in autonomous driving to unprecedented levels. These use cases illustrate that systems based on ANNs are no longer a vision but reality across mission-critical areas. Despite this, problems remain. Deep models' black-box character is a source of concern regarding interpretability and accountability, particularly in high-stakes contexts. Data bias can cascade into systemic bias. Computational costs are high and exacerbate environmental degradation. Privacy issues make data sharing difficult. Solving these problems necessitates interdisciplinarity across AI research, ethics, law, and policy. In the future, research should emphasize the development of light, energy-efficient, and interpretable models that are suitable for edge devices and privacy-driven ecosystems. Advances in neuromorphic computing, few-shot learning, and federated systems are set to define the next wave of smart technologies. Finally, for ANNs to continue being useful, deployment has to be human-centered, ethically sound, and sustainable. They can only then fully be capitalized on to bring about equal societal benefit and environmentally friendly industrial innovation.

Author details

Niyas Ahamed Sirajudeen[1]*, C.S. Sree Thayanandeswari[2]* and Abdul Malik Maheen[1]*

1 Independent Researcher, Tamil Nadu, India

2 PET Engineering College, Tamil Nadu, India

*Address all correspondence to: niyas.ece@gmail.com; sreethaya.cs@gmail.com; am03malik03@gmail.com

References

[1] Taye MM. Understanding of machine learning with deep learning: Architectures, workflow, applications and future directions. Computers. 2023; **12**(5):91

[2] Chava K, Saradhi KS. Emerging applications of generative AI and deep neural networks in modern pharmaceutical supply chains: A focus on automated insights and decision-making. South Eastern European Journal of Public Health. 2024;**XXII**:20-45. DOI: 10.70135/seejph.vi.4441

[3] Bishop CM, Bishop H. Deep Learning: Foundations and Concepts. Switzerland: Springer Nature; 2023

[4] Nanda N, Lee A, Wattenberg M. Emergent linear representations in world models of self-supervised sequence models. Association for Computational Linguistics. 2023. pp. 16-30. arXiv preprint arXiv:2309.00941

[5] Plathottam SJ, Rzonca A, Lakhnori R, Iloeje CO. A review of artificial intelligence applications in manufacturing operations. Journal of Advanced Manufacturing and Processing. 2023;**5**(3):e10159

[6] Tudisco A, Volpe D, Ranieri G, Curato G, Ricossa D, Graziano M, et al. Evaluating the computational advantages of the variational quantum circuit model in financial fraud detection. IEEE Access. 2024;**12**: 102918-102940

[7] Atasever S, Azginoglu N, Terzi DS, Terzi R. A comprehensive survey of deep learning research on medical image analysis with focus on transfer learning. Clinical Imaging. 2023;**94**:18-41

[8] Ahmad T, Katari P, Pamidi Venkata AK, Ravi C, Shaik M. Explainable AI: Interpreting deep learning models for decision support. Advances in Deep Learning Techniques. 2024;**4**(1):80-108

[9] He K, Zhang X, Ren S, Sun J. Delving deep into rectifiers: Surpassing human-level performance on ImageNet classification. 2023. pp. 1026-1032. arXiv. 2015; 1502.01852. View Article

[10] Jang R. Learning representations by forward-propagating errors. 2023. pp. 1-5. arXiv preprint arXiv:2308.09728

[11] Ernst D, Louette A. In: Feuerriegel S, Hartmann J, Janiesch C, Zschech P, editors. Introduction to Reinforcement Learning. 2024. pp. 111-126

[12] Patra B, Ranjan R, Debnath S. A comprehensive review of convolutional neural networks for defect detection in industrial applications. Journal of Industrial Automation. 2023;**34**(2):56-68

[13] Tayal A, Gupta J, Solanki A, Bisht K, Nayyar A, Masud M. DL-CNN-based approach with image processing techniques for diagnosis of retinal diseases. Multimedia Systems. 2022;**28** (4):1417-1438. Available from: https://link.springer.com/article/10.1007/s00530-021-00769-7

[14] Kong Y, Wang Z, Nie Y, Zhou T, Zohren S, Liang Y. Unlocking the power of LSTM for long term time series forecasting. In: Proceedings of the AAAI Conference on Artificial Intelligence. Vol. 39, No. 11. Apr 2025. pp. 11968-11976

[15] Xu Y, Wang H. Extreme event adaptive GRU for hybrid time-series forecasting. Nature Scientific Reports. 2024;**14**:13472

[16] Geethanjali R, Valarmathi A. A novel hybrid deep learning IChOA-CNN-LSTM model for modality-enriched and

multilingual emotion recognition in social media. Scientific Reports. 2024;**14**(1):22270. Available from: https://www.nature.com/articles/s41598-024-73452-2

[17] Sakib S, Mahadi MK, Abir SR, Moon AM, Shafiullah A, Ali S. Attention-based models for multivariate time series forecasting: Multi-step solar irradiation prediction. Heliyon. 2024;**10**(6). Available from: https://www.cell.com/heliyon/fulltext/S2405-8440(24)03826-X

[18] Mnih V, Kavukcuoglu K, Silver D. Human-level control through deep reinforcement learning. Nature. 2015;**518**(7540):529-533

[19] Igl M, Ciosek K, Li Y, Tschiatschek S, Zhang C, Devlin S. Generalization in reinforcement learning with selective noise injection and information bottleneck. Advances in Neural Information Processing Systems. 2019;**32**. Available from: https://proceedings.neurips.cc/paper_files/paper/2019/hash/e2ccf95a7f2e1878fcafc8376649b6e8-Abstract.html

[20] Jia Z, Wang M, Zhao S. A review of deep learning-based approaches for defect detection in smart manufacturing. Journal of Optics. 2024;**53**(2):1345-1351

[21] Zheng S, Li S, Wang Y. A novel BDPCA-SMLSTM algorithm for fault diagnosis of industrial process. Chemical Engineering Science. 2025;**305**:121172

[22] Javaid A, Niyaz Q, Sun W, Alam M. Deep learning vs. machine learning for intrusion detection. Applied Sciences. 2023;**15**(4):1903

[23] Nawaz K, Zanib A, Shabir I, Li J, Wang Y, Mahmood T, et al. Skin cancer detection using dermoscopic images with convolutional neural network. Scientific Reports. 2025;**15**(1):7252

[24] Hama T, Alsaleh MM, Allery F, Choi JW, Tomlinson C, Wu H. Enhancing patient outcome prediction through deep learning with sequential diagnosis codes from structured electronic health record data: Systematic review. Journal of Medical Internet Research. 2025;**27**:e57358. Available from: https://www.jmir.org/2025/1/e57358/

[25] Nama FA, Obaid AJ. Financial fraud identification using deep learning techniques. Al-Salam Journal for Engineering and Technology. 2024;**3**(1):141-147. Available from: http://journal.alsalam.edu.iq/index.php/ajest/article/view/195

[26] Mohan R, Roselyn JP, Uthra RA. LSTM based artificial intelligence predictive maintenance technique for availability rate and OEE improvement in a TPM implementing plant through industry 4.0 transformation. Journal of Quality in Maintenance Engineering. 2023;**29**(4):763-798

[27] Pagano D. A predictive maintenance model using long short-term memory neural networks and Bayesian inference. Decision Analytics Journal. 2023;**6**:100174

[28] De Fauw J, Ledsam JR, Romera-Paredes B, Nikolov S, Tomasev N, Blackwell S, et al. Clinically applicable deep learning for diagnosis and referral in retinal disease. Nature Medicine. 2018;**24**(9):1342-1350

[29] Chia MA, Antaki F, Zhou Y, Turner AW, Lee AY, Keane PA. Foundation models in ophthalmology. British Journal of Ophthalmology. 2024;**108**(10):1341-1348

[30] Vallarino D. Detecting financial fraud with hybrid deep learning: A mix-of-experts approach to sequential and anomalous patterns. arXiv. 2025. arXiv preprint arXiv:2504.03750

[31] Singh MT, Prasad RK, Michael GR, Kaphungkui NK, Singh NH. Heterogeneous graph auto-encoder for CreditCard fraud detection. 2024. pp. 1-27. arXiv preprint arXiv: 2410.08121

[32] Tesla AI Team. Tesla AI Day 2021–2022 [Online]. Available from: https://www.tesla.com/AI

[33] Lundberg SM, Lee S-I. A unified approach to interpreting model predictions. Advances in Neural Information Processing Systems (NeurIPS). 2017;**30**:4765-4774

[34] Ribeiro MT, Singh S, Guestrin C. Why should I trust you? Explaining the predictions of any classifier. In: Proceedings of the 22nd ACM SIGKDD International Conference on Knowledge Discovery and Data Mining (KDD). 2016. pp. 1135-1144

[35] Obermeyer Z, Powers B, Vogeli C, Mullainathan S. Dissecting racial bias in an algorithm used to manage the health of populations. Science. 2019;**366**(6464): 447-453

[36] Hurley M, Adebayo J. Credit scoring in the era of big data. Yale Journal of Law and Technology. 2016;**18**(1):148-216

[37] Angwin J, Larson J, Mattu S, Kirchner L. Machine bias: There's software used across the country to predict future criminals. And it's biased against blacks. ProPublica. May 23, 2016. Available at: https://www.propublica.org/article/machine-bias-risk-assessments-in-criminal-sentencing

[38] Han S, Mao H, Dally WJ. Deep compression: Compressing deep neural networks with pruning, trained quantization and Huffman coding. 2015. pp. 1-14. arXiv preprint arXiv: 1510.00149

[39] Davies M, Srinivasa N, Lin TH, Chinya G, Cao Y, Choday SH, et al. Loihi: A neuromorphic manycore processor with on-chip learning. IEEE Micro. 2018;**38**(1):82-99

[40] Wang Y, Yao Q, Kwok JT, Ni LM. Generalizing from a few examples: A survey on few-shot learning. ACM Computing Surveys (CSUR). 2020; **53**(3):1-34

[41] Yang Q, Liu Y, Chen T, Tong Y. Federated machine learning: Concept and applications. ACM Transactions on Intelligent Systems and Technology (TIST). 2019;**10**(2):1-19

[42] Strubell E, Ganesh A, McCallum A. Energy and policy considerations for modern deep learning research. In: Proceedings of the AAAI Conference on Artificial Intelligence, February 7-12, 2020. Vol. 34. No. 9. New York Hilton Midtown, New York, USA; 2020. pp. 13693-13696

[43] Wu Z, Pan S, Chen F, Long G, Zhang C, Yu PS. A comprehensive survey on graph neural networks. IEEE Transactions on Neural Networks and Learning Systems. 2020;**32**(1):4-24

Chapter 2

Training and Inference Time Dynamics of Artificial Neural Networks

Shreyas Subramanian

Abstract

This chapter examines the computational mechanics underlying artificial neural network training and inference, analyzing the fundamental algorithms, optimization strategies, and resource allocation patterns that govern these two distinct phases of neural network operation. We explore the evolution from basic stochastic gradient descent to modern optimizers like AdamW, investigating how hyperparameters such as learning rates, batch sizes, and scheduling strategies influence convergence behavior and computational efficiency. The discussion covers the transition from training's memory-intensive backpropagation requiring simultaneous storage of activations and gradients to inference's streamlined forward-pass computation, highlighting how this shift fundamentally alters optimization objectives from loss minimization to throughput and latency optimization. We analyze the unique challenges posed by large language models, where autoregressive generation transforms inference from fixed-cost operations into iterative, variable-cost processes that scale with output length and introduce complex memory bandwidth constraints through attention mechanisms and key-value caching. The chapter investigates scaling laws governing both training and inference phases, revealing how optimal resource allocation strategies differ dramatically between these phases, with inference time compute often favoring smaller models combined with sophisticated generation strategies over simply scaling model parameters. Through comprehensive analysis of distributed training dynamics, hardware acceleration patterns, and inference optimization techniques, we demonstrate how understanding the computational trade-offs between training and inference phases proves essential for practitioners navigating the complex landscape of modern neural network deployment, where inference costs frequently dominate the total computational budget over a model's operational lifetime.

Keywords: training, inference, hyperparameters, scheduling, scaling laws, inference time compute

1. Introduction

The lifecycle of artificial neural networks unfolds across two fundamentally distinct phases, each presenting unique challenges in resource allocation, algorithmic design, and performance optimization. Training and inference represent opposing computational paradigms: while training demands extensive computational resources to iteratively adjust ("learn") billions of parameters through gradient-based optimization, inference requires rapid, efficient execution of the learned model to produce predictions reliably in production environments.

The computational dynamics governing these phases have evolved dramatically with the emergence of large-scale models, where training costs can reach millions of dollars and inference must serve billions of requests daily. This has lead to innovations around specialized hardware architectures, advances in training and inference algorithms, and inference-specific accelerators emphasizing throughput and energy efficiency. Understanding the intricate interplay between training and inference dynamics proves essential for practitioners navigating the complex landscape of model development, deployment, and maintenance. The exponential growth in model sizes—from millions to potentially trillions of parameters—has fundamentally altered the computational calculus, necessitating novel approaches to distributed computing, memory management, and algorithmic efficiency that transcend traditional boundaries between these phases.

This chapter provides a comprehensive examination of these computational phases, beginning with the fundamental mechanics of backpropagation that underpin neural network training. We explore how modern frameworks like PyTorch have abstracted away low-level implementation details while exposing powerful primitives for distributed computation and automatic differentiation. The discussion progresses through the critical hyperparameters that govern learning dynamics—from learning rate schedules to batch size selection—and their profound impact on convergence behavior and computational efficiency.

We then delve into the transformative realm of distributed training, where data and model parallelism strategies enable the training of models that exceed the memory capacity of individual accelerators. The emergence of scaling laws has provided principled approaches to resource allocation, revealing precise relationships between model size, dataset size, and computational budget that guide the development of foundation models. These massive architectures, trained on unprecedented scales of data and compute, exhibit emergent capabilities that have redefined the boundaries of machine learning applications.

The transition from training to inference marks a fundamental shift in optimization objectives: from minimizing loss functions to maximizing throughput and minimizing latency under strict resource constraints. We examine the arsenal of techniques—quantization, pruning, and knowledge distillation—that compress models by orders of magnitude while preserving their predictive capabilities. The chapter concludes with emerging paradigms in inference-time compute, where adaptive processing and test-time optimization blur the traditional boundaries between training and deployment, pointing toward a future where models continuously adapt to their computational environment and task requirements.

2. Revisiting the basics of training

Today, we frequently mention models that contain Billions of parameters (like the Llama 405B parameter model). To set the context, lets consider a simple three-layer linear network (x is the input, and $\hat{y}$ is the output):

$$x \rightarrow W_1 \rightarrow h_1 \rightarrow W_2 \rightarrow h_2 \rightarrow W_3 \rightarrow \hat{y}$$

where each layer performs $h_i = W_i h_{i-1}$ (with $h_0 = x$). During the forward pass, we compute

- $h_1 = W_1 x$,
- $h_2 = W_2 h_1$, and
- $\hat{y} = W_3 h_2$, storing each intermediate activation.

The backward pass then computes gradients:

- $\partial L/\partial W_3 = \partial L/\partial \hat{y} \cdot h_2^T$,
- $\partial L/\partial W_2 = (W_3^T \partial L/\partial \hat{y}) \cdot h_1^T$, and
- $\partial L/\partial W_1 = (W_2^T W_3^T \partial L/\partial \hat{y}) \cdot x^T$.

Each weight update $W_i \leftarrow W_i - \eta \partial L/\partial W_i$ requires both the gradient flowing backward and the activation flowing forward from the previous layer, demonstrating why both must be simultaneously available in memory.

The backpropagation algorithm represents one of the most computationally intensive operations in modern machine learning, requiring careful orchestration of memory allocation and computation scheduling. During the forward pass, neural networks compute activations layer by layer, with each layer's output serving as input to the next. These intermediate activations must be stored in memory because they are essential for gradient computation during the backward pass. For a network with L layers and hidden dimensions of size d, the memory requirement grows as $O(L \times d \times \text{batch\_size})$, creating substantial memory pressure that scales directly with model depth and batch size.

The backward pass transforms this stored computation into gradient information through systematic application of the chain rule. Starting from the loss function, gradients flow backward through each layer, requiring access to the corresponding forward pass activations to compute parameter gradients correctly. This creates a fundamental dependency: the memory footprint of training is determined not just by model parameters (which can be large for billion-parameter models), but by the intermediate activations that must be maintained throughout the forward pass until their corresponding backward computations complete.

The computational complexity of each training iteration scales as O(parameters + activations), where the activation term often dominates memory usage while the parameter term dominates computation time. Modern transformer architectures exemplify this challenge, where attention mechanisms create activation tensors that grow quadratically with sequence length, and deep networks require storing activations across dozens of layers. This dual pressure on both computation and memory has driven the development of sophisticated scheduling algorithms that decide when to compute, store, or recompute activations to balance memory constraints against computational overhead.

2.1 Stochastic gradient descent and learning rate dynamics

Once gradients have been computed through backpropagation, the fundamental question becomes how to use this information to update the model parameters effectively. Stochastic Gradient Descent (SGD) provides the algorithmic foundation for this process, but its apparent simplicity—updating parameters in the direction opposite to the gradient—masks profound complexities that determine whether training converges to useful solutions or fails entirely.

The basic SGD update rule:

$$W_i \leftarrow W_i - \eta \frac{\delta L}{\delta W_i} \tag{1}$$

introduces the learning rate η as perhaps the most critical hyperparameter in neural network training. This scalar value controls the magnitude of parameter updates and fundamentally shapes the trajectory of optimization through the high-dimensional loss landscape. Too large a learning rate causes the optimizer to overshoot optimal regions, potentially leading to divergent behavior where loss values oscillate wildly or grow without bound. Too small a learning rate results in painfully slow convergence, where the model may require thousands of additional iterations to reach the same level of performance, dramatically increasing computational costs.

The "stochastic" nature of SGD emerges from its use of mini-batches—small subsets of the training data—to compute gradient estimates rather than exact gradients over the entire dataset. This introduces noise into the gradient estimates, but this noise often proves beneficial for escaping local minima and finding flatter, more generalizable solutions. The batch size directly influences this gradient noise: larger batches provide more accurate gradient estimates but reduce the stochastic exploration that helps optimization, while smaller batches increase noise at the cost of computational efficiency and convergence stability.

Let us look at the pseudo code of SGD with momentum to dive deeper (this is based on the official PyTorch implementation that can be found here - https://docs.pytorch.org/docs/stable/generated/torch.optim.SGD.html):

```
Input: parameters θ, learning rate η, momentum μ, weight decay λ
Initialize: momentum buffers b_i = 0 for all parameters
For each training step:
  For each parameter θ_i with gradient g_i:
    // Add weight decay directly to gradient
    g_i ← g_i + λ · θ_i
    // Update momentum buffer and use as effective gradient
    if first step:
      b_i ← g_i
    else:
      b_i ← μ · b_i + g_i
    // Parameter update using momentum buffer
    θ_i ← θ_i - η · b_i
Return: updated parameters θ
```

The SGD algorithm with momentum operates by maintaining velocity buffers that accumulate gradient information across training iterations, providing inertia that helps optimization navigate through the loss landscape more effectively. At each step, the algorithm first incorporates L2 regularization by adding the weight decay term directly to the computed gradients, encouraging smaller parameter values to prevent overfitting. The momentum mechanism then updates exponentially-weighted moving averages of gradients in the momentum buffers, where the momentum coefficient μ controls how much historical gradient information is retained—higher values create stronger inertia that can help the optimizer barrel through small local minima and oscillations. On the first iteration, the momentum buffer is simply initialized to the current gradient, but in subsequent steps it combines the previous momentum (scaled by μ) with the current gradient. Finally, parameters are updated using these momentum buffers rather than raw gradients, creating smoother optimization trajectories that tend to accelerate in consistent directions while dampening oscillations in directions where gradients frequently change sign.

`From the above pseudocode we can see that the successive iterates, starting from θ_0 should ideally progress toward the solution, or "converge". However, this completely depends on the loss landscape. Take the following example from [1] which shows a 3D visualization of the SGD dynamics. In a non-convex loss landscape. The green dotted line shows the general direction in which the iterates are progressing, but the blue points are the actual iterates. Given that we cannot calculate the *actual* gradients, the noise estimates of gradients lead the successive iterates to bounce around erratically.

When multiple parameters are being updated according to Eq. (1), each parameter follows a different trajectory. We can visualize these changes for simple networks; int eh example below, when training a 2 layer ReLU network without biases, weight updates with small learning rates tend to stay close to their randomly initialized values (orange dots), but tend to move toward ideal weight vectors (gray dots moving closer to the red lines).

Here is another view of the progress these iterates make from [2]. The authors highlight how a network trained using SGD resulting in different weights that are close to each other may generalize very differently in terms of performance with unseen data. While all the blue dots represent optima that achieve near-perfect train accuracy, the test accuracy for all these points range from 37 to 53%. SGD avoids these bad minima in this specific case, and reaches a final optimum (yellow star) that achieves high train and test accuracy.

2.2 Improvements over SGD: Adam and AdamW

While SGD forms the foundation, several other optimization algorithms for training models have been developed. A full list of other algorithms can be found on the PyTorch documentation page [3].

Loshchilov and Hutter [4] developed what is now one of the most popular algorithms used for training—AdamW. AdamW represents a significant evolution from SGD, addressing several fundamental limitations while introducing adaptive learning rates that adjust independently for each parameter. The development of AdamW stems from a critical insight by Loshchilov and Hutter: the widespread confusion between L2 regularization and weight decay in adaptive gradient methods like Adam was severely hampering their generalization performance.

To understand AdamW's innovations, we must first examine the Adam algorithm that preceded it. Adam (Adaptive Moment Estimation) introduced two key improvements over SGD: it maintains exponentially decaying averages of both past gradients (first moment) and their squared values (second moment), using these statistics to adapt the learning rate for each parameter individually. This adaptive mechanism allows parameters with historically large gradients to receive smaller updates, while parameters with consistently small gradients receive larger updates—a form of automatic learning rate tuning that can dramatically improve convergence in practice.

However, Adam's original formulation suffered from a subtle but critical flaw in how it handled regularization. The standard implementation applied L2 regularization by adding the weight decay term $\lambda\theta$ directly to the gradient before computing the adaptive updates. This approach works perfectly for SGD due to a mathematical equivalence between L2 regularization and weight decay, but this equivalence breaks down catastrophically for adaptive gradient methods.

The core issue lies in how Adam's adaptive mechanism interacts with regularization. When L2 regularization is applied to Adam, the regularization term gets mixed with the actual loss gradients before being processed by the adaptive scaling mechanism. This means that parameters with large historical gradients—which should arguably be regularized more aggressively—actually receive less regularization because their updates (including the regularization component) get scaled down by Adam's adaptive denominator. Conversely, parameters with small historical gradients receive disproportionately large regularization effects. This creates an inconsistent and suboptimal regularization pattern that undermines the model's ability to generalize.

AdamW solves this problem through a deceptively simple but profound modification: it decouples weight decay from the gradient-based updates entirely. Instead of adding the weight decay term to the gradient before adaptive scaling, AdamW applies weight decay directly to the parameters after the adaptive gradient update has been computed. This separation ensures that all parameters receive consistent regularization proportional to their magnitudes, regardless of their gradient histories.

Let us examine the AdamW algorithm in detail to see exactly where it differs from both SGD and standard Adam:

```
Input: parameters θ, learning rate η, momentum coefficients β₁, β₂,
weight decay λ, epsilon ε
Initialize: moment estimates m₀ = 0, v₀ = 0, time step t = 0

For each training step:
  t ← t + 1

For each parameter θᵢ with gradient gᵢ:
  // First moment (momentum) update
  m_{t,i} ← β₁ · m_{t-1,i} + (1 - β₁) · gᵢ

  // Second moment (variance) update
  v_{t,i} ← β₂ · v_{t-1,i} + (1 - β₂) · gᵢ²

  // Bias correction for moments
  m̂_{t,i} ← m_{t,i} / (1 - β₁ᵗ)
  v̂_{t,i} ← v_{t,i} / (1 - β₂ᵗ)

  // AdamW's key innovation: decoupled weight decay
  θᵢ ← θᵢ - η · (m̂_{t,i} / (√v̂_{t,i} + ε) + λ · θᵢ)

Return: updated parameters θ
```

The critical difference between AdamW and both SGD and standard Adam lies in the final parameter update line. In SGD with momentum, we saw that weight decay was added to the gradient before momentum accumulation. In standard Adam, weight decay would be added to the gradient before adaptive moment estimation. But in AdamW, the weight decay term $\lambda \cdot \theta_i$ is added directly to the final parameter update, completely separate from the adaptive gradient computation.

This architectural change has profound implications for optimization dynamics. The adaptive gradient component $\left(\hat{m}_{t,i}/\left(\sqrt{\hat{v}_{t,i}} + \varepsilon\right)\right)$ handles the direction and magnitude of updates based on loss gradients, while the weight decay component $(\lambda \cdot \theta_i)$ provides consistent regularization across all parameters. Parameters with large magnitudes receive proportionally larger decay regardless of their gradient behavior, creating a more principled and effective regularization scheme.

AdamW's superior performance stems from this combination of adaptive per-parameter learning rates and proper weight decay decoupling. AdamW makes the hyperparameter optimization process significantly more manageable by decoupling the learning rate and weight decay parameters—practitioners can tune these hyperparameters independently rather than dealing with the complex interdependencies that plague other methods. This makes AdamW particularly effective for training large neural networks where different parameters may have vastly different scales and gradient behaviors, and where generalization performance is critical for practical applications.

These algorithms are being continuously improved as shown in the figure below, and developed in open source frameworks like PyTorch, but the fundamentals are still largely based on SGD that we covered previously. While data for 2021–2024 is not available in any source, we can see through manual search that the mentions of these optimizers have proportionately continued to increase until today.

2.3 Importance of schedulers

In the previous sections we explore details of the SGD and AdamW algorithms for training. In both these algorithms, the last line is the update to the parameters θ, using a fixed learning rate η. Modern practitioners rarely use fixed learning rates throughout training. Learning rate schedules have become essential tools for achieving optimal performance, typically starting with higher values to make rapid initial progress and gradually decreasing to enable fine-grained convergence. Common scheduling strategies include step decay (reducing the learning rate by a fixed factor at predetermined intervals), exponential decay (continuously decreasing according to an exponential function), and cosine annealing (following a cosine curve that naturally provides warm restarts). State-of-the-art models being developed by large corporations still use AdamW optimizer with a basic cosine scheduler. For example, the Meta Llama 3 technical report [5] mentions the following about their experimental set up—"We pre-train Llama 3405B using **AdamW** with a peak learning rate of 8×10^{-5}, a linear warm up of 8000 steps, and a cosine learning rate schedule decaying to 8×10^{-7} over 1,200,000 steps." A visual representation of some schedulers that are commonly used today are shown in the figure below:

The choice of schedule can dramatically impact final model performance, with some models requiring thousands of additional training steps to recover from suboptimal scheduling decisions. Therefore, it is important to experiment as no scheduler is proven to work well for all kinds of problems and datasets. Let us take a look at the figure below comparing different learning rate schedules (constant, cosine, cosine with warm restarts, and trapezoidal) across varying computational budgets (one-shot, small, medium, and large budget) and their relative performance improvements over baseline one-shot tuning without scheduling. In this work from

Schmidt et al. [6], the experimental setup was remarkably comprehensive, testing 53,760 unique training runs across a 4-dimensional matrix of 8 problems, 15 optimizers, 4 tuning budgets, and 4 learning rate schedules. The problems ranged from simple quadratic optimization to complex tasks like VAEs, CNNs, and RNNs, providing good coverage of deep learning applications. Regarding learning rate schedulers specifically, the results revealed several key insights. Schedules provided meaningful improvements, with the best combination (large budget + trapezoidal schedule) achieving about 5.2% median improvement over defaults. However, these gains were incremental rather than transformative. The most striking finding was the enormous variability in schedule effectiveness across different optimizer-problem combinations. While schedules helped on average, individual cases showed wildly different responses - some benefited substantially while others saw minimal or even negative effects. This can be seen in the main results below:

The figure demonstrates that while increased budgets and proper scheduling generally lead to performance improvements on average (shown by the orange median line), the benefits are not guaranteed for individual cases, as evidenced by the wide spread of gray lines representing different optimizer-problem combinations. Some configurations show substantial gains while others remain unaffected or even decrease in performance, highlighting the importance of empirical testing across different scheduling approaches.

The interaction between learning rate and batch size reveals deeper principles about optimization dynamics. Larger batch sizes typically require proportionally larger learning rates to maintain the same convergence speed, following heuristics like linear scaling (doubling the batch size doubles the learning rate) or square root scaling. However, these relationships break down at extreme scales, where very large batch sizes can lead to poor generalization even with carefully tuned learning rates—a phenomenon that has driven extensive research into understanding the generalization properties of different batch size regimes.

The learning rate's influence extends beyond simple convergence speed to affect the fundamental nature of the solutions discovered during training. High learning rates tend to find flatter minima in the loss landscape—regions where small perturbations to parameters cause minimal changes in loss. These flatter solutions often generalize better to unseen data, suggesting that the learning rate acts as an implicit regularizer that influences not just training efficiency but also model quality. This connection between optimization dynamics and generalization has profound implications for hyperparameter selection and has motivated the development of adaptive learning rate methods that automatically adjust based on local loss landscape properties.

Understanding learning rate dynamics becomes even more critical in the context of today's large-scale models, where the computational cost of hyperparameter search becomes prohibitive. A single training run for a large transformer model might consume thousands of GPU-hours, making extensive learning rate tuning experiments impractical. This has driven the development of learning rate range tests and other diagnostic tools that can predict optimal learning rates from short preliminary runs, as well as adaptive methods that automatically adjust learning rates during training based on observed optimization progress. Practitioners should treat schedule selection as part of the broader optimizer selection process rather than as a universal enhancement. Testing multiple schedule-optimizer combinations during training with modest computational budgets often outperformed intensive tuning of any single approach.

2.4 Advanced training considerations: Beyond core algorithms

While the fundamental algorithms of SGD and AdamW form the backbone of neural network training, the computational mechanics of modern large-scale training involve several critical considerations mentioned below, that extend beyond our current scope but warrant some coverage here for completeness.

- *Gradient clipping and numerical stability*: As models scale to billions of parameters, gradient magnitudes can become unstable, leading to explosive growth that destroys training progress. Gradient clipping—limiting gradient norms to a maximum threshold—has become standard practice, particularly for transformer architectures. This technique directly affects the training dynamics we have discussed, as it modifies the effective learning rate on a per-step basis and interacts complexly with learning rate schedules and optimizer momentum.

- *Mixed precision training and memory optimization*: Modern training increasingly relies on mixed precision techniques, where different numerical precisions (float16, bfloat16, float32) are used strategically throughout the training process. This approach can nearly double training throughput while maintaining model quality, but introduces subtle dynamics in gradient computation and parameter updates that modify the optimization behavior described in our SGD and AdamW analysis.

- *Distributed training and scaling dynamics*: The computational demands of large-scale models necessitate distributed training across multiple accelerators, introducing complexities in gradient synchronization, communication overhead, and load balancing that fundamentally alter the training dynamics. Data parallelism, model parallelism, and pipeline parallelism each create different computational patterns that influence both training efficiency and the characteristics of the resulting models.

- *Checkpointing and gradient accumulation*: Large models often exceed available memory even with advanced optimization techniques, requiring sophisticated memory management strategies. Gradient checkpointing trades computation for memory by recomputing intermediate activations during the backward pass rather than storing them, while gradient accumulation simulates larger batch sizes by accumulating gradients across multiple forward passes before updating parameters. These techniques modify the effective training dynamics and can influence the relationship between batch size, learning rate, and convergence behavior.

These advanced considerations, while essential for large-scale training implementations, represent specialized topics that extend beyond the fundamental training dynamics covered in this chapter. Readers working with distributed systems, memory-constrained environments, or extreme-scale models will find these areas worthy of deeper exploration through specialized literature on high-performance computing for machine learning.

The training dynamics explored throughout this section—from gradient computation through parameter updates—represent only the first half of the neural network lifecycle. Once training converges and produces a model with optimized parameters, these billions of learned weights must transition from the iterative optimization environment to the production serving environment. This transition marks a fundamental shift in computational objectives: from loss minimization through gradient-based learning to efficient utilization of fixed parameters for prediction generation. The inference phase we examine next operates under entirely different constraints and performance metrics, requiring a complete reconceptualization of how we approach neural network computation.

3. Inference time dynamics

Our discussion now transitions from the parameter learning phase to the parameter utilization phase, where the computational priorities shift dramatically from iterative optimization to efficient execution. The inference dynamics we will explore next build directly upon the training foundation established here, but operate under fundamentally different constraints and objectives that reshape how we approach neural network computation. The billions of parameters learned through the training algorithms discussed above must now be deployed efficiently to serve predictions at scale —a challenge that requires entirely different computational strategies while preserving the essential knowledge encoded during the training process.

While training requires maintaining both forward activations and backward gradients simultaneously in memory, inference eliminates the entire backward pass, transforming the computational profile from one dominated by memory pressure and gradient synchronization to one focused purely on efficient parameter utilization and activation computation. This transformation has profound implications for system design and optimization strategies. The computational complexity shifts from training's O(parameters + activations + gradients) to inference's O(parameters), but this apparent simplification masks new bottlenecks that emerge at scale. Modern inference workloads must balance competing demands: maximizing throughput for batch processing scenarios while minimizing latency for real-time applications, all while efficiently utilizing the massive parameter sets that define today's state-of-the-art models. Understanding these dynamics becomes critical as models grow from millions to hundreds of billions of parameters, where inference costs can dominate the total computational budget over a model's deployment lifetime.

3.1 Fundamentals of model inference: Using trained models in production

Returning to our simple three-layer network from **Figure 1**, inference computation follows the forward path exclusively: $x \to W_1 \to h_1 \to W_2 \to h_2 \to W_3 \to \hat{y}$. Each layer computes $h_i = W_i h_{i-1}$ sequentially, but unlike training, no intermediate activations need persistent storage beyond their immediate use in the next layer. This elimination of activation storage represents the most dramatic memory reduction from training to inference, where memory requirements drop from $O(L \times d \times batch\_size)$ for storing all layer activations to $O(d \times batch\_size)$ for storing only the current layer's output (**Figures 2-9**).

The computational pattern of inference creates a fundamentally different optimization landscape than training. Where training optimization focuses on gradient computation efficiency and memory management for backpropagation, inference optimization centers around optimizing the ratio of computation to memory access to provide fast, effective inference. Each parameter must be loaded from memory exactly once per inference pass, making parameter access patterns and cache efficiency critical

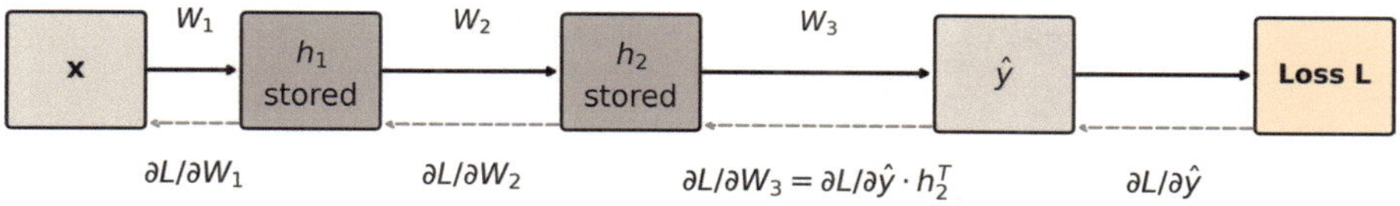

Figure 1.
Forward and backward propagation in a simple neural network.

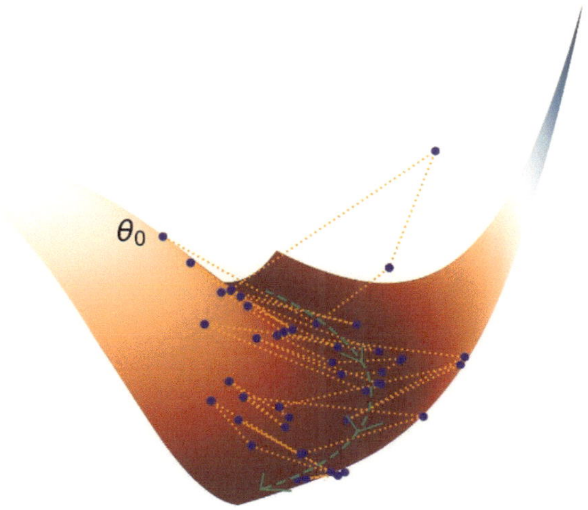

Figure 2.
Sample 3D visualization of SGD dynamics through a smooth non-convex surface.

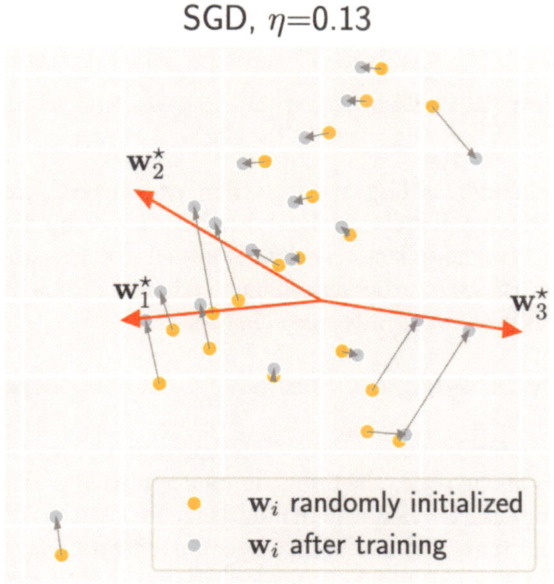

Figure 3.
Multiple parameters being updated using SGD.

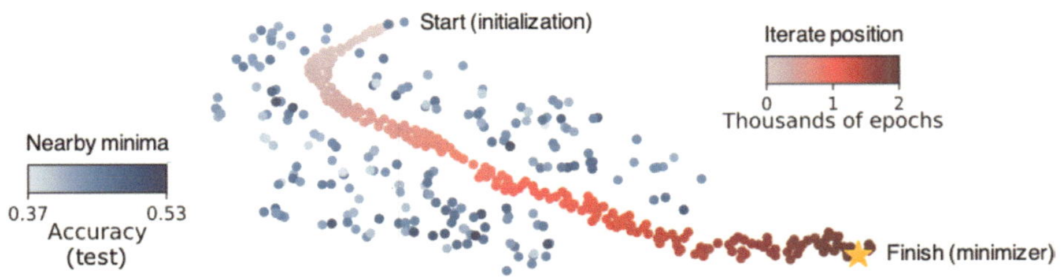

Figure 4.
Parameter updates over thousands of epochs leading to the optimum.

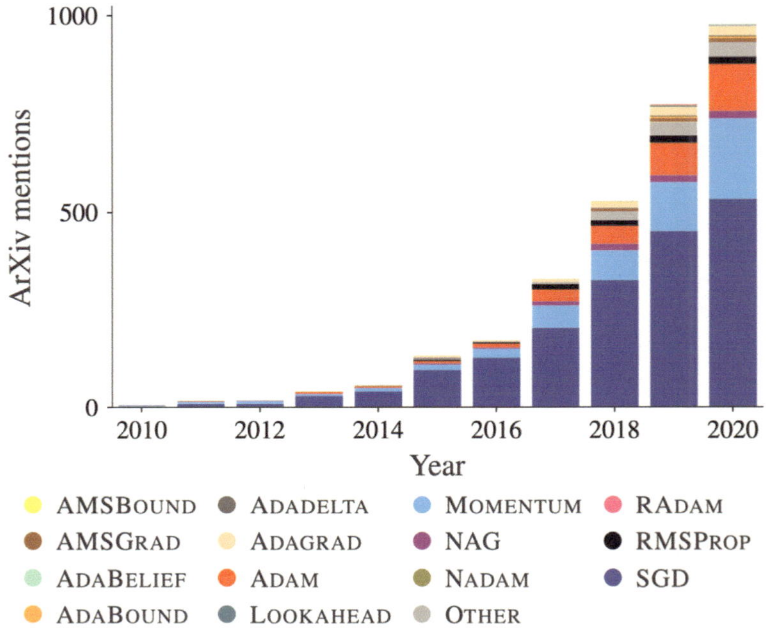

Figure 5.
Various optimizer algorithms used in training from 2010 to 2020 (source: https://icml.cc/media/icml-2021/Slides/8645.pdf).

performance determinants. For large models where parameters exceed cache capacity, inference becomes memory-bandwidth bound rather than compute-bound, fundamentally altering the performance characteristics compared to training's compute-intensive gradient calculations. Of course, the underlying mechanics of this has been largely commoditized via easily available inference engines.

3.1.1 Inference engines: The software infrastructure behind AI applications

Practitioners today rely heavily on these "inference engines" to deploy machine learning models efficiently and at scale. The most common approach is to use inference engines as the core of Inference as a Service, where models are exposed as APIs or microservices, allowing other systems to request predictions over the network. Major cloud providers like AWS, Google Cloud, and Azure have made this process even more accessible by offering managed inference platforms that handle scaling, hardware acceleration, and high availability, letting teams focus on model quality rather than infrastructure.

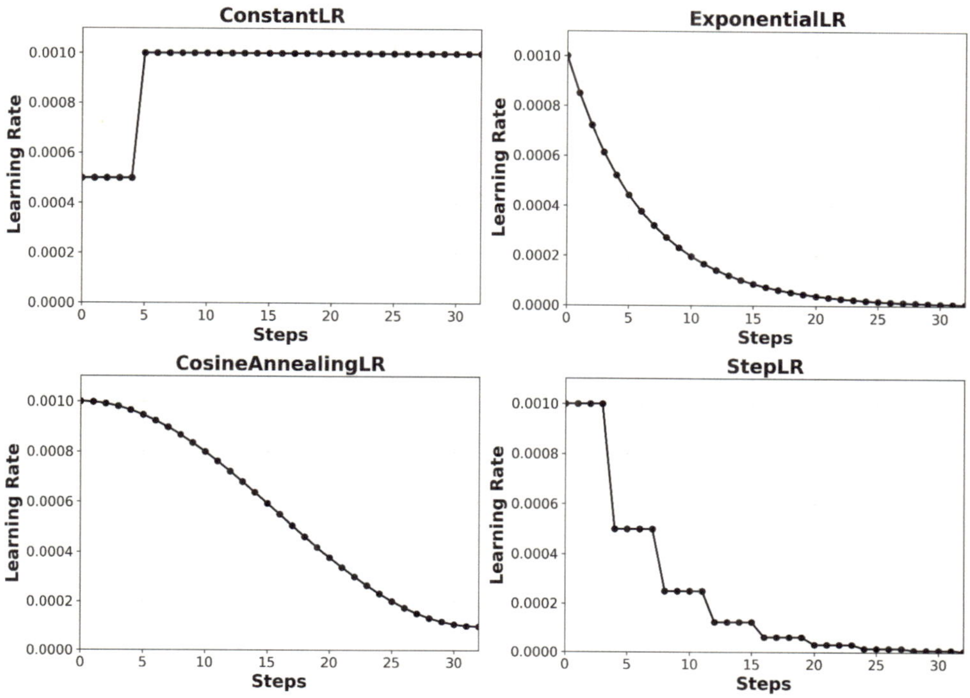

Figure 6.
Commonly used schedulers (source: adapted from https://towardsdatascience.com/a-visual-guide-to-learning-rate-schedulers-in-pytorch-24bbb262c863/).

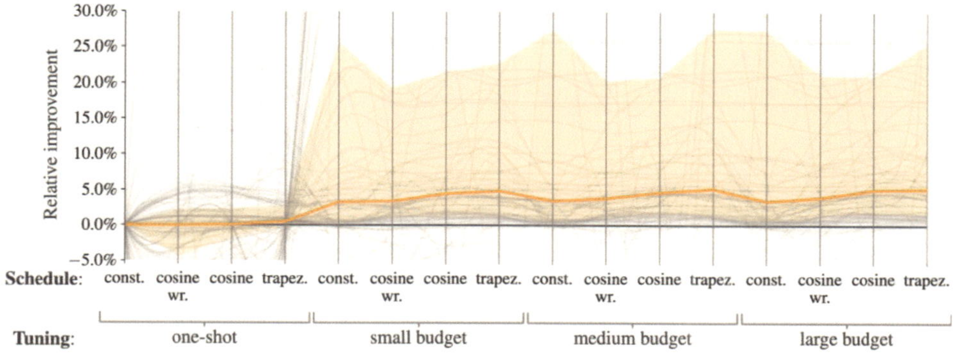

Figure 7.
Relative improvement across different schedulers and tuning budgets.

For applications that require low latency or need to function without constant internet connectivity, practitioners often deploy models directly onto edge devices or embedded systems. This is especially relevant in areas like IoT, augmented reality, or mobile applications, where real-time performance and data privacy are critical. In other scenarios, such as large-scale data processing or analytics, batch inference is preferred, allowing practitioners to process vast amounts of data efficiently and cost-effectively by leveraging hardware resources to their fullest.

Modern inference engines have evolved into sophisticated software stacks. They not only load and execute models but also manage request routing, caching, and resource allocation, often integrating seamlessly with orchestration tools like

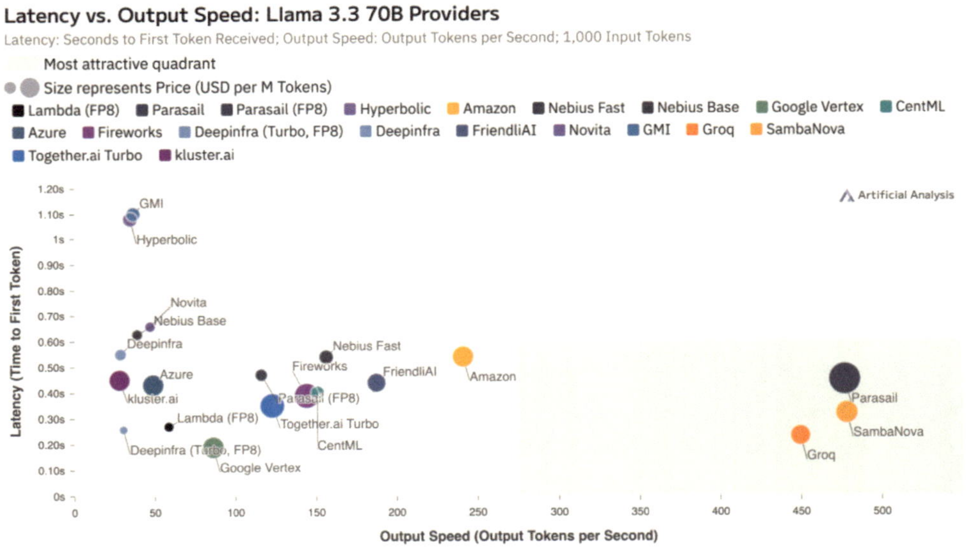

Figure 8.
Latency vs. output speed for the Llama 3.3 70B parameter model across model providers (source: artificialanalysis.com).

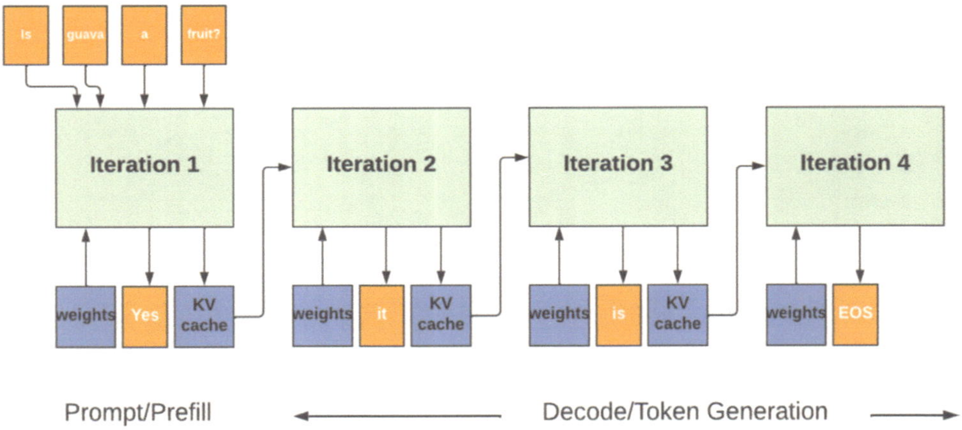

Figure 9.
Iterative inference for LLMs (source: https://community.juniper.net/blogs/sharada-yeluri/2024/02/20/llm-inference-hw-sw-optimizations).

Kubernetes. Practitioners frequently apply post-training optimizations—such as quantization or pruning—to make models faster and more resource-efficient, ensuring smooth operation even on less powerful hardware.

MLOps practices are now integral to model deployment, automating the entire lifecycle from continuous integration and delivery to monitoring and version control. This automation ensures that models remain accurate and reliable as data and requirements evolve, and enables rapid updates or rollbacks with minimal disruption. As the field advances, there is a growing trend toward inference-as-a-service platforms, support for multi-modal and agent-based models, and solutions that prioritize privacy and compliance by enabling on-premises deployments.

3.1.2 Batch processing vs. real-time serving: The throughput-latency trade-off

One of the most fundamental trade-offs in inference system design is to decide whether batch or real-time inference processing is suitable for an application or use case, with each paradigm optimizing for different computational objectives that directly impact hardware utilization and economic efficiency. Batch processing maximizes throughput by amortizing the fixed costs of parameter loading across multiple examples, exploiting the parallelizable nature of matrix operations where W_1X (with X containing a batch of multiple input vectors x) achieves significantly higher arithmetic intensity than individual W_1x computations. The mathematical advantage becomes pronounced for large models: loading a weight matrix W of size $d \times d$ incurs the same memory cost whether computing Wx for a single example or WX for a batch of B examples (up to some limit), but the latter provides B times more computation per memory access.

This throughput optimization comes at the cost of latency, as individual examples must wait for the entire batch to complete processing. Real-time serving prioritizes latency by processing examples immediately upon arrival, accepting lower hardware utilization in exchange for responsiveness. The efficiency gap between these approaches scales with model size: for billion-parameter models, batch processing can achieve 10-100x higher throughput per dollar of compute infrastructure, but individual request latencies may increase by similar factors. This creates a fundamental tension in production systems between serving cost efficiency and user experience requirements.

The batch size selection process involves complex interactions with hardware architecture and model characteristics. Modern GPUs achieve peak efficiency with batch sizes that fully utilize their parallel processing units, typically requiring hundreds to thousands of examples for large models. However, memory constraints limit maximum achievable batch sizes, particularly for models with large intermediate activations like transformers processing long sequences. The optimal batch size often represents a compromise between hardware utilization (favoring larger batches), memory constraints (limiting maximum batch size), and latency requirements (favoring smaller batches), creating a three-way optimization problem that varies significantly across different deployment scenarios. This benchmarking is often resource intensive, but a necessary step to be explored before productionizing any application.

3.1.3 Hardware accelerators: Optimizing silicon for inference workloads

The architectural differences between CPUs, GPUs, and specialized accelerators create dramatically different computational patterns for the same matrix operations that define neural network inference. CPUs excel at sequential processing with sophisticated branch prediction and large caches, making them efficient for small batch sizes where the overhead of parallelization exceeds its benefits. For operations like W_1x with small vectors, CPUs can achieve near-optimal performance through vectorized instructions (AVX-512) and efficient memory hierarchies, but their limited parallel execution units become bottlenecks as batch sizes increase. The CPU's strength lies in its flexibility and low-latency memory access, making it ideal for real-time serving scenarios where single-example inference latency matters more than aggregate throughput. Today, most inference is done on accelerators like GPUs.

GPUs transform the computational dynamics by exposing thousands of parallel cores optimized for the highly parallel matrix operations inherent in neural network inference. The same W_1X operation that might utilize 4–16 CPU cores can simultaneously engage thousands of GPU cores, achieving order-of-magnitude improvements in arithmetic throughput. However, GPUs require substantial parallelism to achieve peak efficiency—the matrix dimensions must be large enough to saturate the available processing units, and memory access patterns must align with the GPU's coalesced memory architecture. This creates a sweet spot for medium to large batch sizes where the parallel nature of inference computation matches the GPU's architectural strengths, but can result in poor utilization for small batches or irregularly shaped computations.

Specialized inference accelerators like Google's TPUs, Intel's Neural Processing Units, and various edge AI chips represent purpose-built solutions that optimize specifically for neural network inference patterns. These accelerators typically feature systolic array architectures that pipeline matrix multiplication operations, achieving higher arithmetic intensity and energy efficiency than general-purpose processors. TPUs, for example, organize computation around 256×256 matrix multiply units that can sustain peak performance on appropriately sized operations, but may underperform on smaller matrices that do not fully utilize the fixed-size processing elements. The key insight is that each architecture class optimizes for different aspects of the inference computation: CPUs for flexibility and low latency, GPUs for high-throughput parallel processing, and specialized accelerators for maximum efficiency on neural network workloads with predictable computational patterns.

Several inference API providers are now working on specialized chips for inference. The image below from artificialanalysis.com shows a comparison of every model provider offering the Llama 3.3 70B parameter model with 128 K context window, comparing the latency vs. output speed (throughput).

As you can tell form the image above, even though the same exact model weights are being used, different providers using different optimizations, inference engines and hardware can yield different results.

3.2 Inference time compute dynamics for large language models (LLMs)

The emergence of large language models has fundamentally transformed inference from the straightforward single-pass computation of traditional neural networks into complex, iterative processes that exhibit computational patterns reminiscent of training dynamics. Unlike the simple pattern of conventional inference, autoregressive language models perform this forward pass repeatedly, using each output token as input for the subsequent generation step. This creates a sequential dependency where the computational cost scales linearly with output length, fundamentally altering the economics of inference from fixed-cost operations to variable-cost processes that depend on generation requirements.

As shown in the figure above, during inference, the model predicts one token at a time in an auto-regressive manner, feeding each new output back as input until a stopping criterion is met. The key components of this process—key, value, and query vectors—enable the attention mechanism to determine which parts of the input sequence are most relevant for generating each output token. The key-value (KV) cache stores intermediate results from previous tokens during inference, enabling the model to efficiently generate subsequent tokens without recalculating attention for the entire sequence. However, as user prompts and model sizes grow, managing the KV cache becomes a major memory bottleneck, requiring careful optimization. The process is computationally intensive, especially given the model's large size and the need for memory to store both parameters and key-value pairs for each user request.

Autoregressive generation, that powers foundation model inference today introduces a unique computational bottleneck where each token generation requires a full forward pass through the entire model, but only produces a single token of output. For a model generating a 1000-token response, this necessitates 1000 separate forward passes, each requiring the full parameter set to be accessed from memory. This pattern creates severe memory bandwidth constraints, as the same billion-parameter model must be loaded repeatedly from memory, often making inference memory-bandwidth bound rather than compute-bound. The iterative nature also prevents the batching optimizations that work well for traditional inference, as each step in the sequence depends on the previous step's output, limiting the parallelization strategies available for throughput optimization.

The attention mechanism compounds these computational challenges by introducing quadratic scaling with sequence length, creating memory and computation patterns that differ dramatically from training. During inference, the attention mechanism must maintain key-value caches for all previously generated tokens, requiring O(sequence_length × hidden_dimension) additional memory per layer that grows with each generated token. This dynamic memory allocation contrasts sharply with training's fixed memory patterns and creates inference scenarios where longer sequences become progressively more expensive in both memory and computation. The combination of autoregressive generation and attention mechanisms transforms inference from a predictable, fixed-cost operation into a complex dynamic process where computational requirements depend on both model architecture and generation characteristics.

Modern LLM inference has thus evolved into a sophisticated resource management problem where traditional inference optimization techniques must be adapted to handle iterative computation patterns, dynamic memory requirements, and sequential dependencies that prevent many standard parallelization approaches. This complexity has driven innovations in inference-specific optimizations like key-value cache optimization, speculative decoding, and dynamic batching strategies and inference time compute scaling that attempt to recover some of the efficiency lost to autoregressive constraints while maintaining the quality of generation that makes these models valuable. Next, let us dive deeper into inference time compute scaling.

3.2.1 Inference time compute dynamics for large language models (LLMs)

The emergence of large language models has fundamentally transformed inference from the straightforward single-pass computation of traditional neural networks into complex, iterative processes that exhibit computational patterns reminiscent of training dynamics. The need to understand and optimize this dynamic execution has been driven by the capabilities and deployment challenges of models across the ecosystem, including general models like GPT-4 and Gemini Flash Thinking, efficiency frameworks like Speculative Decoding utilizing a Draft Model and kNN-LM, and specialized reasoning architectures such as DeepSeek-R1, OpenAI o1, K1.5, and s1. A wide array of experiments have been conducted on these and other specific LLMs to validate the utility of techniques such as Chain-of-Thought (CoT) Prompting, ReAct, Self-Consistency, and sophisticated search frameworks like Tree-of-Thoughts (ToT), RAP, and LLM-A*. These studies [7–9] collectively demonstrate how computation must be scaled or re-architected at test time to fully elicit the models' encoded intelligence.

As mentioned earlier, unlike the simple pattern of conventional inference, autoregressive language models perform this forward pass repeatedly, using each output token as input for the subsequent generation step. This creates a sequential dependency where the computational cost scales linearly with output length, fundamentally altering the economics of inference from fixed-cost operations to variable-cost processes that depend on generation requirements. Autoregressive generation introduces a unique computational bottleneck where each token generation requires a full forward pass through the entire model, yet produces only a single token of output. This often necessitates hundreds or thousands of separate forward passes for a single complex response, requiring the full parameter set to be accessed repeatedly from memory. This pattern frequently makes LLM inference memory-bandwidth bound rather than compute-bound. The iterative nature also restricts the utility of batching optimizations common in traditional inference, as each step depends on the previous output, limiting parallelization strategies. Furthermore, the attention mechanism compounds these challenges by introducing quadratic scaling with sequence length. During inference, the model must maintain a dynamic Key-Value (KV) cache to store intermediate results for all previously generated tokens, requiring memory that grows dynamically with each generated token, which includes components like DOLA and DEXPERTS for improved decoding.

To fully elicit the problem-solving capabilities encoded within the frozen parameters of LLMs, additional computation is deliberately allocated during inference, a paradigm known as *Test-Time Scaling (TTS)*. The following operational map categorizes strategies based on *what* computational pattern is expanded or adjusted to enhance model performance.

3.2.2 Operational map: Test-time scaling paradigms

Test-Time Scaling strategies carefully allocate extra processing time that is necessary to boost performance on complex, reasoning-intensive tasks without requiring additional training or parameter updates. Test-Time Scaling strategies can be organized into an operational map based on how the model's computational capacity is expanded or adjusted. This map classifies methods by whether the model scales thinking by generating many samples simultaneously, structuring thought into iterative steps, blending exploration and refinement, or learning to autonomously determine its own computational budget. Let us take a brief look at these different paradigms:

1. *Internal scaling*. This paradigm represents strategies where the LLM is explicitly trained to autonomously determine its required reasoning effort using its internal parameters, without requiring external human-guided strategies at inference time. The model learns a policy, often through Reinforcement Learning (RL) techniques leveraging outcome-oriented reward modeling, that controls when to halt or extend its internal reasoning steps. This internal management of computational budget defines highly capable systems today, exemplified by the autonomous reasoning behaviors of DeepSeek-R1 and the OpenAI o1 models.

2. *Sequential scaling*. This approach is an external orchestration method that explicitly directs later computations based on intermediate, iterative steps, effectively simulating human deliberation. It addresses the limitation of single-

pass generation by requiring the model to iteratively update its partial solution state through refinement or decomposition. This began with foundational prompt strategies like Chain-of-Thought (CoT) Prompting, which demands step-by-step reasoning. It evolved into adaptive, iterative refinement methods such as Self-Refine, where the model critiques its own output, and ReAct, which dynamically integrates reasoning steps with external actions, allowing the process to alternate between thinking and acting.

3. *Parallel scaling*. This paradigm enhances performance by generating multiple candidate outputs in parallel and subsequently aggregating them into a final decision. This ensemble method relies on achieving high coverage (the likelihood of generating at least one correct response) and a robust consensus mechanism to aggregate the results. The core implementation relies on repeated sampling, where the correct final answer is often determined by consensus, exemplified by the widely used technique Self-Consistency. Other techniques include Best-of-N selection, which uses an external verifier or metric to choose the superior candidate from the batch.

4. *Hybrid scaling*. Hybrid methods strategically blend the broad exploration of parallel scaling with the deep, iterative refinement of sequential techniques, often formalized using search algorithms adapted for language models, known as LLM Inference via Search (LIS). This approach mirrors human divergent and convergent thinking. Key examples include Tree-of-Thoughts (ToT), which generalizes CoT by exploring multiple reasoning paths at decision points before filtering or pruning, and frameworks utilizing complex search algorithms like Monte Carlo Tree Search (MCTS) or A* search, as seen in RAP and LLM-A*. These LIS frameworks structure reasoning as a sequential decision-making process where the LLM can adopt specific roles like Policy, Evaluator, or Transition Model.

3.2.3 Supporting inference optimization mechanisms (ITSI)

Complementing the high-level scaling paradigms, specific mechanisms, termed Inference-Time Self-Improvement (ITSI), dynamically adjust the decoding process to enhance performance or efficiency without altering the original LLM parameters [7–9]:

1. *Independent self-improvement*. This category includes methods that maximize performance purely using the model's frozen weights by manipulating the internal decoding process. Techniques include Constrained Decoding (e.g., NEUROLOGIC* enforcing rules), adjusting next-token probabilities through Contrastive Decoding (e.g., DOLA for factuality), and increasing efficiency via Parallel Decoding (e.g., Lookahead Decoding).

2. *Context-aware self-improvement*. This category utilizes auxiliary external context or knowledge. Examples include specialized Prompting methods beyond basic sequential scaling, using Disturbed Prompt methods (e.g., CAD to contrast probability distributions for hallucination reduction), and employing Retrieval-based systems (e.g., kNN-LM or REST) to ground generation in external knowledge.

3. *Model-aided self-improvement*. This involves collaboration with external agents or auxiliary models, often specialized or smaller, to guide the main LLM. This approach is critical for efficiency and quality assurance. Examples include using a Draft Model in Speculative Decoding (e.g., SEQUOIA) for accelerated inference, employing specialized models like DEXPERTS to adjust output logits for tasks like toxicity reduction, or using Reward Models (e.g., RAD or ARGS) to evaluate responses during decoding.

3.2.4 Inference-time scaling laws: Optimizing compute after training

Training time scaling laws have been extensively studied and well-established in the field of large language models, demonstrating that model performance follows predictable power-law relationships with respect to the number of parameters, the size of the training dataset, and the available compute during training. These laws, exemplified by the Chinchilla scaling law, show how to optimally choose model size and number of training tokens under a given training compute budget, providing clear guidance for resource allocation during the model development phase.

Inference time scaling laws, in contrast, examine how model performance changes when varying the computational resources allocated during inference rather than training. This involves analyzing the trade-offs between model sizes and generating additional tokens through different inference strategies while keeping the inference compute budget fixed. The fundamental question addressed is how to select an optimal model size and effective inference strategy to maximize performance given a specific computational constraint at test time.

The authors of [10] conduct comprehensive experiments across multiple mathematical reasoning benchmarks, specifically GSM8K and MATH500, using various model families including Pythia, Mistral, and math-specialized *Llemma* models ranging from 410 M to 34B parameters. They evaluate different inference strategies including greedy search, majority voting, best-of-n sampling, weighted voting, Monte Carlo Tree Search, and their novel REBASE algorithm. The experiments systematically vary both model size and inference compute budget to establish empirical relationships between computational resources and problem-solving accuracy. They also provide theoretical analysis of the convergence behavior of voting-based methods, showing that sampling strategies eventually saturate to performance limits determined by the underlying model's probability distributions.

The research yields several significant findings that challenge conventional assumptions about optimal resource allocation. Most notably,

1. smaller models combined with sophisticated inference strategies often outperform larger models when operating under the same computational budget, suggesting that traditional approaches of simply scaling model size may be suboptimal for deployment scenarios with inference compute constraints.

2. the right inference algorithm can consistently achieve Pareto-optimal performance across all tested scenarios, outperforming both standard sampling methods and Monte Carlo Tree Search while requiring significantly less computational overhead.

3. sampling-based voting methods inevitably saturate to performance limits determined by the underlying model's probability distributions, indicating diminishing returns from simply increasing sample counts and highlighting the necessity for more sophisticated inference algorithms.

4. the benefits of advanced inference strategies are most pronounced on difficult problems.

These findings have profound implications for real-world deployment, suggesting that practitioners should consider deploying smaller models with advanced inference algorithms rather than simply scaling to larger models, potentially achieving better cost-performance trade-offs while maintaining or improving accuracy.

4. Conclusion

In this chapter, we have explored how the computational requirements and optimization strategies for neural networks fundamentally diverge between training and inference phases, creating distinct engineering challenges that practitioners must navigate as models scale to unprecedented sizes. The evolution from simple gradient descent to sophisticated optimizers like AdamW, combined with careful learning rate scheduling, represents decades of refinement in understanding how to efficiently navigate high-dimensional loss landscapes. Yet these training innovations, while critical for achieving state-of-the-art performance, represent only half of the computational story that defines modern machine learning systems.

What emerges from our analysis is that the traditional view of training as the computationally expensive phase and inference as the simple application phase no longer holds for today's large-scale models. The autoregressive nature of modern language models transforms inference into an iterative, memory-intensive process where the cost of serving predictions can quickly exceed training costs over a model's deployment lifetime. This shift demands a complete rethinking of how we approach model development, where decisions made during training about architecture, parameter count, and optimization strategy have cascading effects on inference efficiency, deployment costs, and user experience that extend far beyond model accuracy metrics.

For practitioners navigating these complexities, several key recommendations emerge from our analysis. During training, AdamW often serves as the default optimizer for most applications, particularly transformer architectures, due to its superior generalization through decoupled weight decay. Similarly cosine annealing schedules with linear warmup provide robust baselines, following patterns established in state-of-the-art models like Llama 3, with warmup periods of 1–5% of total training steps and peak learning rates around 1e-4 to 1e-5 for large models. Memory planning must account for training requirements scaling as $O(\text{parameters} + L \times d \times \text{batch\_size})$, with gradient checkpointing offering 40–60% memory reduction at the cost of 20–30% computational overhead when memory constraints bind. These "settings" have become commonplace in research/academic as well as industry settings today.

The inference phase requires fundamentally different optimization strategies. For deployment scenarios with compute constraints, practitioners should seriously consider smaller models combined with sophisticated inference algorithms rather than defaulting to the largest available model—our analysis demonstrates that models with

10x fewer parameters can achieve comparable performance with appropriate inference strategies while providing significantly better latency and cost characteristics. Hardware selection should align with serving patterns: CPUs for real-time, low-latency applications with small batch sizes; GPUs for medium to high-throughput scenarios with moderate batch sizes; and specialized accelerators like TPUs for predictable, high-throughput workloads with large batch sizes. Empirical benchmarking remains essential for identifying optimal batch sizes, as these vary dramatically across model architectures and hardware configurations.

The following table summarizes the critical trade-offs and recommendations that practitioners must navigate when designing neural network systems (**Table 1**).

Critical trade-offs practitioners must navigate include the tension between training memory requirements versus inference throughput optimization, the contrast between iterative gradient updates during training and sequential token generation

Aspect	Training phase	Inference phase	Key recommendation
Performance Metric	Minimize loss; optimize for convergence	Maximize throughput or minimize latency	Training: focus on generalization; Inference: focus on efficiency
Optimizer	AdamW for most applications; SGD + momentum for extensive tuning scenarios	N/A	Start with AdamW; use cosine annealing with 1–5% warmup
Memory Pattern	O(parameters + L × d × batch_size) - **high** due to activations + gradients	O(parameters + KV cache) - **moderate** but can grow with factors like sequence length	Plan for 3-5x more training memory; use gradient checkpointing if needed
Batch Size	Limited by GPU memory	Limited by latency requirements	Empirically benchmark optimal sizes for your hardware
Hardware Choice	GPUs/TPUs for parallel gradient computation, distributed, cluster-based training for high throughput	CPUs for small models; right-size the GPUs/TPUs for large models. Distributed inference for high throughput	Match hardware to serving pattern, not just raw performance
Cost Structure	Generally easy to estimate; Fixed upfront investment plan per training run	Variable cost scaling with requests and other factors like sequence length	Consider smaller models + advanced inference over larger models
Computational Pattern	Highly parallelizable (data/ model parallel)	Sequential dependencies, e.g. in autoregressive generation	Training favors parallelism; inference requires sequential optimization
Scaling Strategy	Larger models generally improve performance	Smaller models + sophisticated inference can outperform larger models	Test compute-optimal inference strategies before scaling model size

Table 1.
Tradeoffs to be considered during training and inference.

during inference, hardware utilization patterns where training and inference have different optimal batch sizes, cost structures that shift from fixed training expenses to variable per-request inference costs, and parallelization opportunities that favor training's highly parallelizable operations over inference's sequential dependencies.

The computational mechanics we have examined point toward a future where the boundaries between training and inference become increasingly fluid, with models that adapt dynamically to their computational environment and task requirements. Understanding these dynamics becomes essential not just for researchers pushing the frontiers of model capability, but for practitioners who must make informed decisions about architecture selection, resource allocation, and deployment strategies in a landscape where computational efficiency increasingly determines the practical impact of AI innovations. For the interested reader, more insights can be obtained by reading material focusing on sharpness aware minimization [11–15], the theory of generalization related to optimizers in the context of model training [16–22], and continuing work on optimizer design [23–31]. The interplay between training and inference dynamics will continue to shape how we build, deploy, and scale neural networks as they become more deeply integrated into the computational infrastructure of modern society.

Author details

Shreyas Subramanian
Amazon Web Services, Washington, D.C., United States of America

*Address all correspondence to: shreyas.f117@gmail.com

References

[1] Andriushchenko M, Varre AV, Pillaud-Vivien L, Flammarion N. Sgd with large step sizes learns sparse features. In: International Conference on Machine Learning. PMLR; 2023. pp. 903-925

[2] Huang WR, Emam Z, Goldblum M, Fowl L, Terry JK, Huang F, et al. Understanding Generalization through Visualizations. PMLR; 2020. pp. 87-97

[3] PyTorch documentation [Internet]. 2025. Available from: https://docs.pytorch.org/docs/stable/optim.html [Accessed: May 5, 2025]

[4] Loshchilov I, Hutter F. Decoupled weight decay regularization. Journal of Computer and Communications. 30 Jan 2017;**13**(1)

[5] PyTorch documentation [Internet]. 2025. Available from: https://ai.meta.com/research/publications/the-llama-3-herd-of-models/ [Accessed: May 5, 2025]

[6] Schmidt RM, Schneider F, Hennig P. Descending through a crowded valley-benchmarking deep learning optimizers. In: International Conference on Machine Learning. PMLR; 2021. pp. 9367-9376

[7] Dong X, Teleki M, Caverlee J. A survey on LLM inference-time self-improvement. arXiv preprint arXiv:2412.14352v1; 2024

[8] Li X. A survey on LLM test-time compute via search: Tasks, LLM profiling, search algorithms, and relevant frameworks. arXiv preprint arXiv:2501.10069v4; 2024

[9] Zhang Q, Lyu F, Sun Z, Wang L, Zhang W, Hua, W., Wu H, Guo Z, Wang Y, Muennighoff N et al. A survey on test-time scaling in large language models: What, how, where, and how well. arXiv preprint arXiv:2503.24235v3; 2025

[10] Wu Y, Sun Z, Li S, Welleck S, Yang Y. Inference scaling laws: An empirical analysis of compute-optimal inference for problem-solving with language models. arXiv preprint arXiv:2408.00724; 2024

[11] Andriushchenko M, Croce F, Müller M, Hein M, Flammarion N. A modern look at the relationship between sharpness and generalization. arXiv preprint arXiv:2302.07011; 2023

[12] Cai Y, Wu J, Mei S, Lindsey M, Bartlett P. Large stepsize gradient descent for non-homogeneous two-layer networks: Margin improvement and fast optimization. Advances in Neural Information Processing Systems. 2024;**37**:71306-71351

[13] Chen Z, Zhang J, Kou Y, Chen X, Hsieh CJ, Gu Q. Why does sharpness-aware minimization generalize better than sgd? Advances in Neural Information Processing Systems. 2023;**36**:72325-72376

[14] D'Angelo F, Andriushchenko M, Varre AV, Flammarion N. Why do we need weight decay in modern deep learning? Advances in Neural Information Processing Systems. 2024;**37**:23191-23223

[15] Andriushchenko M, Bahri D, Mobahi H, Flammarion N. Sharpness-aware minimization leads to low-rank features. Advances in Neural Information Processing Systems. 2023;**36**:47032-47051

[16] Lin Y, Tan L, Hao Y, Wong H, Dong H, Zhang W, Yang Y, Zhang T.

Spurious feature diversification improves out-of-distribution generalization. arXiv preprint arXiv: 2309.17230; 2023

[17] Wu J, Bartlett PL, Telgarsky M, Yu B. Large stepsize gradient descent for logistic loss: Non-monotonicity of the loss improves optimization efficiency. In: The Thirty Seventh Annual Conference on Learning Theory. PMLR; 2024, June. pp. 5019-5073

[18] Sclocchi A, Wyart M. On the different regimes of stochastic gradient descent. Proceedings of the National Academy of Sciences. 2024;**121**(9): e2316301121

[19] Zhang J, Bottou L. Learning useful representations for shifting tasks and distributions. In: International Conference on Machine Learning. PMLR; 2023. pp. 40830-40850

[20] Keskar NS, Socher R. Improving generalization performance by switching from adam to sgd. arXiv preprint arXiv: 1712.07628; 2017

[21] Zhou Y, Liang Y, Zhang H. Understanding generalization error of SGD in nonconvex optimization. Machine Learning. 2022;**111**(1):345-375

[22] Zhu T, He F, Zhang L, Niu Z, Song M, Tao D. Topology-aware generalization of decentralized sgd. In: International Conference on Machine Learning. PMLR; 2022. pp. 27479-27503

[23] Elshamy R, Abu-Elnasr O, Elhoseny M, Elmougy S. Improving the efficiency of RMSProp optimizer by utilizing Nestrove in deep learning. Scientific Reports. 2023;**13**(1):8814

[24] Kaddour J, Key O, Nawrot P, Minervini P, Kusner MJ. No train no gain: Revisiting efficient training algorithms for transformer-based language models. Advances in Neural Information Processing Systems. 2023; **36**:25793-25818

[25] Metz L, Harrison J, Freeman CD, Merchant A, Beyer L, Bradbury J, Agrawal N, Poole B, Mordatch I, Roberts A, Sohl-Dickstein J. Velo: Training versatile learned optimizers by scaling up. arXiv preprint arXiv: 2211.09760; 2022

[26] Kasimbeg P, Schneider F, Eschenhagen R, Bae J, Sastry CS, Saroufim M, Feng B, Wright L, Yang EZ, Nado Z, Medapati S. Accelerating neural network training: An analysis of the AlgoPerf competition. arXiv preprint arXiv:2502.15015; 2025

[27] Zhao R, Morwani D, Brandfonbrener D, Vyas N, Kakade S. Deconstructing what makes a good optimizer for language models. arXiv preprint arXiv:2407.07972; 2024

[28] Kingma DP, Ba J. Adam: A method for stochastic optimization. arXiv preprint arXiv:1412.6980; 2014

[29] Reddi SJ, Kale S, Kumar S. On the convergence of Adam and beyond. arXiv preprint arXiv:1904.09237; 2019

[30] Zhang Z. Improved Adam optimizer for deep neural networks. In: 2018 IEEE/ ACM 26th International Symposium on Quality of Service (IWQoS). IEEE; 2018. pp. 1-2

[31] Bock S, Weiß M. A proof of local convergence for the Adam optimizer. In: 2019 International Joint Conference on Neural Networks (IJCNN). IEEE; 2019. pp. 1-8

Chapter 3

Bioinspired Vision Systems: From Insect Neural Mechanisms to Advanced Visual Sensors

Jiewei Chen, Tao Zheng, Jiayang Xiao, Junyi Li, Jing Wang, Xinyi Wu, Zhiyu Zhang, Shuliang Zhou, Jiexiong Li, Yuhao Liang and Tianyue Wang

Abstract

Bioinspired vision systems are revolutionizing next-generation visual sensors through their unique neural mechanisms, offering great potential for power-efficient and real-time perception. This chapter explores the remarkable visual systems of insects and their transformative potential for advanced visual sensors. Specifically, we focus on the neural mechanisms of insect vision, particularly the adaptive signal processing by graded neurons and direction-selective circuits, we examine how these biological systems achieve unparalleled efficiency in motion detection, object tracking, and optic flow analysis. The chapter systematically bridges biological principles with engineering applications, detailing the design and implementation of bioinspired vision sensors that replicate these capabilities. Furthermore, we present cutting-edge developments in neuromorphic hardware and adaptive processing architectures while evaluating their performance against conventional systems. The discussion extends to industrial applications such as high-speed defect detection and unmanned aerial vehicle obstacle avoidance and concludes with the future directions and challenges in this interdisciplinary field. This chapter aims to provide researchers and engineers with neurobiology-inspired design principles and practical guidance for developing next-generation visual technologies.

Keywords: bioinspired vision sensors, neural mechanisms of insect vision, motion detection, neuromorphic hardware, autonomous applications

1. Introduction

Recently, the integration of image sensors has reached a high level, and the pixel size in state-of-the-art image sensors has reached the scale of the wavelength of light. The number of cables connecting the image sensor to the backend processing equipment has also reached millions. Nevertheless, this traditional architecture still encounters obstacles such as high power consumption and high time latency when pursuing high-quality images. It seems to be a hard nut to crack, achieving a balance between power consumption and performance in the traditional architecture.

The insect vision system features an efficient and compact neural structure along with a unique processing mechanism. It outperforms the most powerful computers in tasks, such as real-time sensory data processing, perception tasks, and motor control. Moreover, it can complete all these tasks with an incredibly small energy budget. These distinct characteristics have transformative significance in the development of low-power and real-time neuromorphic vision systems for resource-constrained edge computing and autonomous robotics. Therefore, engineers have set their sights on biological visual systems, especially the compound eyes of insects. They have found that the insect compound eye system offers a more satisfactory solution compared to traditional architectures. This chapter aims to expound on the current development status of existing insect-inspired visual devices and bionic visual processing architectures. At the same time, it also intends to compare them with the processing architectures of conventional devices to evaluate their performance. Finally, it discusses the practical application of the bionic vision system and summarizes the future development directions and challenges in this field.

2. Results and discussion

2.1 The basic structure of the insect visual system

2.1.1 Ocelli

Ocelli are simple-structured photoreceptors that exist in many invertebrates. Insect ocelli are composed of visual cells, hexagonal corneas, and conical lenses. They are capable of perceiving the intensity of light but lack the ability to resolve visual objects. Insect ocelli are divided into two types: dorsal ocelli and lateral ocelli. The former are located on the back of the head region in both adults and nymphs, usually occurring in a set of three and arranged in a triangle pattern. The latter are found exclusively in larvae, located on both sides of the head region, usually with 1–7 per side.

2.1.2 Compound eyes

In contrast to ocelli, compound eyes are positioned prominently on the insect's head. They are composed of many ommatidia, each containing corneas, crystalline cones, rhabdoms, retinal cells, as well as pigment cells. The cornea is the outermost structure of the compound eyes and serves to protect the compound eyes. The crystalline cone is a conical transparent structure located beneath the cornea. Together with the cornea, it forms a refractive organ, performing the function of refraction, similar to the crystalline lens of the human eye. The shape of the crystalline cone will adapts to light variations. The rhabdom is formed by the close arrangement of microvilli on the inner side of retinal cells, presenting a central columnar shape, which has a large surface area and strong refraction performance. After the light reaches the rhabdom and propagates downward, the absorption of visual pigments can be enhanced. The rhabdom can also detect the intensity and the angle of light. Particularly, rhabdoms at different positions can sense light waves in different directions and then integrate them. Therefore, the rhabdom has a complex visual orientation function. Pigment cells are mainly distributed around the rhabdom and the crystalline cone. Their primary function is to absorb and disperse the light reaching the ommatidia. As a result, the compound eyes regulate the amount of light entering through the movement of pigment particles between the rhabdom and crystalline cone, thereby adapting to the changes in light in the environment [1].

As shown in **Figure 1**, insect compound eyes can be classified into apposition eyes and superposition eyes based on the distance between pigment cells and crystalline cones. The superposition eyes have a focusing effect and can sense low-intensity light, but the resolution is relatively low. The apposition eyes have no focusing effect while having a higher resolution. Most diurnal insects have apposition eyes, while nocturnal insects have superposition eyes.

2.1.3 Visual neural pathway

The visual neural pathway is a signal transmission network that connects the compound eyes, ocelli, and the central nervous system. Firstly, photoreceptor cells can convert the received light signals into electrical signals and then transmit them to primary sensory neurons (such as cone cells), initially integrating the brightness information of adjacent areas and enhancing the contrast. Secondly, preliminary processing is performed by intermediate neurons (such as bipolar cells and horizontal cells) to regulate the spatial integration of signals and suppress background noise. Finally, the signals are integrated by ganglion cells and then transmitted to the visual processing center of the insect brain (optic lobe), in which they cooperate with other regions of the brain to make behavioral decisions (such as tracking prey).

2.2 The types and functions of neurons in insect vision system

2.2.1 Directional selective neurons

Direction selective neurons (DSNs): DSNs are a class of neurons in the insect visual system that function to detect and encode the direction of movement. DSNs can be found in both invertebrates (e.g., flies and locusts) and vertebrates (such as rabbits and mice). Based on complex neural computing mechanisms in DSNs, insects can quickly perceive movement information, thereby completing key behaviors such as navigation, predation, and obstacle avoidance.

Photoreceptor: One side of compound eyes includes two groups of photoreceptors (peripheral photoreceptors and central photoreceptors). Motion vision mainly relies

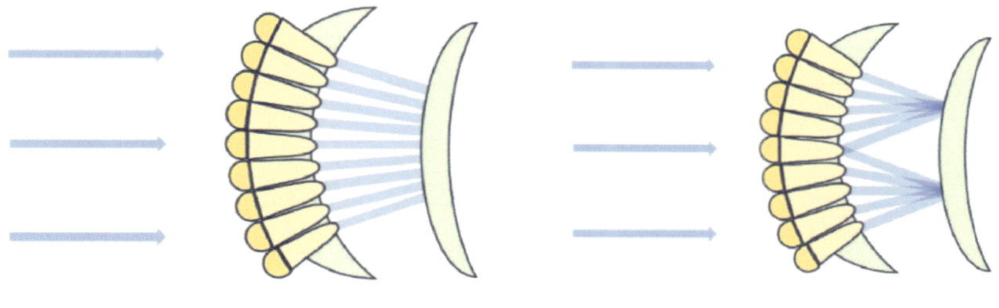

Figure 1.
Insect compound eye structure. Apposition eyes (left) and superposition eyes (right).

on the peripheral photoreceptors, and they are the primary input source of DSNs. Signals of these photoreceptors are divided into two parallel motion circuits, which can be utilized to process the motion information of brightness increase (ON channel) and brightness decrease (OFF channel), respectively.

Lamellar neurons: In **Figure 2**, L1 and L2 are the two prominent target neurons of peripheral photoreceptors and are two large unipolar cells of the lamellar layer. Specifically, L1 mainly transmits the information of increased brightness (ON channel), while L2 mainly transmits the information of decreased brightness (OFF channel).

Tangential cells: The tangential cells are neurons in the visual motor pathway of Drosophila. They have complex dendritic structures and are able to integrate local motion information from multiple visual columns.

Interneurons (T4 and T5 cells): As shown in **Figure 2**, T4 and T5 cells process the motor signals of the ON and OFF channels, respectively. Their output signals converge in four different layers of the lobula, each corresponding to a specific direction of motion.

2.2.2 Lobula Giant Movement Detector

The Lobula Giant Movement Detector (LGMD) is a key neuron located in the optic lobe of the insect visual system (such as locusts). Its function is to detect rapidly approaching objects (such as predators or obstacles) within the field of vision and to avoid collisions by triggering an escape response. This structure is divided into the following three parts (**Figure 3**).

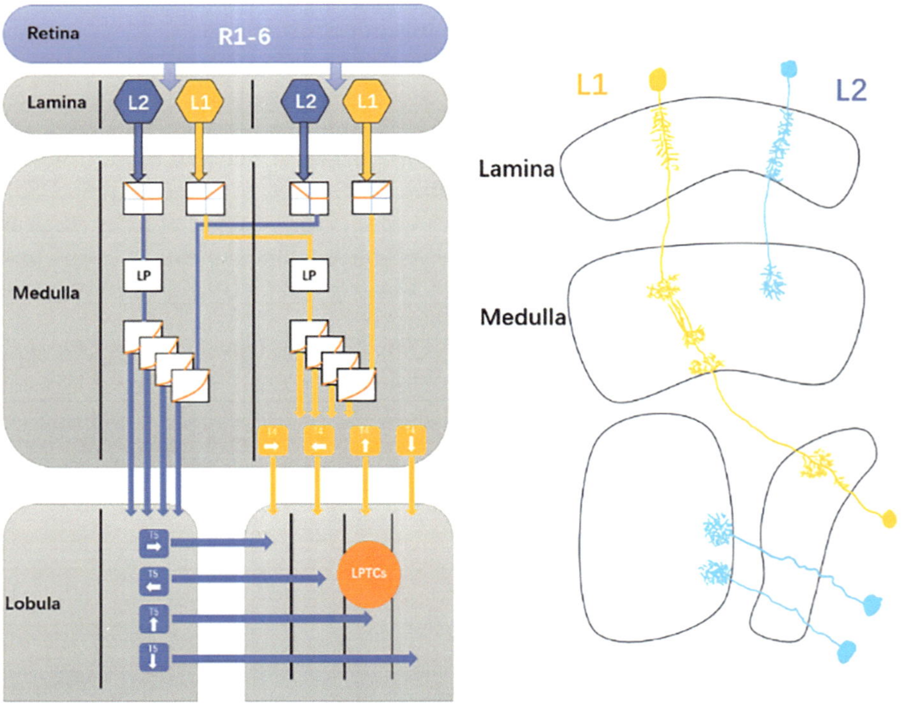

Figure 2.
Circuit diagram of the basic motion detector for flies (left) and some involved neurons (right) [1].

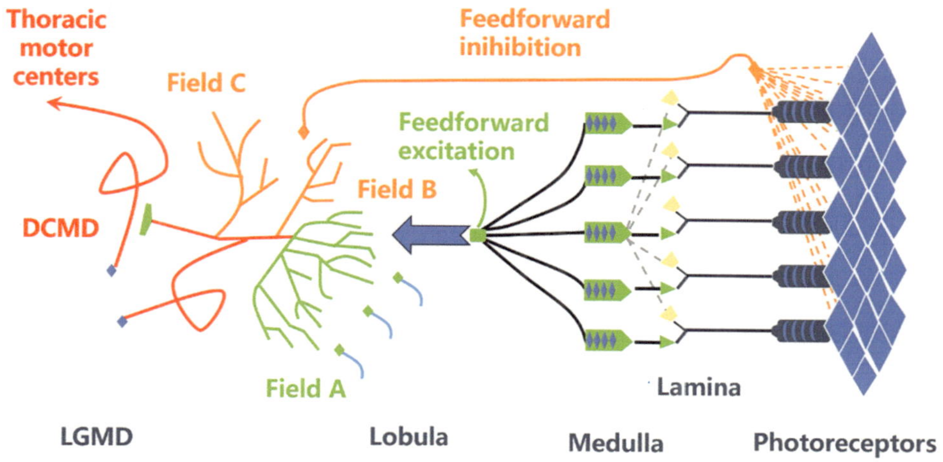

Figure 3.
Structural diagram of LGMD neurons [2].

1. Input pathway: The feedforward excitation, lateral inhibition, and feedforward inhibition are received through hexagonal array photoreceptors in the compound eyes and retinal topological layers of the lamina, medulla, and lobula. These signals are then transmitted to the LGMD via these retinal topological layers.

2. Dendrite domains: They are divided into excitatory dendrites (receiving angular velocity θ' signals) and inhibitory dendrites (receiving angular size θ signals).

3. Output pathway: Connecting with Descending Contralateral Movement Detector (DCMD) neurons and transmitting signals to the motor center.

2.2.3 Graded neurons

Graded neurons can efficiently encode dynamic visual information through multilevel responses and time-domain accumulation characteristics. This type of neuron is particularly common in the insect visual system. Their basic characteristics are as follows:

1. The amplitude is proportional to the intensity of the stimulus: The voltage variation range of the graded potential directly reflects the intensity of the stimulus (such as light intensity and odor concentration). For example, the degree of depolarization of photoreceptors in Drosophila is positively correlated with light intensity (weak light $\rightarrow$ slight depolarization, strong light $\rightarrow$ significant depolarization).

2. No action potential propagation: The graded potential only propagates locally, and its amplitude rapidly decays with increasing distance, making it impossible to be transmitted over a long distance. Such a feature makes signal processing more dependent on the integration of space and time (such as the superposition of inputs from multiple photoreceptors).

3. Sustainability and adaptability: The graded potential can be maintained for a long time (such as the resting potential in the dark) and can quickly adapt to changes in stimuli through the dynamic regulation of ion channels (such as sodium and chlorine channels).

The core functions of graded neurons mainly include three parts: encoding visual information, dynamic adaptation and signal regulation, and energy conservation and efficient processing:

1. Encoding visual information: graded potential allows neurons to continuously and analogously encode light intensity rather than binary (action potential only transmits "presence or absence" signals). For example, under low light, photoreceptors slightly depolarize and release a small amount of histamine, and the Lamina Monopolar Cells (LMCs) slightly depolarize. Under strong light, photoreceptors are significantly depolarized, histamine release surges, and LMCs are strongly hyperpolarized.

2. Dynamic adaptation and signal regulation: After strong light adaptation, photoreceptors reduce neurotransmitter release through sodium ion depolarization, and the chloride ion efflux mechanism of LMCs is enhanced, resulting in a temporary enhancement of postsynaptic responses.

3. Energy conservation and efficient processing: The graded potential transfer has low energy consumption (avoiding frequent action potentials), making it suitable for compact, efficient neural computing in small insects and animals.

The differences between graded potential neurons and action potential neurons are compared in **Table 1**. In summary, graded potential neurons achieve local, short-range integration through analog signals and have low power consumption and dynamically adjustable sensitivity. Action potential neurons, on the other hand, conduct long-range and high-speed transmission via skip conduction with all or no pulse signals and have the characteristics of high power consumption and reliance on frequency coding.

Characteristics	Graded potential neurons	Action potential neurons
Signal form	Continuously changing voltage (the amplitude is strongly correlated with the stimulus)	Electrical pulses with or without (fixed amplitude)
Transmission mode	Local diffusion, and the amplitude will decay with distance	Skip conduction along the axon
Adaptability	Dynamic adjustment sensitivity (such as light intensity adaptation)	Dependent on frequency coding (pulse rate variation)
Energy consumption	Lower	Higher
Typical functions	Analog signal processing (such as vision, smell)	Digital signal transmission (Such as motion control)

Table 1.
Comparison chart of graded potential neurons and action potential neurons.

2.3 Signal processing mechanism in insect vision system

The signal processing mechanism of the insect vision system is a multilevel and complex process, involving a series of process stages from optical signal perception to advanced neural computing.

2.3.1 Photoreceptor physiology

Photoreceptors of insects are the starting point of their visual signal processing and are mainly distributed in compound eyes and ocelli. Different photoreceptors lead to different behavioral tendencies. In Drosophila, peripheral photoreceptor cells are responsible for detecting luminance and motion information and have wide-spectral sensitivity. Central photoreceptor cells, including R7 and R8, express ultraviolet and green light-sensitive opsins, respectively, and are involved in the encoding of color vision. This division of labor enables insects to process both movement and color information at the same time, supporting complex behaviors such as foraging and avoiding enemies.

2.3.2 Neural signal encoding and processing

Neural signal encoding in the insect visual system is a multilevel parallel processing procedure involving a complex network from peripheral ganglia to the higher center. In the lamina layer and medulla layer of compound eyes, neurons enhance contrast through lateral inhibition and spatiotemporal filtration, thereby highlighting the edge and texture features of moving objects.

In the primary motion detection of the insect visual system, DSNs are core components of motion vision. These neurons show selective responses to movements in specific directions, and the mechanism relies on asymmetric synaptic inputs and inhibitory feedback [3]. For example, T4 and T5 neurons of Drosophila specifically process the motion information of opposing contrasts: T4 neurons detect light-ON edges (the forward movement of the light-dark boundary), while T5 neurons respond to light-OFF edges (the backward movement of the dark-bright boundary). These outputs from T4 and T5 neurons are integrated in the optic lobe of the central brain to form global motion perception.

After primary signal processing, LGMD specifically responds to approaching objects. The activation of LGMD depends on the dynamic balance of synaptic inhibition and excitation signals: when an object approaches, the excitatory input increases rapidly, while the inhibitory input is delayed, thereby generating explosive discharges [4]. This "asymmetric inhibition" mechanism enables insects to trigger evasive behaviors rapidly.

2.4 Mechanism of motion control and object tracking in insect vision system

2.4.1 The motion mechanism of DSNs

R1–R6 cells are the main photoreceptors on the periphery of the ommatidia of compound eyes, which are sensitive to blue-green light (approximately 480–550 nm) and are responsible for color vision and luminance perception under a wide spectral range. They convert light signals into electrical signals through rhodopsin, providing local light intensity variation signals, thereby obtaining motion signals. The output signals of R1–R6 are transmitted to the medulla through unipolar cells (such as L1, L2, and L5). L1 and L5 receive the ON and OFF channel signals of R1–R6, respectively, forming the initial movement direction characteristics. For example, L1 cells of Drosophila are sensitive to horizontal movement, and L5 cells are sensitive to vertical movement. Tm3/Mi1 neurons in the medulla receive input signals from unipolar cells and enhance the optical flow signal in a specific direction through lateral inhibition. For example, the Tm3 neuron of Drosophila responds strongly to the clockwise rotating optical flow, while the Mi1 neuron responds strongly to the counterclockwise rotation. Medullary signals are further transmitted to tangential cells in the lobules, such as horizontal cells and vertical cells. The signals are further transmitted to T4 and T5 cells. The dendrites of T4 and T5 cells receive signals from adjacent photoreceptors and integrate signals through synaptic interactions. These signals undergo complex interactions within the dendrites to generate local motion signals.

2.4.2 The motion mechanism of LGMD

The LGMD is a giant single neuron, specifically designed to detect the rapid movement of approaching objects and trigger an escape response. As shown in **Figure 3**, the LGMD collision system is composed of four layers of neural networks: Peripheral photoreceptor cells (R1–R6) sense changes in environmental brightness and generate primary visual signals. These signals are then transmitted to the lamina layer, where unipolar cells decompose the signals into ON and OFF channels. The background noise is suppressed through the center-surround antagonism mechanism to enhance target detection. The medulla layer further processes the ON/OFF channel signals and then extracts the motion direction and speed information through the parallel pathway. Finally, in the lobula plate, multisource information is integrated through LGMD neurons to output collision warning signals. LGMD neurons have two input branches:

1. Visual input branch: Receives the brightness change signal sent by the compound eyes and distinguishes the direction in which the object is approaching or moving away through the ON/OFF channel.

2. Angular velocity input branch: Perceives the relative motion velocity of the target object and calculates the collision time in combination with visual signals [5].

The signal processing process of LGMD is a nonlinear calculation process, as shown in **Figure 4**. Visual signals are processed in the excitation layer (E layer, processing the ON channel) and the inhibition layer (I layer, processing the OFF channel) to form a dynamic balance. When approaching the object, the excitation signal is enhanced while the suppression signal is weakened. When the integrated signal exceeds the preset threshold, LGMD neurons release spike pulses and send emergency obstacle avoidance instructions to the downstream motor control center. This response has extremely low time latency (about 200 ms).

2.4.3 The motion mechanism of graded neurons

The graded potential neuron in the insect visual system is a kind of non-pulsed neuron. Taking the peripheral photoreceptors R1–R6 and output neurons of

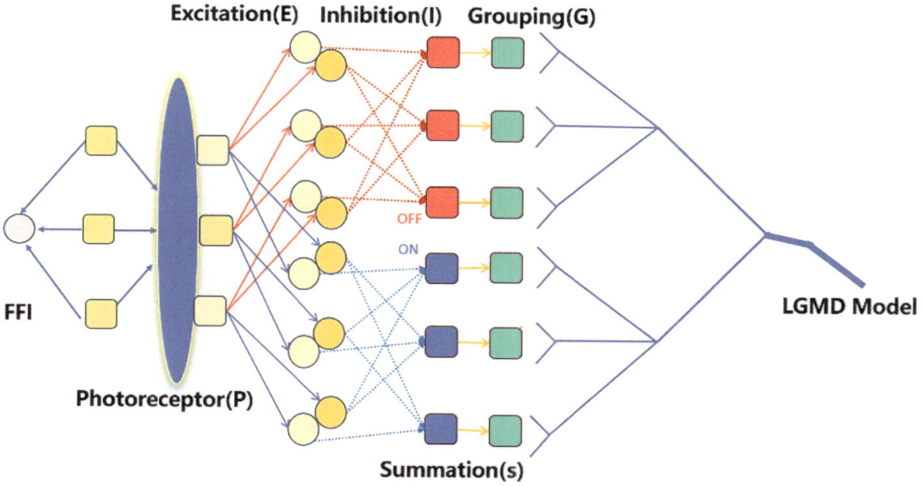

Figure 4.
LGMD signal processing model.

Drosophila as examples, this system can be regarded as R-LMC-R, composed of feed-forward and feedback synaptic networks, forming forward and backward processing units of information. It can be known that the visual information coding in the LMC output is efficient within a few seconds. When photoreceptors encounter a new stimulus pattern again, the LMC enhances its sensitivity to the signal. Visual signals do not respond adequately to the new stimulus pattern for the first time. By increasing the dimension of time, the signal-to-noise ratio of the signal stimulus output by LMCs can be increased.

Analyzed from the time-domain perspective, as shown in **Figure 5(a)**, visual signals are input from the peripheral photoreceptors R1–R6 and output from the LMC. As shown in **Figure 5(b)**, the amplitude statistics of LMC outputs under 20-second stimuli of dim, medium, and bright intensities revealed that the gain varies dynamically with stimulus intensity. This relationship is not a simple static nonlinearity but rather exhibits gain reduction across different luminance levels. **Figure 5(c)** displays the energy output under bright-intensity stimulation for 1, 2, and 20 seconds durations. It can be observed that the gain progressively increases with repeated stimulation. This result indicates that the output of LMC depends on the continuous changes in intensity and time, altering synaptic gain. As shown in **Figure 6**, the standard deviation distribution plots of R1-R6 and LMC responses demonstrate that repeated stimulation of R1-R6 enables LMC to generate a greater voltage response from the weakened voltage response of photoreceptors.

2.5 The current development status of existing hardware

It is a vital method to observe and extract the merits of biological systems in biomimetic design. The insect compound eye system is a typical representative of natural biological visual systems. Its advantages of the wide field of view angle (FOV) and rapid motion tracking provide great value for practical applications. Based on this, Dawei Zhang's group has designed a biomimetic apposition compound eye (BAC-eye) system based on microfluidic-assisted 3D printing technology. The production process is as follows: Firstly, a mold containing hemispherical pits and micropores was

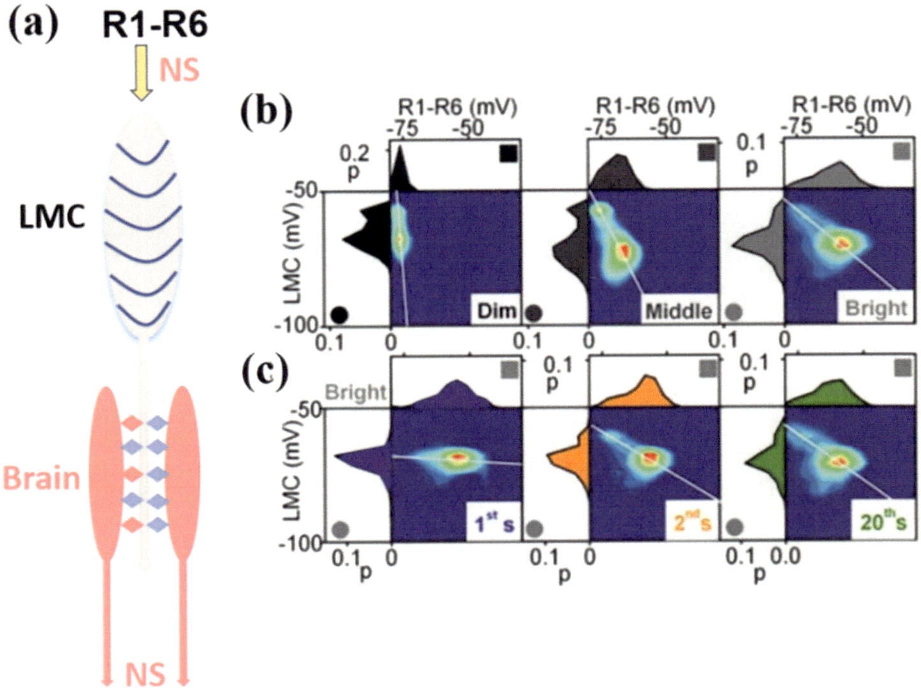

Figure 5.
(a) Structure diagram of photoreceptors (R1–R6) and output neurons (LMC). (b) Probability density function diagrams of R1–R6 and LMC under different light intensities. (c) Probability density function diagrams of R1–R6 and LMC at different times and with the same intensity [3].

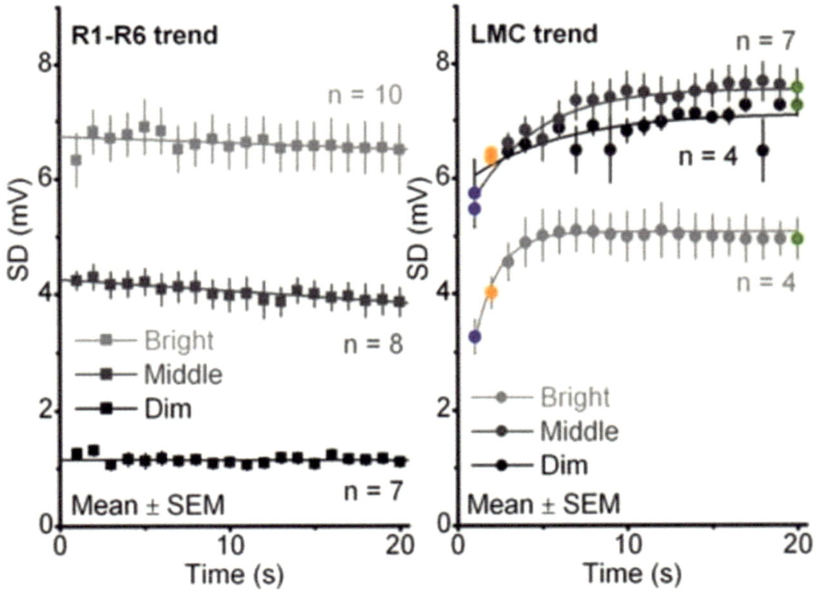

Figure 6.
Distribution standard deviation graphs of R1–R6 and LMC [6].

designed and 3D printed. Secondly, 522 microlens molds were formed in micropores by microfluidic-assisted forming technology. Finally, the compound eye structures were fabricated through photosensitive polymer and silica gel curing. This fabrication process has high scalability. Furthermore, the cost of source materials and equipment is relatively low, and the fabricating procedure is economical and efficient. **Figure 7** shows the comparison between the insect compound eye system and the BAC-eye system. This BAC-eye system has been successfully demonstrated in applications such as panoramic imaging and tracking [5]. This technology still has limitations. For example, the optical properties of microlenses may be limited by 3D printing resolution and microfluidic operation. The imaging quality is easily affected by the optical properties of the material, and redundant microlenses may lead to optical crosstalk. In addition, its application scenarios mainly focus on panoramic imaging and point light source positioning, and the demand for high-resolution or complex optical processing may need to be further optimized or combined with other technologies.

Xuming Zhang's group pointed out that the previous artificial compound eye systems did not faithfully replicate the structures of natural compound eye systems, thus lacking some of the advantages of the insect compound eye system. They have designed an artificial compound eye (ACE) device based on an optical fiber, which was realized by 3D printing technology, as shown in **Figure 8**. The fabrication method is as follows: Firstly, a hemispherical dome and a beam splitter are manufactured using 3D printing technology. Then, 271 plastic optical fibers with tapered microlenses are installed in the through-holes of the dome and the beam splitter. Finally, the light is transmitted from the curved surface of the dome to the planar imaging sensor chip through an imaging lens [7]. The resolution can be improved by increasing the number of optical fibers or reducing the fiber diameter. This ACE device can employ 3D printing technology to adjust the size of the compound eye to adapt to different application scenarios. In addition, material and equipment costs are relatively low. This group studied its static imaging capabilities and dynamic detection capabilities, with results showing a wide FOV, large depth of field, and extremely fast motion detection ability. Although significant progress has been made in the ACE device, there are still some limitations in the optical performance, resolution improvement, and imaging quality of microlenses.

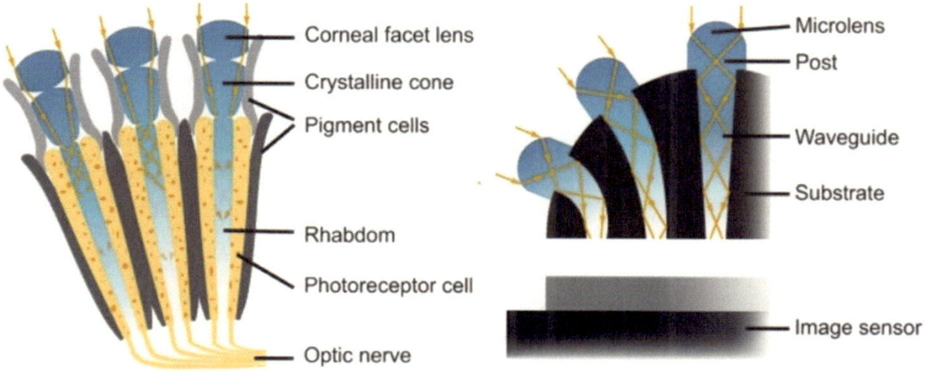

Figure 7.
The nature compound eye system (left). The BAC-eye system (right).

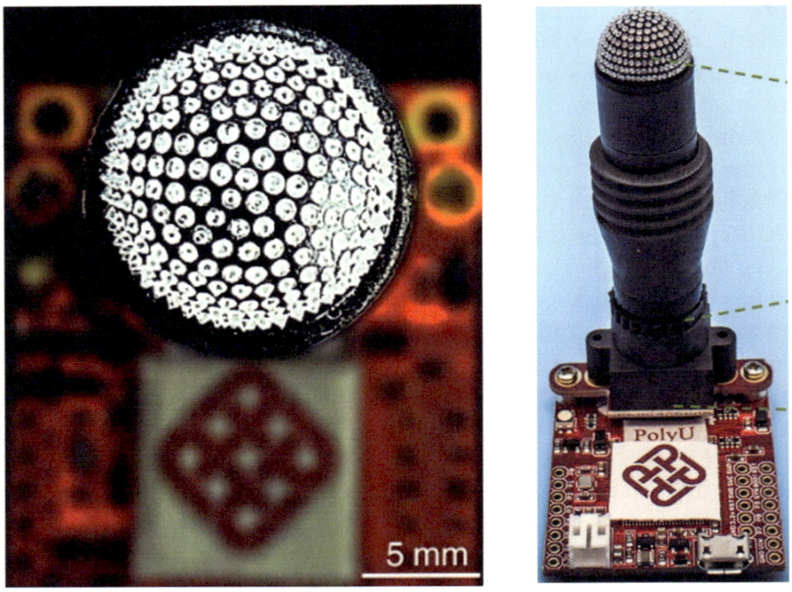

Figure 8.
The artificial compound eye (ACE). The left picture shows the lens on the optical fibers. The right picture shows the ACE on the hardware development platform.

In contrast to previous studies, Zhiyong Fan's group eschewed the use of lenses when designing the optical imaging component and developed an artificial compound eye vision system without a lens [8]. This system integrates a 3D-printed pinhole array optical device with an inherently convex hemispherical image sensor embedded with a high-density perovskite nanowire array. The fabrication process is as follows: Firstly, a hexagonal hole array with an accuracy of 10 microns was fabricated using high-precision 3D printing technology, and the size and layout of holes are optimized through optical simulation to eliminate blind spots and improve light efficiency. Then, a hemispherical aluminum shell was formed from a 500-μm-thick aluminum sheet. A porous alumina film (PAM) was formed on the surface by a two-step anodization process. Next, lead nanowires were formed by electrodeposition in the PAM channel, and perovskite nanowires were grown in a tube furnace. The quality of the nanowires was improved by ion milling and regrowth processes. A layer of organics was evaporated as a passivation layer, and a layer of indium tin oxide was sputtered as a common electrode. Finally, the hemispherical perovskite nanowire imaging sensor was aligned with the keyhole array, fixed with a 3D printing bracket, and connected to a printed circuit board through a copper wire to complete device integration. **Figure 9** illustrates the schematic diagram of the integrated pinhole compound eye (PHCE) system and its magnified details.

The PHCE system can achieve an FOV of approximately 140°. Impressively, when utilized in a binocular configuration, the FOV can be expanded to 220°. And this system possesses outstanding positioning accuracy and high-efficiency motion detection, showcasing significant potential for advanced applications. However, the current signal processing relies on external circuits and computer-controlled multiplexers, which are not conducive to the real-time ability and portability of this system.

Additionally, there are also some works that simulate the human vision system. For the human eye, the retina in the visual system usually exhibits a hemispherical

Figure 9.
The integrated pinhole compound eye system (left). Exploded view of the PHCE system (right).

shape. This feature provides humans with a wide FOV, high resolution, and excellent adaptability to the optical environment. However, such a nearly perfect system also has its drawbacks. In the human vision system, the nerve fiber layer is located in front of the human retina, which leads to light loss and blind spot issues. In order to solve these challenges, Zhiyong Fan's group designed a bionic visual system. The design of this bionic vision system with a hemispherical retina composed of high-density perovskite nanowire arrays is inspired by the human eye. The fabrication method includes preparation of a hemispherical aluminum shell, formation of PAM on an aluminum shell, growth of perovskite nanowires at the bottom of the PAM channel, preparation of a liquid metal contact array, integration of an electrode and ionic liquid, and development of a microneedle-based electrochemical image sensor [9]. As schematically illustrated in **Figure 10**, the bionic visual system is mainly composed of three main parts: the lens, a large number of photosensors on a hemispherical substrate representing the retina of the human visual system, and the thin liquid-metal wires serving as electrical contacts for transmitting the signals from the "artificial

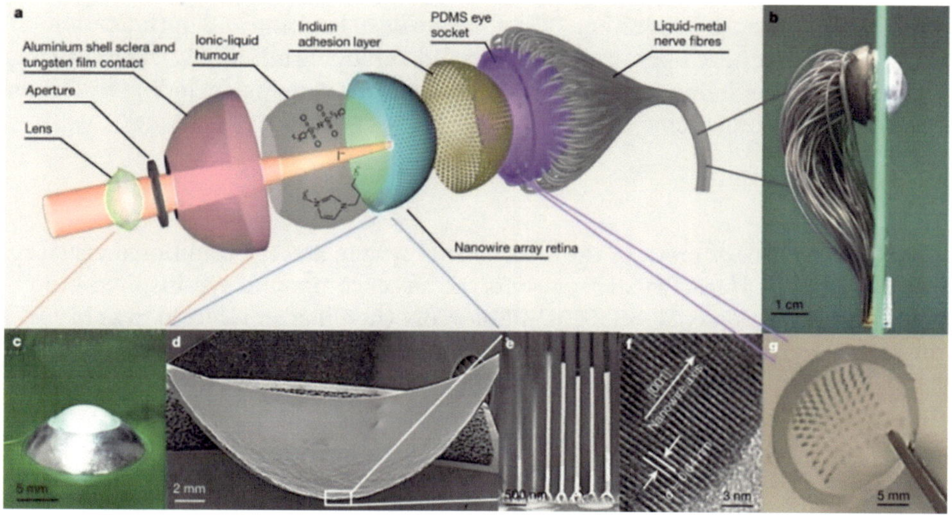

Figure 10.
The diagram of the bionic visual system according to human eyes.

retina" to the backend. This artificial system not only replicates key components of the human visual system but also moves the nerve fibers behind the bionic retina, avoiding the inherent limitations of the natural system. Although this system performs well in image sensing, it still needs to be further improved in terms of pixel size and resolution, electrode alignment strategy, and ionic liquid optimization to achieve wider application.

2.6 The current situation of the existing adaptive processing architectures

In terms of the processing architecture of the visual system, the type of transmitted signal is the major difference between neuromorphic computing and traditional computing. In detail, the signal in traditional computing is generally continuous, while the signal in neuromorphic computing usually appears in the form of pulses. This difference makes the processing tools of traditional computing impossible to be directly applied. Therefore, it is necessary to construct a framework that is almost centered on pulse signals. A typical neuromorphic computing framework is "Nengo." As a Python library, "Nengo" is able to construct and simulate neural cognitive systems. The design of "Nengo" revolves around a concept called "Ensembles," which is a group of neurons that can work together to perform computational tasks. Users can define functions for these sets, such as addition, multiplication, or more complex functions. Additionally, "Nengo" also provides a set of connection rules and learning algorithms, which can customize the connection mode between neurons to achieve dynamic learning and adaptation. "Nengo" not only provides a built-in graphical interface tool but also supports multiple backends, which enables it to run efficiently on different platforms and enables user development of neuromorphic systems.

On the other hand, there is also a framework named "Lava," which is similar to "Nengo." "Lava" provides the "Process" class, with which users can either construct neural networks by using the existing "Processes" or build neural networks by writing their own "Processes." The "Processes" can provide interfaces for each other, run in the local memory, and pass messages between one another through channels. Different "Processes" can carry out asynchronous operations simultaneously, which reflects the inherent and high parallelism of neuromorphic hardware and avoids the side effects of memory interaction. "Lava" offers deep learning and optimization libraries that assist developers in developing and deploying efficiently. "Lava" also has the characteristic of being supported by heterogeneous systems, including traditional CPUs and Intel's Loihi architecture.

2.7 Evaluating

Next, the figures of merit of the insect visual system and the traditional visual system are compared. Here, PHCE represents the insect compound eye-inspired vision system, and Hikvision's MV-SC3016C-06M-WBN (hereinafter referred to as MV) represents the traditional vision sensor. **Figure 11** shows a rough assessment of some figures of merit. It should be noted that the data here is normalized; that is, the original data of the same indicator for the two devices is normalized. In detail, regarding the FOV, the single-eye FOV of the PHCE system reaches 140°, while the FOV of the MV-SC3016C-06M-WBN can be calculated to be approximately 63°. Regarding the frames per second (FPS), the performance of the PHCE here refers to the frame rate measured when this device is installed on a commercial drone, which is 25 Hz, while the FPS of the MV-SC3016C-06M-WBN reaches 60 Hz. Regarding the size per pixel,

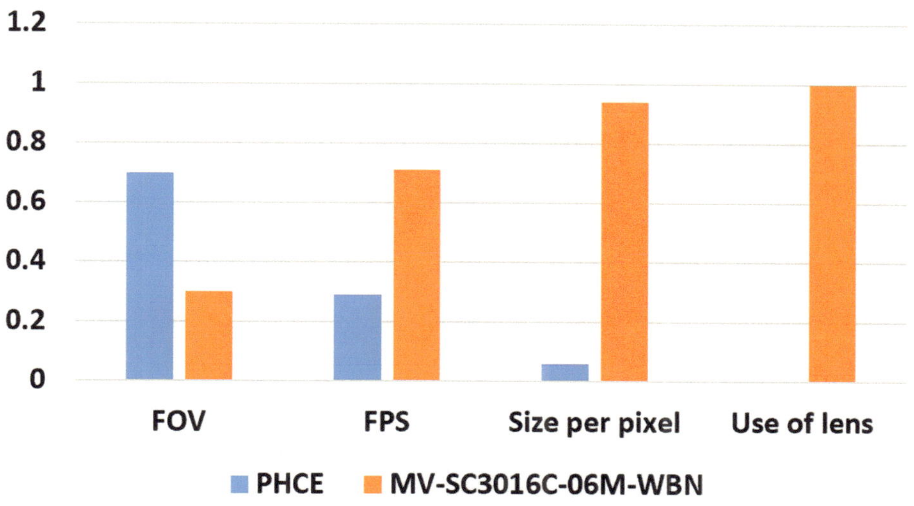

Figure 11.
Rough evaluation of the insect-inspired visual system compared to the traditional visual system.

the performance of the PHCE here refers to the diameter of the nanowire, which is approximately 300 nm. In the data sheet, the pixel size of the MV-SC3016C-06M-WBN is 3.45 μm × 3.45 μm, and here we compare the length of the pixel's diagonal. In terms of the use of lenses, the PHCE is a non-lens system, while the MV-SC3016C-06M-WBN uses a lens group. Accordingly, the key performance parameters of PHCE comprehensively surpass those of the MV-SC3016C-06M-WBN.

2.8 Bioinspired vision in robotics and autonomous systems

2.8.1 Dynamic visual perception

The insect vision system has an efficient motion perception capability due to its compound eyes consisting of a large number of independent imaging units, which are capable of responding quickly to local light changes. An optoelectronic graded neuron sensor developed based on the insect compound eye vision system is able to achieve 92.2% accuracy in action recognition by efficiently encoding spatial-temporal information [10]. This system can capture a large amount of dynamic information and subsequently realize real-time and rapid motion detection and processing through neural networks. This efficient motion perception capability has inspired the design of a variety of bionic vision sensors, such as the Dynamic Vision Sensor (DVS), as shown in **Figure 12**. The DVS can capture sudden luminance events in a scene in millisecond timescales by imitating the extreme sensitivity of insect compound eyes to changes in light intensity. These sensors greatly break through the frame rate limitations of traditional cameras and record dynamic information in an event-driven manner, making them especially suitable for high-speed sports scenes. In this way, the DVS is able to capture the rapid movement of obstacles in real time, providing key information for unmanned aerial vehicle (UAV) obstacle avoidance and robot motion planning and improving the system's dynamic response ability. Currently, these types of vision sensors have achieved large-scale industrial applications. For example, the compound eyes obstacle avoidance system has been developed by DJI using a Sony

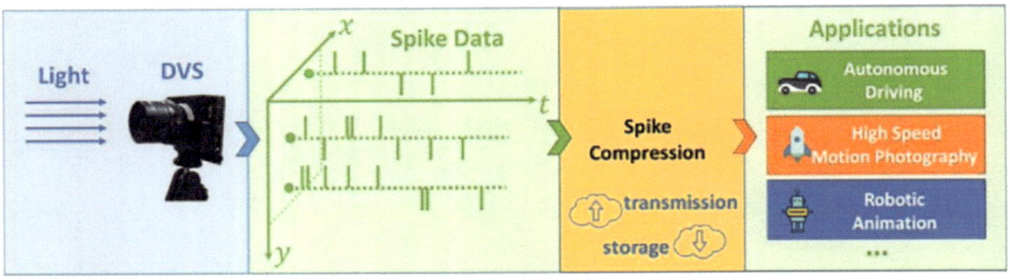

Figure 12.
Pulse data compression based on DVS and its application.

curved CMOS array and Prophet see event camera fusion solution, which can realize sub-millisecond obstacle detection when the UAV is flying at a high speed of 40 m/s. Prophesee and Sony jointly developed the "car-event-camera-fusion scheme," which deeply integrated Prophesee's Metavision event sensor with Sony's global shutter CMOS sensor to form an "event stream-image frame" dual-modal collaborative perception, improving the real-time and reliability of dynamic visual perception in complex scenes. The pixel-level-fusion chip "ALPIX-Pilatus," based on "Hybrid Vision" technology developed by Ruisi Zhixin, can switch between 120-frame-global-exposure mode and ultra-high-frame-rate event perception mode in milliseconds. In addition, the multi-viewing angle characteristic of the bionic compound eyes also allows DVS to realize a wide range of field of view coverage, which reduces the power consumption of the traditional mechanical scanning strategy and improves the overall efficiency of the robotic system.

2.8.2 Target tracking

Bionic vision sensors can mimic motion-sensitive properties and neural processing mechanisms of insect compound eyes to effectively recognize and continuously track high-speed moving objects [11]. In an automated production line application, robotic arms equipped with bionic vision sensors are able to quickly adapt to different positions and postures of targets on the assembly line and are able to flexibly and accurately grasp targets. For example, the flexible grasping system (mGrip+3D) based on the "bionic hand-eye collaborative vision" technology is developed by Soft Robotics. This system has a spatial resolution of >0.1 mm and real-time modeling capability in millisecond timescales. Combined with the adaptive pressure control of the gripper, the system can handle irregular and vulnerable items with a success rate of more than 99%. Additionally, in order to improve the reliability of target tracking, current research introduces the polarized light perception technique. By integrating micro-polarization arrays, the bionic vision sensor can sense and extract the polarization information of the target, accurately distinguish between the target and the background under complex lighting conditions, and enhance the anti-interference ability for target tracking.

2.8.3 Autonomous navigation

The navigational ability of insects relies heavily on their compound eyes and sensitivity to polarized light. For example, the Saharan silver ants perceive naturally polarized light for orientation and combine it with methods such as path integration for navigation. Such a navigation method has the advantages of strong anti-interference ability, high precision, and non-accumulating errors over time, which is suitable for long-distance autonomous navigation in complex environments. Similarly, the bionic polarized light navigation sensor mimics the navigation method of the insect vision system and realizes the autonomous navigation function by detecting the polarized light pattern after atmospheric scattering and extracting the direction information from it. These sensors can be further combined with spectral sensing modules to obtain a wealth of information in environments with complex lighting conditions, such as 3D terrain features and surface material properties. In disaster rescue, these sensors can help robots quickly identify structural collapse areas and detect hazardous surfaces, thereby facilitating safer and more efficient mission execution. In addition, insects also achieve autonomous navigation by combining "odometry" and "snapshot"-based visual guidance behaviors. Researchers at Delft University of Technology have drawn inspiration from the visual navigation mechanisms of ants, enabling microrobots to move flexibly and navigate autonomously in confined areas (**Figure 13**). Their "CrazyFlie" small UAV, weighing only 56 g, is equipped with an omnidirectional camera and is able to combine "odometry" with the "snapshots" to achieve autonomous return flights of up to 100 m. This UAV is able to find the locations where it has left "snapshots" in conjunction with "odometry," allowing it to return home autonomously over distances up to 100 m. Meanwhile, the underwater bionic polarized light navigation system (Seapath-Polar) is proposed by Kongsberg Maritime. By combining underwater polarized light perception and a multi-sensor fusion algorithm, this system realizes sub-meter-level positioning and heading correction in complex marine environments (such as low illumination and turbid water).

2.9 Applications of bioinspired visual sensors in industrial inspection

The visual system of insects has a special neural processing architecture. A hierarchical network composed of neurons in compound eyes can complete an effective parsing function of visual information based on the three-stage signal processing method: lower-order

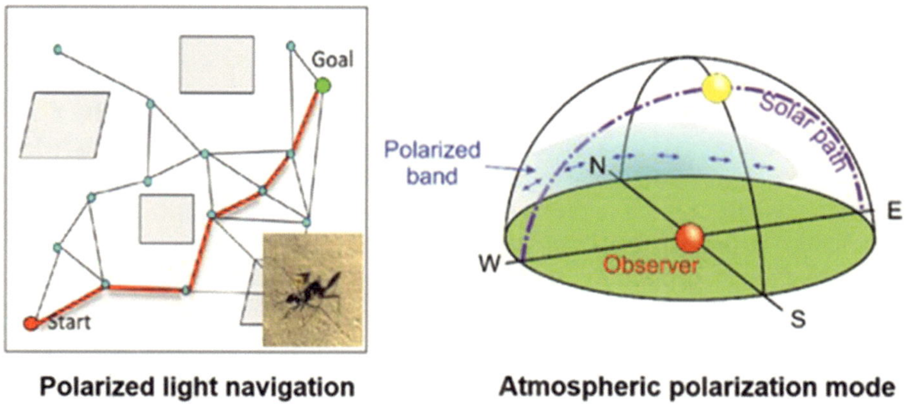

Figure 13.
Biomimetic polarization light navigation and polarization information reconstruction.

neurons complete the detection work about the basic signal, such as light intensity or color; middle-order neurons integrate these elementary images to finish the edge discrimination and judgment work about object shape; higher-order neurons use nonlinear calculation methods to accurately identify motion targets and forecast target tracks.

Drosophila has dozens of thousands of ommatidia per compound eye, which can make them obtain important characteristics of critical flicker frequency, reaching 96 Hz, four times that of the human single-eye system's dynamic response capacity (24 Hz). On the basis of combining neurobiology with bionics, researchers have proposed the concept of "bionic visual sensor technology." This approach incorporates (a) micro/nano-optical arrays mimicking the ommatidial structure of insect compound eyes and (b) hierarchical signal-processing algorithms that replicate neural computation patterns derived from biological behaviors. Therefore, the bionic visual sensor can realize accurate weak-light difference detection below one-thousandth ($<10^{-3}$ lux) and sub-millisecond target-capture dynamics capability. Contrary to the limited frame rate and resolutions of machine vision, the bionic visual sensor provides nanometer- and millisecond-level spatial-temporal precision for the inspected item during industrial inspection applications, so it can be widely used in various industrial inspection fields.

2.9.1 Real-time quality monitoring on high-speed production lines

The conventional visual system has an image acquisition frame rate of only 10–20 FPS in computer, communication, and consumer electronics products. When facing chip mounters with a maximum production speed of up to 30,000 chips/hour, the conventional visual system is difficult to capture instantaneous offset and welding faults, resulting in a fault recognition false negative rate of 5–8%. Conversely, bioinspired visual sensors are inspired by the compound eyes of Drosophila. Multi-channel parallel acquisition technology enables it to achieve ultra-high frame rates of 120 FPS. At the same time, combined with a motion vector algorithm analysis technology, bioinspired visual sensors can realize real-time detection of placement deviation and welding fault information at a resolution of 0.1 mm, and the detection accuracy is as high as 99.2%. Through actual testing, the product defect rate of the smartphone motherboard was reduced by 4.3%, which significantly improved the productivity of mobile phone manufacturing.

2.9.2 Sub-micron defect detection in precision manufacturing

The inspection of the surface quality of aircraft engine blades has very strict requirements, while traditional visual systems cannot detect cracks and pores below 5 μm. The bioinspired visual sensor utilizes multispectral imaging and polarization analysis technologies similar to the spectral perception characteristics and the polarization-sensitive features of insect vision systems, realizing three-dimensional reconstruction of microdefects. Combining actual test data from an aircraft engine manufacturer, this device detects cracks as low as 3 μm, achieving a defect recognition accuracy rate of 98.7%, reducing aviation accident hazards caused by material defects (**Figure 14**).

As for automotive manufacturing, critical automotive parts such as engine blocks directly relate to the reliability and safety of the entire car's powertrain. Its surface quality tolerance reaches the micron level. Bioinspired visual sensors have the high-resolution perceptual characteristics of insect vision systems. These sensors take advantage of the characteristic that the structure of the fly's compound eyes captures multiple-angle lighting

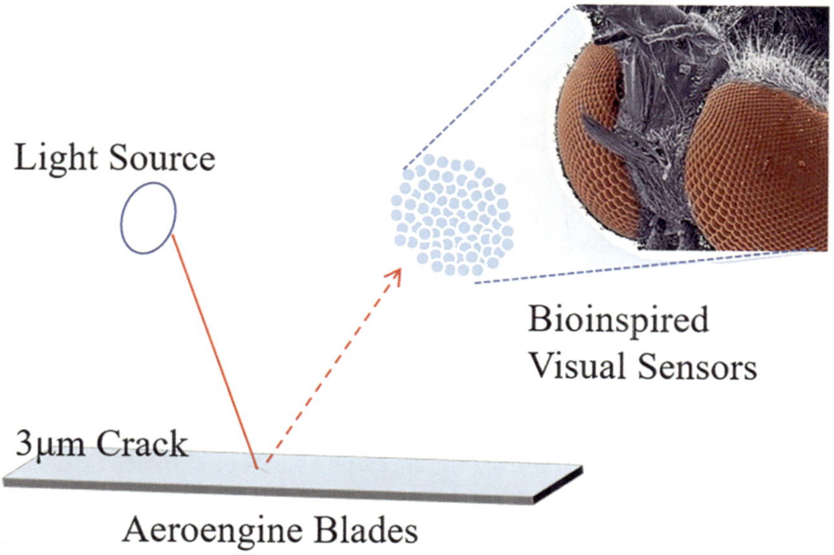

Figure 14.
Applications of bioinspired visual sensors in industrial defect detection.

and combines the defect feature recognition model based on deep learning to quickly discover and reconstruct 3D images of microdefects (including scratches within 0.1 mm^2 and holes <50 μm) on the surface of some engine blocks of automobile bodies. This method effectively ensures the precision manufacturing of the engine block and provides important technical guarantees for the reliability and driving safety of automobile parts.

2.9.3 Dynamic sorting optimization in automated systems

Bioinspired visual sensors have also been widely used in the automated warehouse and logistics system due to their fast processing capabilities. According to the quick target tracking mechanism of the insect visual system, these artificial sensors are able to quickly track goods passing through complicated logistics areas. Inside an automated warehouse system, it is very important to monitor how many products are in each shelf slot using instant bioinspired sensors that respond to the required number of items. Upon detecting insufficient quantities or location deviations, they send an alert message to all control systems so that all control systems can send orders for filling up actions. When workers deal with a large number of packages containing different items, the packages flow very fast on the conveyor belts, so workers usually spend a lot of time sorting out their deliveries before releasing each package to the appropriate destination. By referencing the effective velocity detection of moving objects observed in insect vision systems, researchers have begun developing novel sensors capable of matching such rapid processing through near-instantaneous information transfer and functional response times. This novel sensor captures and archives label images of each package passing through the designated conveyor system, enabling real-time comparison between expected values and acquired data to facilitate automated decision-making. Therefore, those pieces of luggage would be directed to the same destination or thrown directly into the bin according to a completely different path. Such automatic sorting operations can go hand-in-hand with several other fast-related applications. Indeed, when inspecting some conveyors under scrutiny during scheduled maintenance checks, these bioinspired visual sensors could detect various problems related to the working status of incoming packages, which may be loaded incorrectly due to human negligence during loading times (e.g., broken cases and lost labels). This additional function triggers automatic decisions so as to prevent possible problems from occurring later. Even if there are multiple failures around some critical points involved in daily workflow plans, everything can stay smooth.

2.10 Outlooks and challenges

Bionic vision sensors are moving toward the direction of engineering applications from basic research, and their future direction will mainly focus on performance optimization, multifunctional integration, and the improvement of cross-modal sensing capability. As for the further performance optimization of bionic vision sensors, researchers are working to improve the sensor's dynamic sensing ability and imaging resolution. The asynchronous pulse sensor developed based on the event-driven mechanism of insect compound eyes has shown better dynamic response characteristics than traditional frame cameras. This kind of sensor can realize microsecond-fast response and operate with low power consumption. However, its dynamic response characteristics and signal-to-noise ratio under complex lighting conditions still have a certain gap when compared to biological systems. Further optimization of its spatial-temporal resolution and noise suppression capability is needed in the future, especially the development of adaptive adjustment algorithms under complex lighting conditions.

Bionic vision sensors are moving toward multifunctional integration and cross-modal sensing capability. On the one hand, neuromorphic computing chips with bionic vision sensors need further collaborative optimization. The efficiency of parallel processing and feature extraction in honeybee vision systems drives the design of specialized integrated circuits in the storage-computing architecture. However, there is still an order of magnitude difference between the operating frequency of existing synaptic devices and the millisecond response of the biological nervous system, which requires the joint optimization of novel amnion materials and pulsed neural network algorithms. On the other hand, current research is attempting to fuse biological properties such as polarized light navigation and multispectral sensing into a single sensor platform, which entails the process challenge of highly integrating physical carriers for different sensing modalities at the micro- and nanoscale. In addition, breakthroughs in energy efficiency can hopefully be realized through the development of integrated photovoltaic-sensing designs, such as visual sensors with self-powered energy supply characteristics by borrowing the light-trapping mechanism from the photonic crystal structure of a butterfly's wing.

3. Conclusion

A comprehensive summary of bioinspired vision systems, bridging neural mechanisms of insect vision with cutting-edge engineering applications, is presented. Insect visual systems exhibit advantages in motion detection, collision avoidance, and dynamic adaptation, making them ideal candidates for next-generation visual sensors. Biological principles, e.g., the direction-selective circuits of DSNs, the collision-detection mechanism of LGMD neurons, and the energy-efficient signal encoding of graded neurons, have inspired innovative hardware designs, including hemispherical compound eye sensors (e.g., BAC-eye, ACE, and PHCE) and neuromorphic processing

DOI: http://dx.doi.org/10.5772/intechopen.1011096

architectures (e.g., Nengo and Lava). These bioinspired systems outperform conventional vision sensors in fields of view, response speed, and power efficiency. Despite the above-mentioned progress, critical challenges remain in the following parts: (1) high fabrication costs for integrated systems; (2) limited robustness in occluded environments; and (3) hardware incompatibility in multimodal sensing. Future breakthroughs will require combining material innovations, neuromorphic computing architectures, and adaptive algorithms to emulate the sophistication of biological vision.

Acknowledgements

This work is supported by the National Key R&D Program of China (No. 2024YFB3614600), the National Natural Science Foundation of China (No. 52402185), the Guangzhou Basic and Applied Basic Research Foundation (No.2025A1515011800), the Research Center for Brain Cognition and Human Development, Guangdong, China (No. 2024B0303390003), State Key Laboratory of Photonics and Communications, Shanghai Jiao Tong University, China (No.2025QZKF022) and the Shenzhen Science and Technology Program (No. JCYJ20241202123712017).

Conflict of interest

The authors declare no conflict of interest.

Appendices and nomenclature

Lamina	The first level of visual neural structure connecting photoreceptors in insect compound eyes.
Medulla	The secondary neural structure that receives lamina signals in insect compound eyes.
Lobula	The third higher visual center located behind the medulla.
DCMD neurons	The core component of the key neural pathway for survival, which converts the threat signal of the contralateral visual field into a rapid escape action.
LMC	The "primary signal processor" of insect vision, which converts the original optical signal into highly efficient encoded neural information.
Fiber	One kind of waveguide, which is usually used for directing light by applying the theory of total internal reflection of light. It is usually made of glass or plastic.
Beam splitter	An optical element used to divide an incident light into two or more beams in a specific proportion, whose core function is to control the energy distribution and propagation direction of the optical path.
FOV	The angle corresponding to the spatial range that an optical system can observe or capture, which describes the "visible range" of the system in the horizontal, vertical, or diagonal directions, and is an important parameter for measuring the observation capability of the optical system.

Author details

Jiewei Chen[1,2]*, Tao Zheng[1,2]*, Jiayang Xiao[1,2], Junyi Li[1,2], Jing Wang[1,2], Xinyi Wu[1,2], Zhiyu Zhang[1,2], Shuliang Zhou[1,2], Jiexiong Li[1,2], Yuhao Liang[1,2] and Tianyue Wang[3]*

1 School of Optoelectronic Science and Engineering, South China Normal University, Guangzhou, P. R. China

2 Future Institute of Technology, Guangdong Provincial Key Laboratory of Nanophotonic Functional Materials and Devices, Guangdong Basic Research Center of Excellence for Structure and Fundamental Interactions of Matter, MOE Key Laboratory of Laser Life Science and Guangdong Provincial Key Laboratory of Laser Life Science, School of Optoelectronic Science and Engineering, South China Normal University, Guangzhou, China

3 Department of Applied Physics, The Hong Kong Polytechnic University, Hong Kong, China

*Address all correspondence to: jwchen@m.scnu.edu.cn; taozheng@m.scnu.edu.cn and ty.wang@connect.polyu.hk

References

[1] Borst A. Neural circuits for elementary motion detection. Journal of Neurogenetics. 2014;**28**:361-373

[2] Wang Y, Gong Y, Huang S, et al. Memristor-based biomimetic compound eye for real-time collision detection. Nature Communications. 2021;**12**:5979

[3] Maisak MS, Haag J, Ammer G, et al. A directional tuning map of Drosophila elementary motion detectors. Nature. 2013;**500**:212-216

[4] Gabbiani F, Krapp HG, Koch C, et al. Multiplicative computation in a visual neuron sensitive to looming. Nature. 2002;**420**:320-324

[5] Dai B, Zhang L, Zhao C, et al. Biomimetic apposition compound eye fabricated using microfluidic-assisted 3D printing. Nature Communications. 2021;**12**:6458

[6] Zheng L, Nikolaev A, Wardill TJ, et al. Network adaptation improves temporal representation of naturalistic stimuli in Drosophila eye: I dynamics. PLoS ONE. 2009;**4**:e4307

[7] Jiang H, Tsoi CC, Yu W, et al. Optical fibre based artificial compound eyes for direct static imaging and ultrafast motion detection. Light: Science & Applications. 2024;**13**:256

[8] Zhou Y, Sun Z, Ding Y, et al. An ultrawide field-of-view pinhole compound eye using hemispherical nanowire array for robot vision. Science Robotics. 2024;**9**:eadi8666

[9] Gu L, Poddar S, Lin Y, et al. A biomimetic eye with a hemispherical perovskite nanowire array retina. Nature. 2020;**581**:278-282

[10] Chen J, Zhou Z, Kim BJ, et al. Optoelectronic graded neurons for bioinspired in-sensor motion perception. Nature Nanotechnology. 2023;**18**:882-888

[11] Lee PL, Szema R. Inspirations from biological optics for advanced photonic systems. Science. 2005;**310**:1148

Chapter 4

Toward Ethical and Transparent Brain-Computer Interfaces: Challenges and Perspectives in EEG-Based AI

Badr Mouazen and Zainab El Bouyed

Abstract

The convergence of electroencephalography (EEG) and artificial intelligence (AI) has transformed brain-computer interfaces (BCI) from experimental medical devices into potential consumer technologies, raising unprecedented ethical challenges. This chapter analyzes ethical and transparency issues in EEG-based BCIs, examining implications for privacy, autonomy, equity, and human dignity. We explore three dimensions: technological foundations, emerging ethical risks, and practical solutions. Key challenges include "neuroprivacy" concerns, threats to mental autonomy, algorithmic bias, informed consent complexities, and security vulnerabilities. Neural data's inferential potential through AI creates new categories of personal information exposure. We propose a framework integrating explainable AI, ethics-by-design principles, adaptive governance, and legal recognition of "neuro-rights." Technical transparency and ethical integration are the essential conditions for responsible BCI development. While EEG-BCIs offer therapeutic potential, preserving human dignity requires ethics-centered innovation. This work provides theoretical frameworks and practical guidelines for navigating brain-machine interface ethics.

Keywords: brain-computer Interface (BCI), electroencephalography (EEG), artificial intelligence (AI), explainable AI (XAI), neuro-rights, neuroprivacy

1. Introduction

What once belonged to the realm of science fiction is now becoming a tangible reality in our laboratories and, progressively, in our daily lives. Brain-computer interfaces (BCI) emerge as one of the most promising and disruptive technologies of our era, paving the way for revolutionary applications: from direct device control through thought to the restoration of sensorimotor functions in people with disabilities, and even the augmentation of human cognitive capabilities. This transformation is no longer a distant promise, but an ongoing reality that redefines the boundaries between mind and machine.

At the heart of this technological revolution lies a remarkable convergence between two major scientific domains: electroencephalography (EEG), which offers us a privileged window into the electrical activity of the human brain, and artificial intelligence (AI), which acts as a powerful interpreter capable of decoding and making sense of complex neural signals. EEG, a non-invasive technique developed nearly a century ago, allows real-time recording of brain electrical activity with exceptional temporal resolution. When coupled with modern machine learning algorithms, it becomes a direct communication tool between the brain and digital systems, transforming mental intentions into exploitable computer commands. Among these capabilities, affective computing—the recognition and interpretation of human emotional states through EEG—represents a particularly promising yet ethically complex domain. The capacity to decode emotions opens possibilities for mental health monitoring and empathic technologies, while raising fundamental questions about emotional privacy and manipulation.

This unprecedented capacity to decode mental states, intentions, and potentially thoughts themselves nevertheless raises ethical, legal, and societal questions of unparalleled magnitude. How can we preserve mental privacy when our thoughts become accessible to machines? What mechanisms should be implemented to guarantee individual autonomy in the face of technologies capable of influencing our cognitive processes? How can we ensure equity in access to these human augmentation technologies and avoid creating new inequalities? These fundamental questions challenge not only the scientific community, but society as a whole, as BCI touch the very essence of what defines humanity: thought, consciousness, and free will.

Faced with these complex and interdependent challenges, this chapter proposes to systematically review and analyze the ethical and transparency issues inherent in the development of EEG-based brain-computer interfaces powered by AI. Our objectives are structured around three main axes. First, we will present the technical foundations of EEG and artificial intelligence, explicating their interaction mechanisms and the innovations that make this technological symbiosis possible. Second, we will conduct an exhaustive mapping of ethical risks and vulnerabilities associated with these technologies, analyzing their implications for privacy, autonomy, equity, and human dignity. Third, we will propose a conceptual and practical framework of solutions to guide the responsible and transparent development of BCI, integrating technical, regulatory, and societal dimensions.

Our analysis will be structured in three main parts that organize the reflection in a progressive and complementary manner. The first part, devoted to the technological revolution, will establish the scientific and technical foundations necessary for understanding EEG-based BCI, describing recent advances in computational neuroscience and machine learning. The second part will present a panorama of the new risk landscape, identifying and analyzing the emerging ethical challenges that this technology poses for individuals and society. Finally, the third part will propose a mapping of solutions, presenting methodological approaches, regulatory frameworks, and best practices necessary to ensure ethical and transparent development of these technologies.

The evolution of brain-computer interfaces spans an extraordinary 150-year journey, from the initial discovery of electrical signals in animals' brains in 1875 to today's sophisticated neural decoding systems capable of producing full sentences of natural speech. This remarkable trajectory, illustrated in **Figure 1**, reveals a fascinating progression through distinct technological eras.

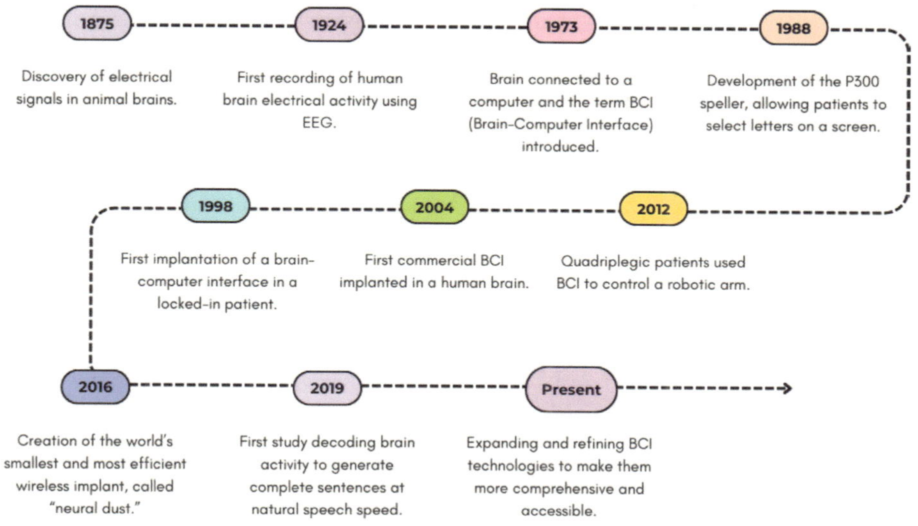

Figure 1.
Timeline of brain-computer interface evolution (from electrical signal discovery to comprehensive neural decoding).

This timeline not only demonstrates the accelerating pace of innovation—with particularly rapid advances in the past decade—but also highlights the critical inflection point we have reached. The convergence of mature EEG technology with advanced artificial intelligence has transformed BCI from the experimental medical devices into potentially ubiquitous consumer technologies, thereby amplifying the ethical stakes and urgency of establishing robust governance frameworks.

2. The EEG-AI revolution: Potentials and technical foundations

A deep understanding of the ethical issues related to EEG-based brain-computer interfaces requires first mastering the scientific and technical foundations that make this technological revolution possible. This first part establishes the essential knowledge base needed to comprehend the ethical challenges emerging from this convergence between neuroscience and artificial intelligence. We will successively examine the capabilities and limitations of EEG as a brain activity measurement technique, the transformative role of AI in neural signal interpretation, and finally the landscape of applications shaping our present and future.

2.1 EEG: A window into the mind

2.1.1 Physiological principle and history

Electroencephalography is based on a fundamental principle: measuring the electrical activity generated by cortical neurons. When neurons communicate with each other, they generate small electrical currents that, when summed at the level of large neuronal populations, become detectable at the skull's surface. This electrical activity, on the order of microvolts, reflects the synchronization and desynchronization processes of underlying neural networks [1].

The history of EEG is rooted in the pioneering discoveries of Richard Caton who, in 1875, first observed brain electrical activity in animals. But it was Hans Berger who, in 1924, performed the first human EEG recording, thus opening an unprecedented window into the functioning of the living brain. This revolutionary discovery enabled the identification of the first brain rhythms, notably alpha waves (8–12 Hz) that Berger observed in occipital regions during eye closure.

2.1.2 What EEG measures

EEG captures a rich palette of neurophysiological information reflecting different brain states and processes. Brain rhythms constitute the fundamental signature of this activity: Delta waves (0.5–4 Hz) dominate during deep sleep [2], alpha waves (8–12 Hz) characterize a relaxed waking state [3], and gamma waves (30–100 Hz) are linked to complex cognitive processes and consciousness [4, 5]. Theta (4–8 Hz) and beta (12–30 Hz) rhythms reflect intermediate states of arousal and attention, each contributing to the rich neurophysiological landscape captured by EEG.

Modern EEG also enables evaluation of complex cognitive states: Attention level can be quantified through alpha and beta rhythm analysis, cognitive engagement translates to specific modifications in frequency bands, and mental workload can be estimated from spectral power in certain brain regions. Emotional states leave distinctive signatures in EEG signals through frontal alpha asymmetries (correlating with emotional valence) [6], theta activity (reflecting arousal), and gamma oscillations (indicating emotional processing) [4, 5]. These patterns enable affective computing systems—AI-driven emotion recognition technologies—that achieve 88–89% accuracy in detecting emotional states [7], transforming EEG into an interface for emotion-aware applications in mental health, entertainment, and human-machine interaction.

2.1.3 Strengths and limitations

EEG presents considerable advantages that explain its growing adoption in BCI applications. Its non-invasive character makes it a safe and acceptable technique for a broad public, unlike approaches requiring surgical intervention [8]. Its portability, thanks to modern wireless systems, enables recordings in natural environments. Its exceptional temporal resolution, on the order of milliseconds, captures rapid dynamics of neural processes. Finally, its relative accessibility in terms of cost favors democratization.

However, EEG suffers from important limitations that constrain its applications [8]. Its limited spatial resolution, on the order of centimeters, does not allow precise localization of signal origins in brain depth. Signals must traverse the meninges, cerebrospinal fluid, and skull bone, which attenuates and distorts them. Moreover, EEG is particularly sensitive to artifacts: muscle contractions (EMG), eye movements (EOG), heartbeats (ECG), and environmental electromagnetic interference can mask signals of interest, requiring sophisticated preprocessing techniques for artifact removal.

2.2 AI: The interpreter of brain signals

2.2.1 Why AI is indispensable

EEG signals present a complexity that defies direct human interpretation and necessitates the use of sophisticated artificial intelligence algorithms. This complexity manifests at several levels: high data dimensionality (several dozen channels sampled at high frequency), considerable inter-individual variability (each brain presents unique neurophysiological characteristics), and intra-individual variability (signals from the same person evolve according to their state, fatigue, attention).

Moreover, neural patterns of interest are often buried in physiological and environmental noise, making their extraction particularly delicate. Complex relationships between different frequency bands, spatiotemporal interactions between electrodes, and nonlinear dynamics of neural networks far exceed manual analysis capabilities [9]. These challenges necessitate automated machine learning approaches capable of discovering latent patterns in high-dimensional neural data.

2.2.2 Evolution of methods

The application of artificial intelligence to EEG signal processing has undergone remarkable evolution over recent decades, marked by successive technological leaps that have revolutionized BCI system performance, and this evolution has been systematically documented in the recent literature reviews [10].

- "Classical" machine learning: Early approaches relied on traditional machine learning techniques, notably support vector machines (SVM) and linear discriminant analysis (LDA). These methods required manual feature extraction from EEG signals: spectral power in different frequency bands, autoregression coefficients, connectivity parameters [11].

- Deep learning: The advent of deep learning marked a decisive turning point in EEG signal processing. Convolutional neural networks (CNNs) proved particularly effective for automatic extraction of complex spatiotemporal features. These architectures can identify subtle patterns in raw data without requiring prior feature definition. 1D CNNs exploit temporal signal structures, while 2D CNNs process time-frequency representations or topographic activation maps. Recurrent networks (RNNs) and their sophisticated variants like Long Short-Term Memory (LSTMs) excel in modeling long-term temporal dependencies, crucial for understanding brain dynamics. These architectures can capture complex sequential relationships between successive neural states [9].

More recently, the adaptation of transformers to EEG signals has opened new perspectives. These architectures, initially developed for natural language processing, exploit attention mechanisms that allow weighting the importance of different brain regions and temporal instants in decision-making.

2.2.3 The challenge of real-time and latency

BCI applications often require real-time EEG signal processing with strict latency constraints. For cursor or prosthetic control interfaces, each additional millisecond of delay degrades user experience and may compromise safety. This requirement imposes important architectural constraints: AI models must be sufficiently lightweight to run on embedded processors while maintaining high accuracy [8]. Real-time optimization involves trade-offs between algorithmic complexity and performance, leading to the development of model compression techniques, weight quantization, and dedicated hardware acceleration.

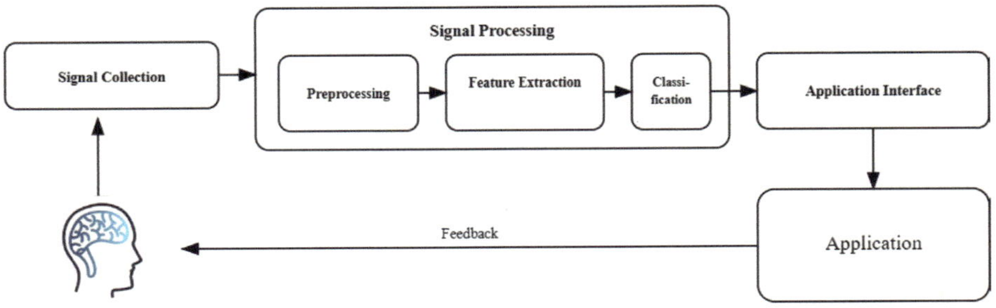

Figure 2.
Architecture of a brain-computer interface (BCI), illustrating signal acquisition, processing, classification, and application feedback.

Real-time optimization involves trade-offs between algorithmic complexity and performance, leading to the development of model compression techniques, weight quantization, and dedicated hardware acceleration (**Figure 2**).

2.3 Application landscape

The convergence between EEG and artificial intelligence has given birth to a remarkably diverse application ecosystem, extending from the traditional medical domain toward previously unexplored sectors. This rapid expansion illustrates the transformative potential of these technologies while raising ethical questions proportional to their societal impact.

2.3.1 Medical and therapeutic domain

The medical sector remains the primary domain for EEG applications, with AI significantly enhancing diagnostic and therapeutic capabilities. In neurological diagnosis, machine learning algorithms are revolutionizing the detection and classification of epileptic seizures, achieving precision levels that surpass traditional human expertise. Recent meta-analyses demonstrate pooled sensitivity of 0.96 (95% CI 0.95–0.97) and specificity of 0.97 (95% CI 0.96–0.98), with area under the curve values reaching 0.99 (95% CI 0.98–1.00), and optimized approaches achieving accuracies of 98–100% in seizure classification [12]. These automated systems can identify subtle patterns in prolonged recordings, drastically reducing diagnosis time [13]. Furthermore, sleep disorder analysis benefits from deep learning algorithms that automatically classify sleep stages and detect apneas with remarkable accuracy [14]. EEG coupled with AI also shows promise for the early diagnosis of cognitive disorders like mild cognitive impairment (MCI) by identifying electrophysiological biomarkers before clinical symptoms appear, and this approach now extends to early diagnosis of Alzheimer's disease, where EEG biomarkers coupled with AI show encouraging results [15]. Therapeutically, numerous studies have shown that BCI therapy can trigger long-lasting neurological changes and improve the motor function of the upper extremity of subacute and chronic stroke patients [16]. BCI-mediated neurofeedback mechanisms enable better engagement of motor areas compared to motor imagery alone and can promote neuroplasticity in brain regions affected by the cerebrovascular accident [17]. It also provides a vital communication pathway for locked-in syndrome patients and enables control of prosthetics through the modulation of brain rhythms.

2.3.2 Affective computing: Wellness and entertainment applications

Affective computing—systems that recognize and respond to human emotions—has emerged as a major EEG-BCI application domain spanning clinical and consumer contexts. In mental health, emotion recognition algorithms achieve approximately 84% accuracy in predicting depression treatment response through analysis of frontal alpha asymmetries and theta patterns [18], enabling objective monitoring where self-reports may be unreliable. These capabilities extend to real-time emotion detection for various applications [7].

In consumer applications, affective BCIs power emotion-aware experiences:

Beyond medicine, EEG-AI technology has expanded into the wellness and entertainment sectors. In personal wellness, neurofeedback experiences a renaissance through AI, offering precise and personalized feedback for assisted meditation and emotional regulation. Systems can detect states of stress, anxiety, or depression and propose tailored interventions. The video game industry is actively exploring EEG interfaces to create deeply immersive experiences where games can adapt in real time to a player's attention, stress, or engagement levels [19]. In some cases, EEG signals serve as a direct control interface. This integration is particularly powerful in virtual reality, where a user's felt emotions can modify virtual landscapes, create empathic interactions, and adapt the narrative flow.

2.3.3 Professional and industrial domain (neuroergonomics)

A third major application area is neuroergonomics, an emerging discipline that uses EEG-AI to optimize human performance in professional and industrial settings. A crucial application is vigilance monitoring for high-risk professions like pilots or drivers, where systems analyze EEG patterns characteristic of drowsiness to trigger preventive alerts [20]. Additionally, cognitive load measurement provides an objective way to evaluate the mental effort required by tasks, informing better workstation design, training programs, and the development of human-machine interfaces. These interfaces can become adaptive, simplifying during cognitive overload or offering more information when the user has sufficient attentional resources [21]. Finally, EEG enables the measurement of pedagogical effectiveness in professional training, allowing for the identification of attentional disengagement and the adaptation of rhythm to an individual's learning capabilities.

3. A new landscape of risks: Ethical and societal challenges

The emergence of EEG-based brain-computer interfaces powered by artificial intelligence is not limited to a simple technological innovation: It inaugurates a new paradigm in the relationship between humans and machines, generating ethical and societal risks of unprecedented nature and magnitude. This technological convergence, by enabling direct access to neural signals and their automated interpretation, crosses fundamental anthropological thresholds and questions the very foundations of our conception of privacy, autonomy, and justice.

The intersection of neuroscience, artificial intelligence, and human-computer interaction creates what philosophers of technology term a "technological assemblage" that fundamentally reconfigures the boundaries between mind and machine, individual and collective, and private and public [22]. Unlike previous technologies that remained external to human cognition, EEG-BCIs create a direct coupling between neural processes and algorithmic interpretation, establishing what we might call a "cyborg epistemology" where human knowledge and machine learning become inextricably intertwined [23].

This section undertakes a systematic and in-depth analysis of these new risks, organized around six critical dimensions that structure the ethical landscape of EEG-BCIs. We examine threats to mental privacy with concrete violations of "neuroprivacy," challenges to human agency through the documented cases of cognitive manipulation, justice issues with empirical evidence of algorithmic bias, the practical breakdown of informed consent in clinical and commercial settings, security vulnerabilities through real-world attack scenarios, and finally the broader implications for human identity and social cohesion in an age of neural surveillance.

3.1 Mental privacy and the emergence of neuroprivacy

3.1.1 The neurological breach of mental sanctuary

EEG signals represent the most intimate category of personal data, transcending traditional information classifications by capturing real-time internal states including emotions, cognitive processes, nascent intentions, and potentially thought content through distinctive neural signatures. Recent advances demonstrate the ability to decode complex mental states: EEG-based emotion recognition systems using frontal alpha asymmetries and other features achieve accuracies of 88–89% [7], gamma oscillations (30–100 Hz) indicate cognitive effort and working memory load [5], and motor cortex patterns can predict the intended movements up to 500 milliseconds before conscious awareness [24]. Affective computing systems specifically target this intimacy, decoding emotions that individuals may deliberately conceal—feelings revealed through neural patterns before conscious awareness or contrary to expressed sentiment [25].

The Libet experiments show that the "readiness potential"—a buildup of electrical activity in the motor cortex—begins approximately 350–500 milliseconds before a person reports being aware of their intention to move [24]. This temporal gap between neural intention and conscious awareness creates what neuroscientist Benjamin Libet called the "free will not" problem: If our brains "decide" before we are consciously aware, what happens to free will when machines can read these unconscious decisions?

Case study—Facebook's neural interface research.

Meta (formerly Facebook) invested significantly in brain-computer interface research through its Building 8 laboratory before discontinuing funding in 2021, with collaborative research achieving speech decoding accuracies up to 75% using invasive electrode arrays [26]. While the project was officially discontinued, the technology demonstrated that consumer-grade EEG devices could potentially access the "inner voice"—the stream of imagined speech that constitutes much of human thinking.

The implications become clear when considering that this technology, developed ostensibly for helping paralyzed patients communicate, could theoretically be deployed in social media platforms to detect users' unspoken reactions to content, advertisements, or political messages. The boundary between thought and expression—fundamental to mental privacy—begins to dissolve when algorithms can decode imagined speech with growing accuracy.

3.1.2 Involuntary neural disclosure and cognitive fingerprinting

Beyond extracting explicit neural information, artificial intelligence can infer undisclosed personal characteristics through what researchers term "brain fingerprinting"—unique neural patterns that can identify individuals and predict personality traits [27]. Research has demonstrated that each individual's brain exhibits distinctive patterns of electrical activity that can serve as biometric identifiers, potentially more informative about internal states than traditional fingerprints [27].

Recent advances in machine learning have enabled the detection of psychiatric conditions using EEG patterns. A 2022 meta-analysis of 15 studies comprising 758 patients demonstrated that EEG-based algorithms could predict depression treatment response with the pooled accuracy rates of approximately 84%, reaching 86% for repetitive transcranial magnetic stimulation (rTMS) and 81% for antidepressant medications [18]. These algorithms identify depression through subtle patterns in frontal theta activity (4–8 Hz) and alpha power asymmetries—neural signatures that individuals cannot consciously control or conceal [18]. More concerning, research has shown that EEG patterns can predict treatment response to antidepressants, essentially revealing not only current mental health status but also biological information about future therapeutic outcomes [18]. This creates scenarios where employers, insurers, or educational institutions could theoretically screen for mental health conditions without explicit testing, simply by analyzing EEG data collected under other pretexts.

3.1.3 The neural data economy: Commodifying consciousness

The commercialization of neural data has created what scholars describe as an extension of "surveillance capitalism" into the realm of consciousness itself [28]. Consumer neurotechnology companies have marketed thousands of EEG devices to consumers, continuously harvesting neural data under broad terms of service that users may not fully understand [29].

3.1.3.1 Privacy concerns in consumer EEG devices

A systematic analysis of privacy practices among consumer neurotechnology companies revealed significant concerns regarding data collection, storage, and use [29]. Studies examining consumer EEG devices found that many collect substantially more data than necessary for their advertised functions, with meditation and wellness apps retaining detailed spectral analysis across multiple frequency bands that could potentially reveal cognitive states, attention patterns, and emotional responses unrelated to their stated purposes [25, 29]. This excess data collection exemplifies what privacy researchers call "function creep"—the gradual expansion of data use beyond original stated purposes.

3.1.3.2 Neuromarketing and consumer manipulation

The application of EEG to marketing research has demonstrated the potential to predict consumer behavior with greater accuracy than the traditional methods. Research in neuromarketing has shown that neural measurements can provide insights into consumer preferences and purchase intentions that subjects themselves may not consciously recognize [30]. Companies have developed EEG-based methodologies for assessing advertising effectiveness, creating "neuromarketing" platforms that promise to optimize advertising by directly accessing consumers' unconscious neural responses. Affective computing amplifies these concerns by enabling "emotion-first" marketing strategies that bypass rational deliberation entirely. Systems that detect micro-expressions of emotional response—positive affect toward product features, anxiety about pricing, desire triggered by imagery—can optimize persuasive content in real-time, exploiting emotional susceptibilities before conscious evaluation occurs [25, 30]. This raises fundamental concerns about bypassing rational decision-making processes and exploiting unconscious responses for commercial gain [31].

3.2 Agency, autonomy, and the dissolution of mental boundaries

3.2.1 Subliminal manipulation and cognitive sovereignty

Brain-computer interfaces may disrupt mental autonomy through mechanisms that operate below the threshold of conscious awareness. These systems can potentially detect moments of cognitive vulnerability—such as attention lapses, decision fatigue, or emotional distress—and theoretically exploit these states to influence behavior [32]. For instance, affective computing systems could identify neural signatures of emotional loneliness, sadness, or anxiety—states that compromise decision-making autonomy—and strategically present content or advertisements designed to exploit those specific affective vulnerabilities.

3.2.1.1 Hypothetical scenario: Adaptive gaming systems

While no documented cases of exploitative commercial BCI gaming systems have been publicly verified, researchers have raised concerns about the theoretical potential for EEG-based adaptive systems in gaming contexts [31]. Current research on BCI gaming remains primarily focused on accessibility and user experience enhancement [33], but the ethical implications of potential misuse warrant careful consideration and regulatory safeguards.

3.2.2 The agency loop: When minds become algorithmic optimization targets

The phenomenon of "neural co-adaptation" occurs when human brains unconsciously modify their activity patterns to improve performance within BCI systems [34]. This creates feedback loops where the distinction between authentic mental states and technologically optimized brain activity becomes increasingly blurred (**Figure 3**).

Research on patients learning to control BCIs has revealed changes in neural patterns over time as users adapt to system requirements [35]. Studies of motor imagery BCIs have documented how users develop novel neural strategies optimized for machine interpretation rather than natural motor planning [36]. This raises philosophical questions about the authenticity of agency when neural processes are shaped by algorithmic feedback.

Long-term BCI users have reported experiences suggesting altered self-perception in relation to their devices. Research indicates that intensive BCI training can lead to what some users describe as the device becoming integrated into their sense of self [37]. As one research participant noted: "Over time, the boundary between my thoughts and the system's interpretation became less clear."

Patient testimonials revealed the psychological impact: "At first, I had to concentrate really hard to move the cursor. But after a few months, it became

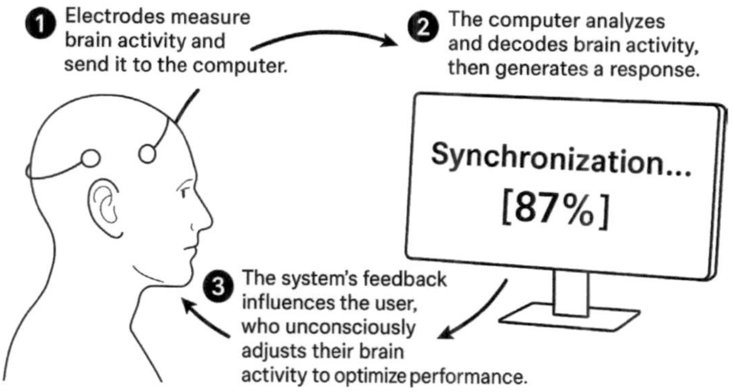

Figure 3.
Agency loop in a brain-computer interface (BCI): EEG signals are acquired, decoded into commands, and returned as feedback, leading to continuous user co-adaptation and potential loss of authentic agency.

automatic—too automatic. I started noticing that even when I wasn't using the system, my thoughts felt different, like they were being shaped by what the computer wanted to see."

3.2.3 Responsibility attribution in human-AI cognitive partnerships

The integration of EEG-BCIs into decision-making processes creates unprecedented challenges for legal and moral responsibility attribution [38]. When algorithmic interpretation of neural signals influences human choices, traditional frameworks of accountability become insufficient. These dynamics create legal responsibility dilemmas involving complex causal chains across multiple actors—users, developers, healthcare providers, and AI systems [39].

Empirical evidence shows that even in relatively simple EEG-based closed-loop systems, users may experience a weakened sense of agency, complicating responsibility attribution when outcomes are contested [38].

3.3 Justice, equity, and algorithmic neurocolonialism

3.3.1 Systemic bias in neural pattern recognition

EEG-BCI systems exhibit documented patterns of algorithmic bias that may systematically disadvantage underrepresented populations. These biases emerge from training datasets that have historically overrepresented certain demographic groups and may fail to account for neuroanatomical and cultural variations [40].

Gender and ethnic disparities in BCI performance Research has revealed consistent performance disparities across demographic groups in EEG-based systems [40]. Studies examining EEG-BCI performance across gender and ethnic groups have documented gender-based differences potentially stemming from anatomical variations (skull thickness affecting signal attenuation), hormonal influences on neural oscillations, and training data imbalances, as well as substantial racial disparities including the following:

- Significant variations in classification accuracy across racial groups
- Higher false-positive rates for certain populations

- Extended training periods required for underrepresented groups
- Higher dropout rates related to usability issues

These disparities correlate with skull morphology variations, cultural differences in cognitive strategies, socioeconomic factors affecting technology exposure, and fundamentally biased training datasets [40].

3.3.2 Neurological colonialism in global health applications

The deployment of Western-developed EEG-BCI systems in diverse global populations has raised concerns about what researchers term "neurological colonialism"—the imposition of culturally biased neural norms that may pathologize natural variations in human brain activity [41].

Studies of EEG-based medical diagnostic systems have revealed concerning patterns when applied to populations different from those on which they were trained. Research has documented:

- Elevated false-positive rates in certain populations
- Systematic misclassification of normal neural variants
- Misinterpretation of physiological variations that occur naturally across different ethnic groups [42].

These algorithmic failures can lead to misdiagnosis, with serious consequences for individuals' employment, healthcare access, and social standing [43].

3.3.3 The myth of neurological objectivity

The perception of neural data as objective and universal masks socially situated bias, making neurotechnological discrimination particularly insidious as it operates under the guise of scientific objectivity while potentially pathologizing natural human neurological diversity [41].

Research in cultural neuroscience demonstrates that cognitive processing patterns vary systematically across cultures [44]. Studies comparing BCI performance across different cultural groups have revealed that participants from different backgrounds may exhibit the distinct patterns of neural activation for similar tasks, reflecting cultural influences on cognitive strategies [45]. When participants use systems trained on data from different cultural populations, accuracy can decrease substantially, with algorithms potentially misinterpreting culturally influenced neural patterns.

3.4 The crisis of informed consent in the age of neural prediction

3.4.1 The complexity barrier and technological opacity

Traditional informed consent frameworks prove fundamentally inadequate for EEG-BCI technologies that generate unpredictable inferences about mental states through machine learning processes that even developers cannot fully explain or control [46]. The "black box" nature of many neural decoding algorithms creates scenarios where users cannot meaningfully consent to all potential uses of their data because those uses may not be fully known at the time of consent [25].

Case study—privacy breaches in neural data.

Data breaches affecting neurotechnology companies have revealed the scope of potential neural data exploitation. In documented incidents, companies collecting consumer EEG data were found to be performing analyses beyond those disclosed to users [29]. These cases illustrate how broad consent language about "improving user experience" or "research purposes" can mask extensive data processing and inference that users may not anticipate.

3.4.2 Vulnerable populations and coercive contexts

Certain populations face particular challenges in providing truly informed consent due to cognitive limitations, coercive circumstances, or therapeutic contexts that may compromise decision-making autonomy [47].

3.4.2.1 Pediatric neurotechnology: The consent paradox

The use of EEG neurofeedback in pediatric populations presents unique ethical challenges. Research indicates that children receiving EEG-based treatments may develop concerns about the technology, including worries about privacy and surveillance [48]. Parents must consent to technologies that may influence their children's neural development, yet long-term consequences of training developing brains to conform to algorithmic expectations of "normal" neural activity remain uncertain [49].

3.4.3 Dynamic consent and technological adaptation

The limitations of traditional consent models have led to proposals for "dynamic consent" systems that allow ongoing permission management [50]. However, implementation presents significant challenges including consent fatigue, technical complexity, and potential economic pressure on users to grant broad permissions [51].

3.5 Neurosecurity and the weaponization of mind-machine interfaces

3.5.1 The unique vulnerability profile of neural data

Neural data presents unprecedented security challenges because it combines permanent, unchangeable biometric characteristics with rich inferential capabilities. Unlike passwords or even traditional biometric data, compromised neural signatures may reveal sensitive information about mental states, cognitive abilities, and psychological conditions.

3.5.1.1 BCI security vulnerabilities

Research has demonstrated multiple attack vectors against EEG-based BCI systems, including side-channel attacks extracting sensitive information from neural signals, injection attacks manipulating BCI control signals, and neural signal spoofing and replay attacks [25]. These vulnerabilities demonstrate that neural interfaces face not only traditional cybersecurity threats but entirely new categories of attacks potentially targeting human cognition itself [25, 52].

3.5.1.2 Systemic vulnerabilities in healthcare settings

Security assessments of medical EEG systems have revealed concerning vulnerabilities, including inadequate encryption, weak authentication, and insufficient incident response protocols for neural data breaches [53]. These systemic weaknesses could enable attacks that alter medical readings or extract sensitive patient information.

3.6 Identity, authenticity, and the transformation of human experience

3.6.1 The cyborg condition and hybrid identity formation

The integration of EEG-BCIs into daily life fundamentally challenges the traditional concepts of personal identity and cognitive authenticity. As neural activity becomes increasingly mediated by algorithmic interpretation, users may experience what philosophers term "hybrid identity"—a form of selfhood that is constitutively technological [54].

3.6.1.1 Longitudinal effects of neural enhancement

Research examining long-term BCI users has documented changes in users' relationship with technology and self-conception. Studies suggest that extended BCI use may alter users' sense of cognitive boundaries, with some describing the technology as becoming integrated into their sense of self rather than remaining an external tool [37].

3.6.2 Collective neural networks and social cognition

Advances in brain-to-brain communication create possibilities for direct neural networking that challenge individualistic concepts of cognition. Research has demonstrated direct brain-to-brain communication using EEG and transcranial magnetic stimulation, enabling transmission of simple signals between individuals [55]. While current capabilities remain limited, these technologies raise profound questions about the boundaries of individual cognition and the potential emergence of networked consciousness.

3.6.3 Cognitive liberty and mental self-determination

The proliferation of EEG-BCI technologies necessitates new legal frameworks protecting "cognitive liberty"—the fundamental right to mental self-determination [56]. Chile became the first country to constitutionally protect neurorights in October 2021, establishing mental privacy, mental integrity, and cognitive liberty as fundamental rights through an amendment to Article 19 of the Chilean Constitution [57]. This legislation was prompted by concerns about rapid commercialization of neurotechnology without adequate protection for neural data and cognitive processes.

The Chilean framework includes protections for:

- Mental privacy (control over access to neural information)
- Personal identity (protection against technological alteration of personality)
- Free will and self-determination
- Equal access to cognitive enhancement technologies
- Protection against algorithmic bias [56]

3.7 Emerging risks and interconnected challenges

3.7.1 Environmental and geopolitical dimensions

The neural data economy has environmental implications through the energy requirements of cloud-based neural signal processing and data storage. Additionally, the concentration of neurotechnology development in a limited number of countries creates technological dependencies with potential geopolitical implications [56].

3.7.2 Long-term societal impacts

Research on the long-term societal implications of widespread neurotechnology adoption remains limited. Concerns include potential effects on:

- Inequality in access to cognitive enhancement
- Normative pressure to adopt neural technologies
- Erosion of cognitive privacy as a social norm
- Potential stigmatization of neurological diversity [56]

These long-term implications require sustained sociological and anthropological research to understand how neurotechnologies may reshape fundamental aspects of human social organization and individual identity [41, 56].

3.7.2.1 Conclusion: Navigating the neural frontier

This analysis reveals that EEG-based brain-computer interfaces represent more than technological advancement—they constitute a fundamental transformation in the relationship between human consciousness and digital systems. The interconnected nature of these risks creates cascading effects: Neural privacy violations enable algorithmic bias, which undermines informed consent, increases security vulnerabilities, and threatens individual agency.

Current ethical and legal frameworks require substantial adaptation to address direct neural interfaces. Traditional concepts of privacy, consent, autonomy, and identity must be reconceptualized for an era where mind-machine boundaries become increasingly permeable [25]. The path forward requires what scholars term "anticipatory governance"—proactive policy development that addresses emerging risks while preserving beneficial potential [58].

The decisions made today about EEG-BCI development will shape the future of human consciousness, social organization, and individual freedom. Society has the opportunity to guide these technologies toward human flourishing while protecting cognitive rights that define our humanity. The question is whether we have the wisdom and collective will to do so.

4. Solutions mapping: Toward responsible and transparent BCIs

4.1 Transparency and explainable AI (XAI)

Algorithmic transparency is the cornerstone of trust, clinical validation, and user autonomy. Applied to EEG data, XAI must tackle spatiotemporal complexity and multidimensionality.

- Backpropagation methods (e.g., saliency maps, Layer-Wise Relevance Propagation) highlight which electrodes and time windows contribute most to classifications [59].
- Ante-hoc models (e.g., attention-based Transformers, interpretable recurrent models) integrate explainability directly in their architecture [60].
- Post hoc methods (e.g., SHAP, LIME) quantify the contribution of EEG features or generate local linear explanations [61].

These techniques help ensure that algorithms rely on neurophysiologically plausible patterns rather than artifacts, enabling debugging, equity checks, and regulatory compliance.

Case Study—SHAP for Epileptic Seizure Prediction.

Recent experimental studies have demonstrated explainable approaches for predicting epileptic seizures from electroencephalograms (EEG) [61]. Models based on convolutional neural networks trained on public datasets integrate SHapley Additive exPlanations (SHAP) to identify, for each prediction, the most contributive electrodes and time windows.

The results showed an *accuracy of 98.14%* and an *F1-score of 98.30%*, while highlighting key EEG channels (notably *P7-O1* and *P3-O1*). This transparency allowed clinicians to validate the *neurophysiological plausibility* of the predictions, thereby reinforcing trust in the model. The study illustrates how explainability tools can foster the clinical acceptance of EEG-AI systems and support the responsible adoption of BCIs in medicine.

4.2 Ethical design principles: "Ethics & Privacy by Design"

Ethics must be embedded from the earliest design stages, not treated as an afterthought. This requires genuine interdisciplinarity among engineers, neuroscientists, ethicists, and ergonomists.

- Privacy by design: end-to-end encryption (even at the sensor level), robust anonymization methods (k-anonymity, l-diversity, differential privacy), homomorphic encryption for secure computation, and strict data minimization [62].
- Fairness by design: diverse and representative datasets, systematic auditing across demographic groups, proactive bias detection, and corrective techniques

including pre-processing (data resampling), in-processing (fairness constraints), and post-processing (threshold adjustment) debiasing approaches [63].

- Human-in-the-loop (HITL): ensuring clinicians and users retain control, with veto options and interfaces designed for clarity and autonomy—a principle fundamental to responsible AI deployment in high-stakeneurotechnology contexts.

A practical checklist helps developers integrate these concerns at each stage: data collection, consent, equity, security, user control, explainability, responsibility, and social impact.

4.3 Governance, regulation and standards: A risk-responsive framework

The governance framework presented here directly addresses the six risk dimensions identified in Section 3: violations of mental privacy (Section 3.1) require frameworks for neural data protection (Section 4.3.1); threats to autonomy (Section 3.2) necessitate the prohibition of manipulative practices (Section 4.3.2); algorithmic biases (Section 3.3) demand standards for fairness and representativeness (Section 4.3.3); failures of consent (Section 3.4) call for dynamic and adaptive mechanisms (Section 4.3.4); security vulnerabilities (Section 3.5) require enhanced neurosecurity protocols (Section 4.3.5); and identity and cognitive liberty concerns (Section 3.6) are protected by the constitutional recognition of neurorights, as illustrated by the pioneering Chilean approach (Sections 4.3.2 and 4.3.6).

4.3.1 Mental privacy protection: Regulatory responses to neuroprivacy violations

4.3.1.1 Current legal frameworks and neural data

The emergence of neural data as an intimate category of personal information requires fundamental reconceptualization of privacy law. Research has highlighted the unique challenges posed by brain data, which differs fundamentally from traditional personal data in its inferential richness and permanence [64].

4.3.1.1.1 European approach: GDPR extensions and limitations

The General Data Protection Regulation (GDPR) provides a foundation for neural data protection by potentially classifying it as "special category data" under Article 9, requiring explicit consent and heightened safeguards [64, 65]. However, scholars have identified significant implementation challenges specific to neurotechnology:

- *Pseudonymization problem*: Neural signatures exhibit unique patterns that enable individual identification through "brain fingerprinting," making traditional anonymization techniques potentially ineffective [64]

- *Inferential privacy gap*: Current frameworks inadequately address AI's capacity to infer undisclosed characteristics (mental health conditions, cognitive abilities, personality traits) from neural patterns [66]

- *Data portability paradox*: The "right to data portability" (GDPR Article 20) becomes problematic when neural data could potentially be weaponized or misused by third parties [64]

4.3.1.1.2 Proposed regulatory solutions

Legal scholars and neuroscientists have proposed several enhancements to existing frameworks [65]:

- *Neural data minimization principle*: Mandatory limitation of EEG data collection to specific, declared purposes with technical enforcement mechanisms
- *Inferential consent framework*: Legal requirement for separate, granular consent for each category of inference derived from neural data
- *Neural right to explanation*: Specific implementation of GDPR Article 22 for neural AI systems with mandatory explainability requirements adapted to neurotechnology contexts.

4.3.1.2 Addressing the neural data economy

The commodification of neural data through consumer neurotechnology requires specific regulatory intervention [29].

4.3.1.2.1 Market structure regulation

Proposed frameworks include [65]:

- *Neural data fiduciary standards*: Companies handling neural data could operate under fiduciary obligations similar to those in financial services, creating heightened duties of care and loyalty.
- *Algorithmic auditing mandates*: Regular third-party audits of neural AI systems for privacy violations and "function creep."
- *Consumer neural rights*: Standardized disclosure mechanisms (analogous to "nutrition labels") informing users of data collection scope, inference capabilities, and third-party sharing practices.

4.3.2 Autonomy and agency protection: Regulating cognitive manipulation

4.3.2.1 Addressing subliminal manipulation

The capacity for neural systems to potentially detect and influence unconscious cognitive processes demands specific regulatory attention [32].

4.3.2.1.1 Prohibited practices framework

Scholars have proposed specific prohibitions [65]:

- *Neural exploitation prohibition*: Legal restrictions on using EEG data to detect and exploit moments of cognitive vulnerability for commercial or manipulative purposes.

- *Unconscious influence disclosure*: Mandatory notification when systems may influence behavior below conscious awareness thresholds.
- *Cognitive sovereignty protection*: Recognition of the right to mental self-determination and neural non-interference.

4.3.2.1.2 Implementation mechanisms

Proposed technical and legal safeguards include [67]:

- *Dynamic consent systems*: Technical requirements for real-time consent mechanisms when neural manipulation risks are detected.
- *Agency preservation protocols*: Mandatory "cognitive firewalls" designed to prevent unconscious behavioral influence.
- *Responsibility attribution frameworks*: Clear legal standards for accountability in human-AI cognitive partnerships where agency boundaries become blurred.

4.3.2.2 Neural co-adaptation governance

The phenomenon of brains unconsciously adapting to algorithmic requirements necessitates regulatory oversight [34].

4.3.2.2.1 Therapeutic context regulation

Proposed clinical governance mechanisms include:

- *Neural training standards*: Clinical protocols designed to prevent harmful neural adaptation patterns
- *Long-term monitoring requirements*: Mandatory follow-up studies tracking cognitive changes in long-term BCI users
- *Therapeutic boundary maintenance*: Strict regulatory separation between therapeutic and enhancement applications [68].

4.3.3 Justice and equity: Bias mitigation and algorithmic fairness

4.3.3.1 Addressing systemic neural bias

Documented disparities in BCI performance across demographic groups require comprehensive regulatory response [40].

4.3.3.1.1 Algorithmic fairness standards

Proposed frameworks include [63]:

- *Demographic parity requirements*: Legal mandates for equivalent BCI performance across protected demographic groups

- *Cultural neurodiversity recognition*: Regulatory acknowledgment of natural neurological variations across populations [44]
- *Bias testing protocols*: Mandatory pre-deployment testing across diverse demographic groups with specific performance benchmarks.

4.3.3.2 Global health equity measures

Scholars have identified the need for [41]:

- *Decolonized neural standards*: Requirements for culturally adapted neural norms in international deployments
- *Training data diversity mandates*: Legal requirements for representative datasets reflecting global neurological diversity
- *Algorithmic justice oversight*: Independent bodies monitoring neural AI deployments in vulnerable populations.

4.3.3.3 Addressing neurological bias in global contexts

The application of Western-developed neural norms in diverse global populations raises concerns about what researchers term "neurological colonialism" [41].

4.3.3.4 International deployment standards

Proposed governance mechanisms include:

- *Cultural neuroadaptation requirements*: Mandatory localization and validation of neural AI systems for different populations
- *Community consent protocols*: Requirements for community-level consultation in addition to individual consent
- *Post-deployment monitoring*: Ongoing surveillance for discriminatory outcomes in international settings

4.3.4 Informed consent evolution: Dynamic and contextual frameworks

4.3.4.1 Addressing consent complexity

Traditional consent models prove inadequate for neural technologies that generate unpredictable inferences through machine learning processes [47].

4.3.4.1.1 Dynamic consent architecture

Researchers have proposed novel consent frameworks [50]:

- *Granular permission systems*: Technical and legal frameworks enabling specific consent for different categories of neural inferences

- *Consent burden mitigation*: Intelligent consent systems designed to reduce user fatigue while maintaining meaningful protection
- *Predictive consent models*: Systems that anticipate future consent needs based on technological evolution.

4.3.4.1.2 Vulnerable population protection

Special considerations are required for populations with limited capacity for autonomous consent [47]:

- *Enhanced pediatric protections*: Specific frameworks for children whose neural development may be influenced by neurotechnology
- *Coercive context identification*: Systematic screening for situations that compromise consent validity (therapeutic pressure, employment contexts)
- *Cognitive impairment accommodations*: Adaptive consent processes for individuals with varying cognitive capacities.

4.3.4.2 Technological opacity solutions

The "black box" nature of many neural decoding algorithms requires specific transparency mandates [46].

4.3.4.2.1 Explainability requirements

Proposed standards include:

- *Neural XAI standards*: Technical specifications for explainable AI adapted to neural contexts
- *User-comprehensible explanations*: Legal requirements for explanations accessible to non-expert users
- *Contestability mechanisms*: Procedures for challenging neural AI decisions affecting individuals.

4.3.5 Security and cybersecurity: Protecting neural infrastructure

4.3.5.1 Addressing novel threat vectors

Neural interfaces create unprecedented security vulnerabilities requiring specialized regulatory response [25].

4.3.5.1.1 Neurosecurity standards

Research has identified the need for [25]:

- *Neural cybersecurity frameworks*: Specific security standards for brain-computer interfaces addressing unique vulnerabilities

- *Adversarial attack prevention*: Requirements for robustness against neural signal manipulation and injection attacks
- *Incident response protocols*: Specialized procedures for responding to neural data breaches, recognizing the permanent nature of compromised neural signatures.

4.3.5.1.2 Critical infrastructure protection

Healthcare and public safety applications require heightened security [53]:

- *Healthcare neural security*: Enhanced security requirements for medical EEG systems in clinical settings
- *Supply chain security*: Regulations ensuring secure neural technology components throughout development and deployment
- *International cooperation*: Frameworks for coordinating responses to cross-border neural security threats.

4.3.5.2 Identity and authentication challenges

The permanent, unchangeable nature of neural signatures requires novel authentication governance:

4.3.5.2.1 Neural biometric governance

- *Revocation impossibility recognition*: Legal frameworks acknowledging that compromised neural signatures cannot be reset like passwords
- *Multi-factor neural authentication*: Standards preventing over-reliance on neural signatures as sole authentication factors
- *Breach notification requirements*: Specific protocols for neural data compromise notification, recognizing long-term implications.

4.3.6 Regional and national approaches: Comparative analysis

4.3.6.1 United States: FDA medical device framework

4.3.6.1.1 Current approach

The U.S. Food and Drug Administration (FDA) regulates BCIs as medical devices, with recent guidance addressing AI-enabled software and implanted brain-computer interfaces [69].

The FDA's 2021 guidance on implanted BCIs provides recommendations for non-clinical testing and clinical study design [28]. In January 2025, the FDA issued comprehensive draft guidance on AI-enabled device software functions, addressing lifecycle management and marketing submission recommendations [69].

4.3.6.1.2 Strengths and limitations

- *Strengths*: Robust clinical trial requirements, clear regulatory pathways for medical devices, emphasis on safety and efficacy
- *Limitations*: Focus primarily on medical applications with limited coverage of consumer neurotechnology, insufficient attention to broader ethical implications including privacy and algorithmic bias.

4.3.6.1.3 Recommended enhancements

- Expanded scope to encompass consumer neural technologies beyond medical contexts
- Integration of privacy assessment and bias evaluation into approval processes
- Development of neural-specific guidance documents addressing unique characteristics of brain data.

4.3.6.2 European Union: Comprehensive rights-based approach

4.3.6.2.1 Current framework

The European Union employs a multi-layered regulatory approach combining the GDPR for data protection with the recently enacted Artificial Intelligence Act (AI Act) [70].

The EU AI Act, which entered into force in August 2024, classifies medical devices incorporating AI as "high-risk" systems subject to stringent requirements, with implementation timelines varying based on device category [70].

4.3.6.2.2 Implementation challenges

Research has identified several challenges [71]:

- Complex compliance requirements that may create barriers for smaller developers
- Unclear enforcement mechanisms for novel neural applications
- Potential for regulatory fragmentation across member states despite harmonization efforts
- Coordination challenges between the AI Act and existing medical device regulations.

4.3.6.2.3 Ongoing developments

- Neural-specific guidance from European data protection authorities
- Integration of neurorights considerations into AI Act implementation
- Harmonization efforts across multiple regulatory bodies (European Medicines Agency, national competent authorities).

4.3.6.3 Chile: Constitutional neurorights pioneer

4.3.6.3.1 Groundbreaking approach

In October 2021, Chile became the first country to constitutionally protect neurorights through an amendment to Article 19 of the Chilean Constitution [57].

The constitutional amendment establishes protections for:

- Mental privacy and control over neural information
- Personal identity protection against technological alteration
- Free will and cognitive self-determination
- Equal access to cognitive enhancement technologies
- Protection against algorithmic bias in neural technologies.

4.3.6.3.2 Global implications

Chile's pioneering approach has influenced international discourse on neural rights [72]:

- Provides a model for constitutional protection of cognitive liberty
- Influences international human rights discussions
- Offers a template for comprehensive neural rights frameworks.

4.3.6.3.3 Implementation challenges

Scholars have noted challenges in operationalizing constitutional neurorights [56]:

- Translating abstract constitutional principles into specific operational law
- Balancing innovation incentives with rights protection
- Ensuring practical enforceability of novel rights concepts
- Developing technical standards that align with constitutional principles.

4.3.6.4 Other national approaches

Canada: Privacy-focused approach building on the Personal Information Protection and Electronic Documents Act (PIPEDA), with growing attention to neurotechnology [65].

Japan: Technology-forward regulation emphasizing public-private collaboration and industry self-governance.

Australia: Healthcare-centered approach with growing privacy considerations under the Privacy Act.

China: State-coordinated development with emphasis on national competitiveness in neurotechnology, raising international human rights concerns.

4.3.7 International standardization and harmonization

4.3.7.1 Technical standards development

4.3.7.1.1 ISO working groups

Multiple International Organization for Standardization (ISO) technical committees are developing standards relevant to neural technologies:

- *ISO/IEC JTC 1/SC 42* (Artificial Intelligence): Developing AI standards applicable to neural data processing
- *ISO/TC 215* (Health Informatics): Addressing medical BCI standardization
- *ISO/IEC 27001* extensions: Considering neural data security requirements.

4.3.7.1.2 IEEE standards activities

The Institute of Electrical and Electronics Engineers (IEEE) has established working groups developing neural technology standards:

- IEEE P2857: Standards for privacy engineering applicable to neural data
- IEEE P7000 series: Addressing ethical considerations in autonomous and intelligent systems, relevant to BCIs
- Ongoing work on bias mitigation and cybersecurity standards for neural interfaces.

4.3.7.2 Regulatory harmonization efforts

4.3.7.2.1 Challenges

International harmonization faces significant obstacles:

- Differing cultural approaches to privacy, autonomy, and cognitive liberty
- Varying technological capabilities and innovation priorities across jurisdictions
- Competing economic interests in neural technology development
- Divergent legal traditions and regulatory philosophies.

4.3.7.2.2 Harmonization mechanisms

Proposed approaches include [65]:

- Bilateral regulatory cooperation agreements between major regulatory authorities

- Multilateral frameworks through existing international organizations (WHO, UNESCO, OECD)
- Industry-driven global standards initiatives with multi-stakeholder participation
- Academic-led international consensus-building efforts.

4.3.8 Enforcement mechanisms and compliance

4.3.8.1 Monitoring and oversight

4.3.8.1.1 Regulatory agency capabilities

Effective governance requires enhanced agency capacities:

- Specialized neural technology expertise within regulatory bodies
- Cross-disciplinary teams combining technical, legal, ethical, and clinical expertise
- Continuous monitoring capabilities adapted to rapidly evolving neural technologies
- International cooperation mechanisms for coordinated oversight.

4.3.8.1.2 Industry compliance

Proposed compliance frameworks include:

- Self-assessment systems with independent verification requirements
- Regular algorithmic auditing protocols
- Whistleblower protection for neural technology concerns
- Transparency reporting requirements.

4.3.8.2 Sanctions and remedies

4.3.8.2.1 Graduated enforcement approach

Regulatory responses should be proportionate [65]:

- Warning systems and corrective action plans for minor violations
- Mandatory remediation measures for systemic issues
- Significant penalties for deliberate harm or negligence
- Product recall or market withdrawal for serious safety or rights violations.

4.3.8.2.2 Victim remedies

Individuals affected by neural technology failures require access to:

- Compensation mechanisms for neural rights violations
- Support services for individuals affected by neural discrimination or privacy breaches
- Clear pathways for legal recourse and dispute resolution.

4.3.9 Adaptive governance for emerging technologies

4.3.9.1 Anticipatory regulation

The rapid evolution of neural technologies requires governance mechanisms capable of responding to emerging challenges through anticipatory approaches that proactively identify and address risks before they fully materialize [65].

4.3.9.1.1 Regulatory sandboxes

Controlled testing environments can facilitate innovation while ensuring safety [73]:

- Temporary regulatory flexibility for novel neural technologies with enhanced monitoring
- Learning-oriented approach enabling evidence-based regulation development
- Stakeholder collaboration in identifying emerging risks.

4.3.9.1.2 Horizon scanning

Proactive identification of future challenges through:

- Systematic monitoring of neural technology development trajectories
- Stakeholder engagement in anticipating future challenges
- Interdisciplinary foresight exercises combining technical, ethical, and social perspectives.

4.3.9.2 Stakeholder engagement

4.3.9.2.1 Multi-stakeholder governance

Effective governance requires diverse participation [65]:

- Patient and disability advocacy organizations in BCI governance
- Neuroscience and engineering communities providing technical expertise

- Ethics committees and civil society organizations
- International cooperation addressing global challenges.

4.3.9.2.2 Public participation

Democratic governance mechanisms include:

- Citizen panels for neural technology policy input
- Public consultation requirements for major regulatory changes
- Transparency in regulatory decision-making processes
- Accessible public education about neurotechnology implications.

4.3.10 Future regulatory challenges and opportunities

4.3.10.1 Emerging governance needs

4.3.10.1.1 Convergent technologies

Future regulatory frameworks must address:

- Neural interfaces combined with other emerging technologies (genetic engineering, nanotechnology)
- Brain-to-brain communication networks raising collective rights questions
- Cognitive enhancement applications blurring therapeutic and enhancement boundaries [70].

4.3.10.1.2 Global coordination

International frameworks are needed for:

- Coordinated neural technology governance across jurisdictions
- Responses to transnational neural security threats
- Harmonized approaches to neural rights protection
- Prevention of regulatory arbitrage and "neural data havens"

4.3.10.2 Building trust through governance

4.3.10.2.1 Transparency requirements

Public confidence requires [65]:

- Public reporting on neural technology development and deployment
- Accessible information about neural AI system capabilities and limitations

- Clear accountability mechanisms for neural technology outcomes
- Regular independent assessments of regulatory effectiveness.

4.3.10.2.2 Democratic oversight

Maintaining democratic control over neurotechnology development through:

- Legislative involvement in neural technology governance
- Judicial review of regulatory decisions
- Public accountability for government neural technology use
- Protection against authoritarian misuse of neural surveillance.

4.3.10.2.3 Conclusion

This expanded governance framework demonstrates how regulatory responses can be systematically aligned with the specific risks identified in Section 3. The multifaceted approach combines the constitutional protections, statutory regulations, technical standards, and adaptive governance mechanisms to create comprehensive oversight of neural technologies.

Effective governance must balance multiple objectives: protecting fundamental rights while enabling beneficial innovation, ensuring safety without stifling research, and harmonizing international approaches while respecting cultural differences. The frameworks emerging in the EU, Chile, and through international standardization efforts provide foundations for this balance, though the significant implementation challenges remain.

The path forward requires sustained commitment from multiple stakeholders—regulatory authorities, technology developers, healthcare providers, civil society organizations, and individuals whose cognitive liberty is at stake. Only through collaborative, anticipatory, and ethically grounded governance can society harness the transformative potential of brain-computer interfaces while safeguarding the neural foundations of human identity, autonomy, and dignity.

4.4 Future perspectives: Toward adaptive governance

4.4.1 Emerging challenges and anticipation

The accelerated pace of EEG-BCI innovation necessitates the governance mechanisms capable of rapidly adapting to emerging technological developments. Traditional regulatory frameworks, designed for relatively stable technologies, show their limits faced with the evolution speed of neurotechnologies and artificial intelligence.

The emergence of new technological paradigms like hybrid BCIs (combining EEG and other modalities), integration with augmented reality, or development of direct brain-to-brain interfaces poses unprecedented ethical challenges that exceed the current regulatory framework. These innovations require continuous prospective monitoring and real-time ethical evaluation mechanisms.

Growing convergence between BCIs and other emerging technologies (artificial general intelligence, biotechnologies, nanotechnologies) will create powerful synergies but also complex systemic risks. Evaluating these risks requires new interdisciplinary approaches that exceed current sectoral silos.

4.4.2 Algorithmic governance and ethical automation

Paradoxically, ethical management of BCIs could itself benefit from intelligent automation to face the complexity and scale of posed challenges. Algorithmic governance systems could automate certain aspects of ethical surveillance, bias detection, and compliance evaluation.

"Ethical algorithms" capable of automatically detecting privacy violations, discriminatory biases, or autonomy infringements could complement human surveillance without replacing it. These systems could continuously analyze usage patterns, identify abnormal behaviors, and alert about emerging risks.

However, this ethics automation itself raises fundamental questions: Can we delegate moral judgments to algorithms? How to avoid algorithmic governance reproducing the biases it is supposed to detect? These questions require deep reflection on appropriate limits of ethical automation.

4.4.3 Responsible innovation and trust ecosystem

Building a trust ecosystem for BCIs requires profound cultural transformation in the technology industry, favoring responsible innovation rather than innovation at any cost. This transformation implies new economic models that integrate ethical and social externalities into profitability calculations.

Economic incentive mechanisms must be aligned with ethical objectives: public subsidies conditioned on ethical compliance, ethical certifications valued by the market, insurance premiums modulated according to the governance practices. This realignment requires coordination between public and private actors.

The emergence of "BCI commons"—shared resources of data, algorithms and knowledge developed according to strict ethical principles—could democratize access to these technologies while maintaining high protection standards. These commons require new collaborative governance models inspired by open source successes.

4.4.4 Education and neural digital citizenship

Development of "neural digital citizenship" represents a major educational issue for coming decades. Tomorrow's citizens will have to navigate a world where their neural data will potentially be collected, analyzed, and used by multiple actors. This navigation requires new skills and a new form of literacy.

Neurotechnology education must begin in primary school, integrating basic understanding of brain functioning, BCI principles, and neural privacy issues. This education must evolve with age to include more complex aspects of governance, applied ethics, and collective decision-making.

Training "neuro-citizens" must also include practical skills: how to evaluate BCI system reliability, how to negotiate privacy preferences, and how to participate in public debates on neurotechnology regulation. These skills become as essential as traditional digital literacy.

4.4.5 International cooperation and harmonization

Neurotechnologies, by their global nature and transborder impact, require reinforced international cooperation to avoid regulatory fragmentation and "neurological havens" where ethical standards would be relaxed.

Establishing an international framework for neuro-rights, modeled on the Universal Declaration of Human Rights, could provide a common basis for national legislation harmonization. This framework should recognize universal principles while allowing appropriate cultural adaptations.

International technical cooperation mechanisms for best practice sharing, ethical research resource pooling, and coordination of responses to emerging crises become crucial. This cooperation can rely on existing international organizations (WHO, UNESCO, OECD) while creating new specialized instances.

This solutions mapping reveals the complexity but also the feasibility of ethical development of EEG-based brain-computer interfaces. The challenges identified in the previous part are not insurmountable, provided we adopt a systemic, proactive, and collaborative approach.

Technical solutions like explainable AI and privacy by design provide necessary tools to build transparent and privacy-respectful systems. Emerging governance frameworks offer institutional structures to appropriately regulate these technologies. Stakeholder involvement and neuro-ethical literacy development create social conditions for responsible adoption.

However, the success of this enterprise depends on collective willingness to place ethics at the heart of innovation rather than on the periphery. It also requires recognition that today's technological choices will shape tomorrow's society, and that it is our responsibility to orient them toward a future that preserves and enriches our humanity.

The future of EEG-BCIs does not reduce to a technical question but to a societal choice: Do we want technologies that augment us while alienating us, or technologies that strengthen us as autonomous and dignified human beings? The answer to this question will determine whether brain-computer interfaces contribute to human flourishing or its diminishment.

Foundations are laid, tools are available, and actors are mobilized. It now remains to transform this vision into reality, with the patience, perseverance, and wisdom that an issue of this importance for our species' future deserves.

5. Conclusion: Humans at the center of the loop

5.1 Synthesis of tensions: Between promise and peril

This chapter has explored the multiple facets of a technological revolution that redefines the boundaries between mind and machine. EEG-based brain-computer interfaces powered by artificial intelligence carry within them transformative potential of historic magnitude: restoring communication for patients in locked-in syndrome, enabling intuitive thought-controlled prosthetics, offering new therapies for neuropsychiatric disorders, and even augmenting human cognitive capabilities beyond their natural limits.

These promises, far from being mere futuristic speculation, are materializing today in our laboratories and clinics. Paralyzed patients are regaining digital voices, amputees are controlling artificial limbs with increasing dexterity, and individuals suffering from attention disorders are benefiting from personalized cognitive training guided by their real-time brain activity. The therapeutic and wellness potential of these technologies is undeniable and legitimately inspires enthusiasm in the scientific and medical community.

However, our analysis has also revealed the emergence of ethical risks of unprecedented nature and depth. The capacity to decode neural signals and infer mental states, intentions, and even thoughts crosses fundamental anthropological thresholds. Affective computing applications exemplify this tension: Emotion recognition offers transformative mental health monitoring yet creates unprecedented emotional surveillance capabilities [7, 29]. The capacity to decode felt experience—traditionally inaccessible to external observation—challenges fundamental assumptions about mental privacy while enabling potentially beneficial clinical interventions [56]. Balancing these dimensions requires recognizing emotional data as uniquely sensitive information deserving heightened protection. For the first time in human history, our most intimate mental spaces become technically accessible to third parties, raising existential questions about the very nature of privacy and autonomy.

The identified risks are not hypothetical but very real: commercialization of brain data, subliminal cognitive manipulation, discrimination based on neuropsychological profiles, and attacks on human agency by systems that blur the boundary between personal intention and algorithmic influence. These risks are all the more concerning as they often operate invisibly, escaping traditional mechanisms of individual and collective defense.

This tension between promise and peril cannot be resolved by a simple cost-benefit calculation. It questions the fundamental values of our civilization: What does it mean to be human in the era of brain-machine interfacing? How do we preserve our humanity while embracing the possibilities of technological augmentation? These questions transcend the technical framework to touch the philosophical, ethical, and political foundations of our societies.

5.2 Central vision: Transparency and ethics as essential requirements

The analysis developed in this chapter leads to a central conviction: technical transparency and ethical integration from the design stage do not constitute desirable options but sine qua non conditions for responsible development of EEG-BCIs. This conviction rests on recognition that technical choices are never neutral and that each line of code, each algorithmic architecture, and each data collection protocol carries within it ethical and social implications.

Technical transparency, embodied in explainable artificial intelligence (XAI), responds to a fundamental democratic imperative: Citizens have the right to understand the systems that analyze their brain activity and make decisions concerning them. This transparency is not merely a matter of psychological comfort but a necessary condition for exercising individual autonomy and collective responsibility. How can a patient give informed consent to BCI treatment if they do not understand how the system interprets their neural signals? How can a society democratically regulate opaque technologies?

XAI for EEG signals must go beyond generic approaches to develop methods specifically adapted to the spatiotemporal and multidimensional nature of brain activity. Saliency map visualizations, layer-wise relevance propagation techniques, and intrinsically interpretable models offer promising avenues but require additional development to achieve a level of explainability accessible to non-experts.

Ethical integration from design (Ethics by Design) transforms ethics from an external constraint into a structuring principle of technological development. This approach recognizes that ethical considerations, when introduced late, can only partially correct biases and vulnerabilities already inscribed in system architecture. Privacy by Design, Fairness by Design, and Human-in-the-loop are not patches but architectural principles that must inform every design decision.

This vision demands profound cultural transformation in the technological ecosystem, replacing the "move fast and break things" ethos with an approach of "move thoughtfully and build trust." This transformation cannot be imposed solely by external regulation but must emerge from collective awareness of the historical responsibility of neurotechnology developers. Explainable AI provides the technical foundation for this transparency [46], while comprehensive governance frameworks establish the institutional structures necessary for accountability [65]. Together, these elements create the conditions for trustworthy neurotechnology development that respects human dignity.

5.3 Neuro-rights perspective: Legal anchoring of mental protection

The emergence of neurotechnologies requires corresponding evolution of our legal frameworks to recognize and protect new fundamental rights related to mental integrity. "Neuro-rights" emerge as a new legal paradigm that extends classical human rights to the era of brain-machine interfacing. Chile's pioneering constitutional amendment [57], comprehensive frameworks proposed by legal scholars [56], and international advocacy efforts [72] demonstrate growing recognition that neural data and cognitive processes require specific legal protections beyond existing privacy and autonomy frameworks.

The right to mental privacy constitutes the central pillar of this legal architecture. This right goes beyond traditional personal data protection to recognize the existence of an inviolable mental space. It implies the right to keep one's thoughts, emotions, and cognitive processes private, as well as control over their potential sharing. This right poses considerable challenges as it must be operationalized in a context where boundaries between mental and digital become blurred.

The right to mental identity protects against non-consensual modifications of personality, memories, or cognitive processes. This right becomes crucial with the development of BCIs capable of influencing neural activity and potentially modifying mental states. It also implies the right to continuity of personal identity in the face of technologies that could alter one's sense of self.

The right to cognitive free will guarantees preservation of decisional autonomy in the face of technologies capable of subtly influencing decision-making processes. This right recognizes that autonomy is not limited to absence of physical coercion but includes protection against subtle cognitive manipulation.

The right to equitable access to neurotechnologies addresses distributive justice issues in a context where BCIs could create new forms of cognitive inequalities.

This right implies not only access to therapeutic technologies but also prevention of social stratification based on cognitive augmentation.

Legal anchoring of these rights requires legislative innovations at several levels: constitutional (like Chile's pioneering amendment), legislative (neurotechnology-specific laws), and regulatory (technical and ethical standards). This legal evolution must be internationally coordinated to avoid fragmentation and neurological havens where protection standards would be relaxed.

Acknowledgement

The author acknowledges the use of Claude.ai for language polishing of the manuscript.

Nomenclature

BCI	brain-computer interfaces
EEG	Electroencephalography
AI	artificial intelligence
XAI	explainable AI
SVM	support vector machines
LDA	linear discriminant analysis
CNN	convolutional neural networks
RNN	Recurrent Neural Networks
LSTM	Long Short-Term Memory
SHAP	SHapley Additive exPlanations
LIME	Local Interpretable Model-agnostic Explanations
HITL	human-in-the-loop
EMG	electromyography
EOG	electrooculography
ECG	electrocardiography
MCI	mild cognitive impairment
SSVEP	Steady-State Visual Evoked Potential
GDPR	General Data Protection Regulation
FDA	Food and Drug Administration
ISO	International Organization for Standardization
IEEE	Institute of Electrical and Electronics Engineers
WHO	World Health Organization
UNESCO	United Nations Educational, Scientific and Cultural Organization
OECD	Organisation for Economic Co-operation and Development

Author details

Badr Mouazen*† and Zainab El Bouyed†
LINP2 Lab, Paris Nanterre University, UPL Paris, France

*Address all correspondence to: bmouazen@parisnanterre.fr

† These authors contributed equally.

References

[1] Kirschstein T, Köhling R. What is the source of the EEG? Clinical EEG and Neuroscience. 2009;**40**(3):146-149. DOI: 10.1177/155005940904000305

[2] Knyazev GG. EEG delta oscillations as a correlate of basic homeostatic and motivational processes. Neuroscience and Biobehavioral Reviews. 2012;**36**(1):677-695. DOI: 10.1016/j.neubiorev.2011.10.002

[3] Klimesch W. Alpha-band oscillations, attention, and controlled access to stored information. Trends in Cognitive Sciences. 2012;**16**(12):606-617. ISSN 1364-6613. DOI: 10.1016/j.tics.2012.10.007

[4] Herrmann CS, Fründ I, Lenz D. Human gamma-band activity: A review on cognitive and behavioral correlates and network models. Neuroscience and Biobehavioral Reviews. 2010;**34**(7):981-992. DOI: 10.1016/j.neubiorev.2009.09.001

[5] Howard MW, Rizzuto DS, Caplan JB, Madsen JR, Lisman J, Aschenbrenner-Scheibe R, et al. Gamma oscillations correlate with working memory load in humans. Cerebral Cortex (New York, N.Y.: 1991). 2003;**13**(12):1369-1374. DOI: 10.1093/cercor/bhg084

[6] Chikhi S, Matton N, Blanchet S. EEG power spectral measures of cognitive workload: A meta-analysis. Psychophysiology. 2022;**59**(6):e14009. DOI: 10.1111/psyp.14009

[7] Mouazen B, Benali A, Chebchoub NT, Abdelwahed EH, De Marco G. Enhancing EEG-based emotion detection with hybrid models: Insights from DEAP dataset applications. Sensors. 2025;**25**(6):1827. DOI: 10.3390/s25061827

[8] Rashid M, Sulaiman N, Majeed APPA, Musa RM, Nasir AFA, Bari BS, et al. Current status, challenges, and possible solutions of EEG-based brain-computer interface: A comprehensive review. Frontiers in Neurorobotics. 2020;**14**:25. DOI: 10.3389/fnbot.2020.00025

[9] Roy Y, Banville H, Albuquerque I, Gramfort A, Falk TH, Faubert J. Deep learning-based electroencephalography analysis: A systematic review. Journal of Neural Engineering. 2019;**16**(5):051001. DOI: 10.1088/1741-2552/ab260c

[10] Mouazen B, Bendaouia A, De Marco G. Leveraging machine learning and clinical EEG data for multiple sclerosis: A systematic review. 2024;**166**:103116. DOI: 10.1016/j.artmed.2025.103116

[11] Koelstra S, Mühl C, Soleymani M, Lee J, Yazdani A, Ebrahimi T, et al. Deap: A database for emotion analysis; using physiological signals. IEEE Transactions on Affective Computing. 2012;**3**(1):18-31. DOI: 10.1109/t-affc.2011.15

[12] Bai L, Litscher G, Li X. Epileptic seizure detection using machine learning: A systematic review and meta-analysis. Brain Sciences. 2025;**15**(6):634. DOI: 10.3390/brainsci15060634

[13] Rajpurkar P, Chen E, Banerjee O, Topol EJ. Ai in health and medicine. Nature Medicine. 2022;**28**(1):31-38. DOI: 10.1038/s41591-021-01614-0

[14] Supratak A, Dong H, Wu C, Guo Y. Deepsleepnet: A model for automatic sleep stage scoring based on raw single-channel EEG. IEEE Transactions on Neural Systems and Rehabilitation

Engineering. 2017;**25**(11):1998-2008. DOI: 10.1109/tnsre.2017.2721116

[15] Mouazen B, Bellakhdar O, Ennair A, Laghdaf K, Bendaouia A, Abdelwahed EH, et al. Transparent EEG Analysis: Leveraging Autoencoders, Bi-LSTMs, and SHAP for Improved Neurodegenerative Diseases Detection. Preprints. 2025;**25**(18):5690. DOI: 10.20944/preprints202507.0639.v1

[16] Ramos-Murguialday A, Broetz D, Rea M, Läer L, Yilmaz O, Brasil FL, et al. Brain-machine interface in chronic stroke rehabilitation: A controlled study. Annals of Neurology. 2013;**74**(1):100-108. DOI: 10.1002/ana.23879

[17] Pichiorri F, Morone G, Petti M, Toppi J, Pisotta I, Molinari M, et al. Brain-computer interface boosts motor imagery practice during stroke recovery. Annals of Neurology. 2015;**77**(5):851-865. DOI: 10.1002/ana.24390

[18] Watts D, Pulice RF, Reilly J, et al. Predicting treatment response using EEG in major depressive disorder: A machine-learning meta-analysis. Translational Psychiatry. 2022;**12**:332. DOI: 10.1038/s41398-022-02064-z

[19] Amores J, Richer R, Zhao N, Maes P, Eskofier BM. Promoting relaxation using virtual reality, olfactory interfaces and wearable EEG. In: 2018 IEEE 15th International Conference on Wearable and Implantable Body Sensor Networks (BSN). Las Vegas, NV, USA: IEEE; 2018. pp. 98-101. DOI: 10.1109/bsn.2018.8329668

[20] Lin C, Chuang C, Huang C, Tsai S, Lu S, Chen Y, et al. Wireless and wearable EEG system for evaluating driver vigilance. IEEE Transactions on Biomedical Circuits and Systems. 2014;**8**(2):165-176. DOI: 10.1109/tbcas.2014.2316224

[21] Mehta RK, Parasuraman R. Neuroergonomics: A review of applications to physical and cognitive work. Frontiers in Human Neuroscience. 2013;7:889. DOI: 10.3389/fnhum.2013.00889

[22] Hayles NK. Unthought: The Power of the Cognitive Nonconscious. Chicago and London: University of Chicago Press; 2017. DOI: 10.7208/chicago/9780226447919.001.0001

[23] Clark A. Supersizing the Mind: Embodiment, Action, and Cognitive Extension, Philosophy of Mind Series. Oxford: Oxford University Press; 2008

[24] Libet B, Gleason CA, Wright EW, Pearl DK. Time of conscious intention to act in relation to onset of cerebral activity (readiness-potential). The unconscious initiation of a freely voluntary act. Brain: A Journal of Neurology. 1983;**106**(Pt 3):623-642. DOI: 10.1093/brain/106.3.623

[25] Ienca M, Haselager P. Hacking the brain: Brain–computer interfacing technology and the ethics of neurosecurity. Ethics and Information Technology. 2016;**18**(2):117-129. DOI: 10.1007/s10676-016-9398-9

[26] Regalado A. Facebook is ditching plans to make an interface that reads the brain. Technology Review. 2021;**14**

[27] Finn ES, Shen X, Scheinost D, Rosenberg MD, Huang J, Chun MM, et al. Functional connectome fingerprinting: Identifying individuals using patterns of brain connectivity. Nature Neuroscience. 2015;**18**(11):1664-1671. DOI: 10.1038/nn.4135

[28] Shoshana Z. The Age of Surveillance Capitalism: The Fight for a Human Future at the New Frontier of Power. New York, Berlin, Heidelberg: Public Affairs, Springer-Verlag; 2019

[29] Genser J, Damianos S, Yuste R. Safeguarding Brain Data: Assessing the Privacy Practices of Consumer Neurotechnology Companies. Columbia University: NeuroRights Foundation; 2024

[30] Plassmann H, Venkatraman V, Huettel S, Yoon C. Consumer neuroscience: Applications, challenges, and possible solutions. Journal of Marketing Research. 2015;**52**(4):427-435. DOI: 10.1509/jmr.14.0048

[31] Murphy E, Illes J, Reiner PB. Neuroethics neuromarketing. Journal of Consumer Behaviour. 2008;7:293-302. DOI: 10.1002/cb.252

[32] Clausen J. Man, machine and in between. Nature. 2009;**457**:1080-1081. DOI: 10.1038/4571080a

[33] Cattan G. The use of brain–computer interfaces in games is not ready for the general public. Frontiers in Computer Science. 2021;**3**:628773. DOI: 10.3389/fcomp.2021.628773

[34] Perdikis S, Tonin L, Saeedi S, Schneider C, Millán JDR. The Cybathlon BCI race: Successful longitudinal mutual learning with two tetraplegic users. PLoS Biology. 2018;**16**(5):e2003787. DOI: 10.1371/journal.pbio.2003787

[35] Collinger JL, Wodlinger B, Downey JE, Wang W, Tyler-Kabara EC, Weber DJ, et al. High-performance neuroprosthetic control by an individual with tetraplegia. Lancet (London, England). 2013;**381**(9866):557-564. DOI: 10.1016/S0140-6736(12)61816-9

[36] Shenoy P, Krauledat M, Blankertz B, Rao RP, Müller KR. Towards adaptive classification for BCI. Journal of Neural Engineering. 2006;**3**(1):R13-R23. DOI: 10.1088/1741-2560/3/1/R02

[37] Gilbert F, Cook M, O'Brien TJ, Illes J. Embodiment and estrangement: Results from a first-in-human "intelligent BCI" trial. Science and Engineering Ethics. 2017;**25**(1):83-96. DOI: 10.1007/s11948-017-0001-5

[38] Haggard P. Sense of agency in the human brain. Nature Reviews Neuroscience. 2017;**18**(4):196-207. DOI: 10.1038/nrn.2017.14

[39] Floridi L, Cowls J. A unified framework of five principles for AI in society. Harvard Data Science Review. 2019;**1**(1). DOI: 10.1162/99608f92.8cd550d1

[40] Webb EK et al. Addressing racial and phenotypic bias in human neuroscience methods. Nature Neuroscience. 2022;**25**(4):410-414. DOI: 10.1038/s41593-022-01046-0

[41] Rose N, Abi-Rached JM. Neuro: The New Brain Sciences and the Management of the Mind. US: Princeton University Press; 2013. Available from: http://www.jstor.org/stable/j.ctt1r2f5p

[42] Obermeyer Z, Powers B, Vogeli C, Mullainathan S. Dissecting racial bias in an algorithm used to manage the health of populations. Science (New York, N.Y.). 2019;**366**(6464):447-453. DOI: 10.1126/science.aax2342

[43] Elfenbein H, Mandal M, Ambady N, Harizuka S, Kumar S. Cross-cultural patterns in emotion recognition: Highlighting design and analytical techniques. Emotion. 2002;**2**:75-84. DOI: 10.1037/1528-3542.2.1.75

[44] Chiao JY, Ambady N. Cultural Neuroscience: Parsing Universality and Diversity across Levels of Analysis. 2007. Available from: https://api.semanticscholar.org/CorpusID:91951788

[45] Hamada H et al. Comparison of brain activity between motor imagery and mental rotation of the hand tasks: A functional magnetic resonance imaging study. Brain Imaging and Behavior. 2018;**12**(6):1596-1606. DOI: 10.1007/s11682-017-9821-9

[46] Rudin C. Stop explaining black box machine learning models for high stakes decisions and use interpretable models instead. Nature Machine Intelligence. 2019;**1**:206-215. DOI: 10.1038/s42256-019-0048-x

[47] Klein E, Ojemann J. Informed consent in implantable BCI research: Identification of research risks and recommendations for development of best practices. Journal of Neural Engineering. 2016;**13**(4):043001. DOI: 10.1088/1741-2560/13/4/043001

[48] Gevensleben H, Holl B, Albrecht B, Vogel C, Schlamp D, Kratz O, et al. Is neurofeedback an efficacious treatment for ADHD? A randomised controlled clinical trial. Journal of Child Psychology and Psychiatry, and Allied Disciplines. 2009;**50**(7):780-789. DOI: 10.1111/j.1469-7610.2008.02033.x

[49] Lotte F, Bougrain L, Cichocki A, Clerc M, Congedo M, Rakotomamonjy A, et al. A review of classification algorithms for EEG-based brain-computer interfaces: A 10 year update. Journal of Neural Engineering. 2018;**15**(3):031005. DOI: 10.1088/1741-2552/aab2f2

[50] Kaye J, Whitley E, Lund D, et al. Dynamic consent: A patient interface for twenty-first century research networks. European Journal of Human Genetics. 2015;**23**:141-146. DOI: 10.1038/ejhg.2014.71

[51] Zhang A, Lin X. Towards secure and privacy-preserving data sharing in e-health systems via consortium blockchain. Journal of Medical Systems. 2018 Jun;**42**(8):140. DOI: 10.1007/s10916-018-0995-5

[52] Ienca M, Andorno R. Towards new human rights in the age of neuroscience and neurotechnology. Life Sciences, Society and Policy. 2017;**13**:5. DOI: 10.1186/s40504-017-0050-1

[53] Rushanan M, Rubin AD, Kune DF, Swanson CM. SoK: Security and privacy in implantable medical devices and body area networks. In: 2014 IEEE Symposium on Security and Privacy. Berkeley, CA, USA: IEEE; 2014. pp. 524-539. DOI: 10.1109/SP.2014.40

[54] Clark A, Chalmers D. The extended mind. Analysis. 1998;**58**(1):7-19. Available from: http://www.jstor.org/stable/3328150

[55] Jiang L, Stocco A, Losey DM, et al. BrainNet: A multi-person brain-to-brain interface for direct collaboration between brains. Scientific Reports. 2019;**9**:6115. DOI: 10.1038/s41598-019-41895-7

[56] Farahany NA. The Battle for your Brain: Defending the Right to Think Freely in the Age of Neurotechnology. New York: St. Martin's Press; 2023

[57] Chile Constitutional Reform. Amendment to Article 19 of the Chilean Constitution Protecting Neurorights. Signed October 25, 2021. Law No. 21.383. 2021

[58] Barben D, Fisher E, Selin CL, Guston DH. Anticipating governance of nanotechnology: Foresight, engagement, and integration. In: Hackett EJ, Amsterdamska O, Lynch M, Wajcman J, editors. The Handbook of Science and Technology Studies. 3rd ed. Cambridge: MIT Press; 2007. pp. 979-1000

[59] Hyeonyeong N, Jun-Mo K, WooHyeok C, Soyeon B, Tae-Eui K. The effects of layer-wise relevance propagation-based feature selection for EEG classification: A comparative study on multiple datasets. Frontiers in Human Neuroscience. 2023;**17**:1205881. DOI: 10.3389/fnhum.2023.1205881

[60] Ruixiang L, Yihu C, Ma X, Xianzheng S, Limin S, Shuo L, et al. ERTNet: An interpretable transformer-based framework for EEG emotion recognition. Frontiers in Neuroscience. 2024;**18**:1320645. DOI: 10.3389/fnins.2024.1320645

[61] Vimbi V, Shaffi N, Mahmud M. Interpreting artificial intelligence models: A systematic review on the application of LIME and SHAP in Alzheimer's disease detection. Brain Informatics. 2024;**11**(1):10. DOI: 10.1186/s40708-024-00222-1

[62] Hong C. Recent advances of privacy-preserving machine learning based on (fully) homomorphic encryption. Security and Safety. 2024;**4**:2024012. DOI: 10.1051/sands/2024012

[63] Mehrabi N, Morstatter F, Saxena N, Lerman K, Galstyan A. A survey on bias and fairness in machine learning. ACM Computing Surveys. 2021;**54**:6. Article 115 (July 2022), 35 pages. DOI: 10.1145/3457607

[64] Rainey S, McGillivray K, Akintoye S, Fothergill T, Bublitz C, Stahl B. Is the European data protection regulation sufficient to deal with emerging data concerns relating to neurotechnology? Journal of Law and the Biosciences. 2020;**7**(1):lsaa051. DOI: 10.1093/jlb/lsaa051

[65] Ienca M, Fins JJ, Jox RJ, Jotterand F, Voeneky S, Andorno R, et al. Towards a governance framework for brain data. Neuroethics. 2022;**15**(2):20. DOI: 10.48550/arXiv.2109.11960

[66] Ienca M, Malgieri G. Mental data protection and the GDPR. Journal of Law and the Biosciences. 2022;**9**(1):lsac006. DOI: 10.1093/jlb/lsac006

[67] Mecacci G, Haselager P. Identifying criteria for the evaluation of the implications of brain reading for mental privacy. Science and Engineering Ethics. 2019;**25**(2):443-461. DOI: 10.1007/s11948-017-0003-3

[68] Ricci G. Pharmacological human enhancement: An overview of the looming bioethical and regulatory challenges. Frontiers in Psychiatry. 2020;**11**:53. DOI: 10.3389/fpsyt.2020.00053

[69] U.S. Food and Drug Administration. Artificial Intelligence-Enabled Device Software Functions: Lifecycle Management and Marketing Submission Recommendations (Draft Guidance). FDA-2024-D-4488. Federal Register. 7 Jan 2025;**90**:1154-1156

[70] Parlamento Europeo. EU AI Act: First Regulation on Artificial Intelligence. 2024. Available from: https://www.europarl.europa.eu

[71] Aboy M, Minssen T, Vayena E. Navigating the EU AI Act: Implications for regulated digital medical products. NPJ Digital Medicine. 2024;**7**(1):237. DOI: 10.1038/s41746-024-01232-3

[72] Yuste R, Genser J, Herrmann S. It's time for neuro-rights. Horizons. 2021;**18**:154-164

[73] Attrey A, Lesher M, Lomax C. The role of sandboxes in promoting flexibility and innovation in the digital age. In: OECD Going Digital Toolkit Notes, No. 2. Paris: OECD Publishing; 2020. DOI: 10.1787/cdf5ed45-en

Chapter 5

Optimized Equalization in IM/DD Optical Communications Using Hardware-Friendly Neural Networks

Zhaopeng Xu and Jinlong Wei

Abstract

The increasing demand for high-speed, low-cost data transmission in short-reach optical interconnects has cemented intensity-modulated direct-detection (IM/DD) optical systems as a practical solution. However, nonlinear impairments stemming from square-law detection under chromatic dispersion channels, as well as the nonideal optoelectronic components, pose significant challenges to signal integrity. To address these issues, neural network (NN)-based equalization techniques have garnered considerable attention due to their inherent capability to model complex channel behaviors. While these approaches offer performance improvements, their deployment is often constrained by computational burden and hardware resource consumption. This chapter focuses on recent advances in hardware-friendly NN designs for IM/DD equalization, highlighting effective complexity reduction strategies such as network pruning, low-precision quantization, and multi-task learning. We examine a range of NN architectures and evaluate their adaptability to low-power, low-latency implementations. Furthermore, this chapter discusses practical trade-offs between accuracy and computational cost, with insights into deployment in real-time systems. We outline future directions toward scalable and resource-efficient NN equalization, paving the way for intelligent digital signal processing in next-generation optical communication links.

Keywords: equalization, short reach, intensity-modulated direct-detection, optical communications, intelligent signal processing, hardware-friendly, complexity, neural network

1. Introduction

With the surging demand for bandwidth-intensive services in cloud computing and artificial intelligence applications, short-reach optical interconnects, particularly those based on intensity-modulated direct-detection (IM/DD) schemes, have become indispensable due to their simplicity and cost-efficiency [1–9]. However, IM/DD short-reach optical systems are inherently susceptible to nonlinear impairments, including the nonlinearity accompanied by the square-law detection of dispersion-impacted signals and the nonlinearity introduced by low-cost transceiver devices such as directly modulated lasers (DMLs). These distortions compromise signal integrity, especially at large data rates, and demand powerful equalization strategies at the receiver side.

Machine learning has seen extensive applications in optical communication. It is utilized in various aspects, such as enhancing signal processing in the physical layer to combat fiber-optic nonlinearity and optimizing network-layer operations such as intelligent routing and resource allocation, greatly promoting the development of optical communications [10–21]. In recent years, neural network (NN)-based equalizers have emerged as compelling solutions to nonlinear channel equalization, offering superior performance over traditional linear and polynomial-based techniques. Variants such as feedforward neural networks (FNNs [22–27], cascade FNN (C-FNN) structures [28–30], recurrent NN (RNN) architectures, including cascade RNN (C-RNN) structures [31–36], and many other NN variants [37–42] have demonstrated notable improvements in bit-error-rate (BER) across a range of transmission scenarios. Nonetheless, the practical deployment of NN equalizers is hindered by their high computational complexity, which directly translates into increased hardware resource demands and energy consumption. These factors are critical in latency-sensitive and power-constrained optical interconnect environments.

To bridge this performance-efficiency gap, research efforts have pivoted toward hardware-efficient NN designs. One of the most effective strategies is weight-pruning, which systematically removes redundant connections within the network [43–49]. For instance, pruning in cascade RNN equalization architectures has been shown to maintain equalization performance while reducing the number of original connections, thereby achieving significant complexity savings without sacrificing BER. Furthermore, inspired by advances in multi-task learning (MTL), recent studies have introduced multi-symbol prediction schemes that allow a single NN to simultaneously equalize multiple consecutive symbols [50–59]. By sharing weights and biases across prediction tasks, these networks achieve comparable BER to single-output models while reducing per-symbol operations by a significant amount. This strategy is also effective for equalization architectures such as C-FNNs and autoregressive RNNs, where additional connections can be leveraged to improve learning efficiency without substantially increasing parameter counts. Another promising approach is quantization, where neural weights are constrained to low-precision formats such as integer values, enabling fixed-point operations that are friendly to digital signal processors (DSPs) and real-time implementations [60–69]. Multi-symbol prediction and quantization can also be combined with pruning techniques to further relax the complexity constraints. These techniques not only minimize memory and computational overhead but also pave the way for energy-efficient and scalable hardware designs.

This chapter aims to provide a structured overview of these complexity-aware NN techniques for nonlinear equalization in short-reach IM/DD optical communication systems. We summarize the key architectural advances, performance trade-offs, and implementation challenges associated with pruning,

MTL, and quantization, as well as their hybrid combinations. We discuss benchmarking metrics and hardware design considerations to guide future research toward deployable, high-throughput optical receivers powered by intelligent NN-aided signal processing.

2. Overview of NNs

NNs are computational models inspired by the structure and function of biological neurons. They are composed of interconnected processing units, called neurons, organized in layers. Each connection between neurons has an associated weight that determines the strength of the transmitted signal. An NN typically consists of an input layer, one or more hidden layers, and an output layer.

Forward propagation is the process by which an NN generates predictions. The input vector is multiplied by a weight matrix, and a bias vector is added. The result is passed through a nonlinear activation function to produce the output of that layer, which then serves as the input to the next layer. This process continues until the final output layer produces the prediction. Forward propagation allows the NN to transform raw inputs into outputs through a sequence of learned transformations, enabling the approximation of highly nonlinear relationships.

Training a NN involves adjusting its weights so that the predictions match the desired outputs as closely as possible. This is achieved by defining a loss function that quantifies the prediction error. The weights of the network are then updated to minimize this loss using backpropagation combined with an optimization algorithm such as stochastic gradient descent or Adam. Backpropagation computes the gradient of the loss with respect to each weight by applying the chain rule of calculus in reverse order, starting from the output layer and moving backward through the network. These gradients indicate how each weight should change to reduce the loss, and the optimizer applies the updates iteratively over many training examples.

While many NN architectures exist, they differ mainly in how layers are connected and how information flows between them. FNNs have strictly one-way connections from inputs to outputs, making them well-suited to tasks where each prediction depends on a fixed-size input. RNNs introduce feedback connections that allow information from previous steps to influence current predictions, making them effective for sequential data with temporal dependencies. Hybrid structures, such as C-FNNs and C-RNNs, integrate linear and nonlinear processing paths to better handle mixed-distortion environments.

3. Principles of FNN, C-FNN, RNN, and C-RNN equalizers for IM/DD optical systems

A great number of NN-aided equalization approaches have been applied in short-reach IM/DD systems for nonlinear signal processing; however, most of them are regarded as too complicated to be applied in real-time optical communication applications. Considering the possibility of practical implementations, this chapter introduces four types of NN-based equalizers, including the traditional FNN and three modified variants (with limited additional complexity involved) based on the FNN structure.

3.1 FNN equalizers

The FNN equalizer is a fundamental NN architecture that processes input signals through a series of layers without feedback connections, as shown in **Figure 1**. In short-reach IM/DD optical communication systems, it takes the received symbols as inputs, which typically include the current symbol and its adjacent past and post symbols to capture inter-symbol interference (ISI). The simplest architecture consists of an input layer, one or more hidden layers, and an output layer, with each layer connected to the next through weight matrices and bias vectors. As illustrated in **Figure 1**, the i-th layer consists of $n^{[i]}$ neurons, where $i = 0, 1, 2$. The weight matrix $\mathbf{W}^{[i]}$ denotes an $n^{[i]} \times n^{[i-1]}$ matrix which consists of all the weights connected from the (i-1)-th layer to the i-th layer. The bias vector $\mathbf{b}^{[i]}$ denotes an $n^{[i]} \times 1$ vector containing all the bias of the i-th layer, and the activation function is represented by $f^{[i]}(\cdot)$. The forward-propagation process of an FNN equalizer can be expressed as follows:

$$\mathbf{h} = f^{[1]}\left(\mathbf{W}^{[1]}\mathbf{x} + \mathbf{b}^{[1]}\right) \tag{1}$$

$$y = f^{[2]}\left(\mathbf{W}^{[2]}\mathbf{h} + b^{[2]}\right) \tag{2}$$

where the NN inputs are denoted by $\mathbf{x}$, and the NN output is denoted by y. After NN processing, the NN output represents the predicted symbol. By employing a sliding window manner, all the received symbols can be equalized sequentially one at a time.

FNNs leverage nonlinear activation functions in hidden layers to approximate complex nonlinear impairments, such as those introduced by square-law detection of dispersion-impaired signals and laser chirp in IM/DD systems. However, their purely feedforward structure may struggle to fully compensate for residual linear impairments, limiting their performance in mixed linear–nonlinear channel conditions.

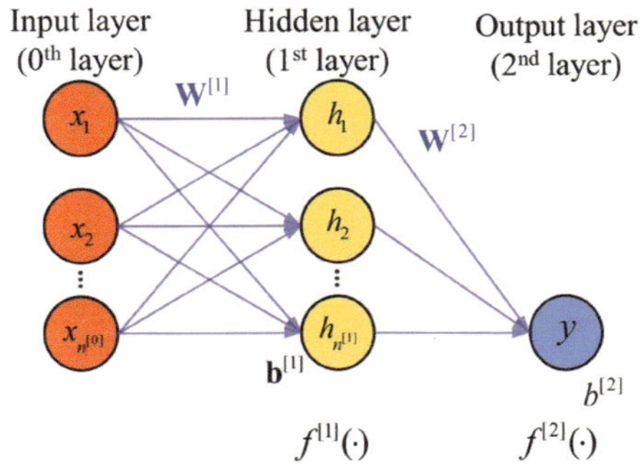

Figure 1.
Schematic of FNN equalizers.

3.2 C-FNN equalizers

As illustrated in **Figure 2**, the C-FNN equalizer extends the traditional FNN by introducing a direct linear path from the input layer to the output layer, known as the cascade structure. This design allows the network to jointly address linear and nonlinear impairments by combining linear mapping with nonlinear approximation. The cascade connection is controlled by a $1 \times n^{[0]}$ weight vector $\mathbf{W}^c$, which establishes a linear mapping from inputs to outputs. The forward-propagation process of a C-FNN equalizer is given by the following:

$$\mathbf{h} = f^{[1]}\left(\mathbf{W}^{[1]}\mathbf{x} + \mathbf{b}^{[1]}\right) \tag{3}$$

$$y = f^{[2]}\left(\left[\mathbf{W}^{[2]},\ \mathbf{W}^{[c]}\right]\left[\mathbf{h}^T, \mathbf{x}^T\right]^T + b^{[2]}\right) \tag{4}$$

where the superscript Tdenotes the transpose of a matrix. Here, the input is concatenated with the hidden layer output to form the input for the output layer, with $\mathbf{W}^{[c]}$ enabling direct linear compensation. By integrating linear and nonlinear processing through joint optimization during training, C-FNNs outperform traditional FNNs in mitigating combined impairments. The cascade structure reduces the “BER floor” by addressing residual linear effects that FNNs may overlook, making it particularly effective in short-reach IM/DD optical systems with mixed linear–nonlinear distortions.

3.3 RNN equalizers

In contrast to the FNN equalizer that processes data in a unidirectional manner from input to output, the RNN equalizer incorporates feedback connections, allowing it to leverage past output predictions to improve current symbol estimation. As depicted in **Figure 3**, this recurrence enables RNNs to model temporal dependencies in the signal, making them well-suited for compensating dynamic impairments. The feedback mechanism endows RNNs with the remarkable ability to model temporal dependencies, making them particularly well-suited for compensating complex effects in optical communication channels such as IM/DD links that exhibit dynamic behaviors. Assuming k output feedbacks are introduced, the forward propagation of a RNN equalizer is defined as follows:

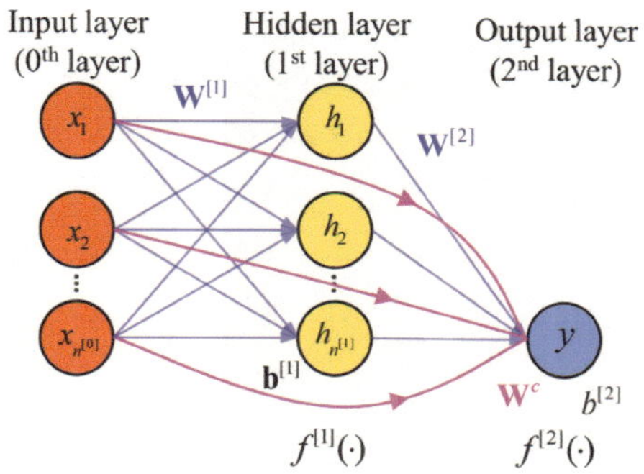

Figure 2.
Schematic of C-FNN equalizers.

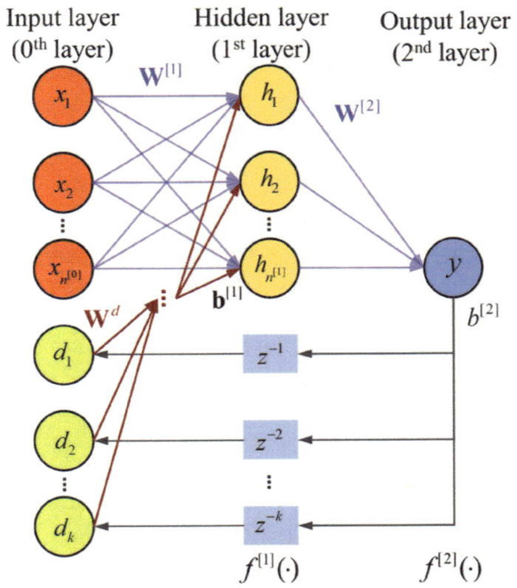

Figure 3.
Schematic of RNN equalizers.

$$\mathbf{h} = f^{[1]}\left([\mathbf{W}^{[1]}, \mathbf{W}^{d}][\mathbf{x}^{\mathbf{T}}, y_d^T]^T + \mathbf{b}^{[1]}\right) \tag{5}$$

$$y = f^{[2]}\left(\mathbf{W}^{[2]}\mathbf{h} + b^{[2]}\right) \tag{6}$$

where the k output feedbacks are represented by $\mathbf{y}_d$ and the recurrent connections are controlled by an $n^{[1]} \times k$ weight matrix $\mathbf{W}$. RNNs excel in capturing long-term dependencies in the signal, leading to better ISI mitigation compared to FNNs. However, their computational complexity is slightly higher due to the feedback mechanism, and the loop structure may also pose challenges for real-time implementation.

3.4 C-RNN equalizers

The C-RNN equalizer combines the strengths of recurrent and cascade structures, integrating feedback connections with a direct linear path from inputs to outputs, as shown in **Figure 4**. This hybrid architecture enables joint compensation of linear and nonlinear impairments while leveraging temporal dependencies through recurrence. The cascade connection weight vector $\mathbf{W}^{[c]}$now has a dimension $1 \times (n^{(0)} + k)$. The forward propagation of a C-RNN equalizer is expressed as follows:

$$\mathbf{h} = f^{[1]}\left([\mathbf{W}^{[1]}, \mathbf{W}^{d}][\mathbf{x}^{\mathbf{T}}, y_d^T]^T + \mathbf{b}^{[1]}\right) \tag{7}$$

$$y = f^{[2]}\left([\mathbf{W}^{[2]}, \mathbf{W}^{c}][\mathbf{h}^{T}, \mathbf{x}_d^T, \mathbf{y}_d^T]^T + b^{[2]}\right) \tag{8}$$

By optimizing the cascade and recurrent components simultaneously, C-RNNs achieve superior performance in mixed impairment scenarios. The cascade path

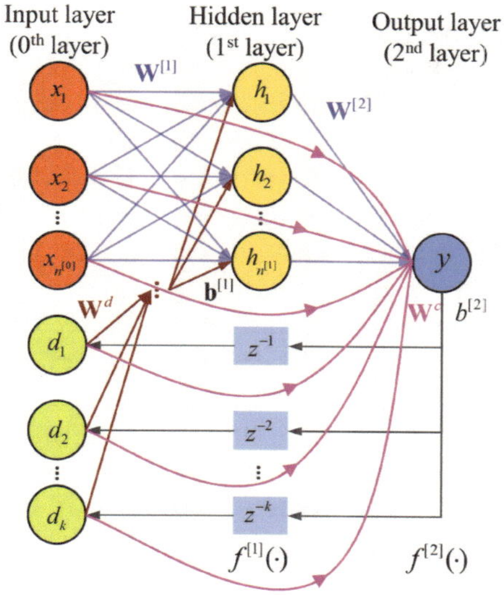

Figure 4.
Schematic of C-RNN equalizers.

addresses linear distortions, while the recurrent path mitigates dynamic nonlinear effects, resulting in lower BER and improved receiver sensitivity compared to standalone RNNs or C-FNNs.

4. Experimental configuration of DML-based IM/DD links

A typical illustration for the DML-based four-level pulse amplitude modulation (PAM4) IM/DD link is depicted in **Figure 5**. In real experiments, it involves a more comprehensive setup designed to evaluate the performance of NN-based equalizers under realistic short-reach conditions. At the transmitter, a 50/100-Gb/s PAM4 signal is generated by an arbitrary waveform generator (AWG, Keysight M8196A) operating at a sample rate of 92 GSa/s. A root-raised cosine (RRC) filter with a roll-off factor of 0.1 is employed for Nyquist pulse shaping. The electrical PAM4 signal is amplified by a 17 dB gain electronic amplifier (SHF 100 BP) before being fed into a 16-GHz DML biased at 55 mA. The DML outputs an optical power of 9.5 dBm, which is transmitted over a 25/15-km standard single-mode fiber.

At the receiver, a variable optical attenuator adjusts the received optical power (ROP), and a 43-GHz photodetector (PD, BPDV2,150 R) performs square-law direct detection of the optical signal. The detected electrical signal is captured by a digital storage oscilloscope (DSO, DSA-X 93304Q) at a sample rate of 80 GSa/s. Post-capture signal processing includes resampling, matched RRC filtering, and

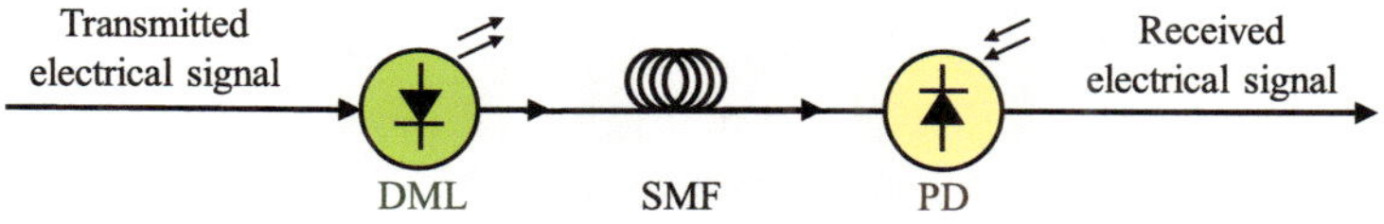

Figure 5.
Illustration of a typical DML-based IM/DD link.

downsampling, after which the signal is fed into the NN-based DSP module for equalization and BER calculation.

For the 50-Gb/s 25-km system, FNN, C-FNN, and RNN equalizers are employed, all of which utilize 15 inputs and nine hidden neurons to achieve the BER floor and perform a fair performance comparison. For the 100-Gb/s 15-km system, only the C-RNN equalizer can support reliable communication, where 23 inputs and 12 hidden neurons are adopted. In terms of the recurrent structure, only two feedback delays are utilized. The 100-Gb/s system requires a larger C-RNN structure to handle the increased nonlinearities and ISI, demonstrating the scalability of NN-based equalizers to higher data rates with appropriate architectural adjustments. Both setups validate the effectiveness of NN equalizers in mitigating complex impairments in DML-based IM/DD optical systems.

5. Key techniques toward hardware-friendly NN equalizers and experimental results

This section will introduce three key optimization techniques, that is, network pruning, multi-symbol processing, and weight quantization, to achieve hardware-friendly NN receiver implementation. The corresponding experimental results for each technique will also be provided, taking both system BER performance and computational complexity into account.

5.1 Network pruning

Network pruning is a NN compression technique aimed at reducing model size and computational cost by removing redundant or insignificant parameters. In a trained network, many weights have very small magnitudes, indicating that they contribute minimally to the final output. Pruning sets these low-importance weights to zero, resulting in a sparser connectivity pattern. This sparsity can substantially lower the number of multiplications and memory accesses required during inference, which is particularly beneficial for real-time, hardware-constrained optical receivers. Common selection criteria include the following: (i) magnitude-based thresholding, where connections with absolute weight values below a predefined threshold are removed because their contribution to the output is negligible; (ii) gradient-based importance scores, which evaluate the sensitivity of the loss function to each weight and prune those with minimal influence on the learning dynamics of the network; and (iii) iterative prune-and-retrain schemes, in which a fraction of the least important weights is pruned in multiple stages, with the network retrained after each pruning step to recover accuracy and allow for higher overall sparsity without significant performance loss. As shown in **Figure 6**, by employing network pruning, a sparsely connected network architecture can be finally obtained, starting from the original fully connected version. The removal of less significant weights allows for network efficiency, making NNs hardware-friendly for practical implementations.

For a fully connected C-RNN, the architecture comprises four types of weights: input-hidden layer weights, hidden-output layer weights, recurrent feedback weights from delayed outputs to hidden neurons, and cascade connection weights from inputs to the output layer. Experimental analysis (the 100-Gb/s 15-km PAM4

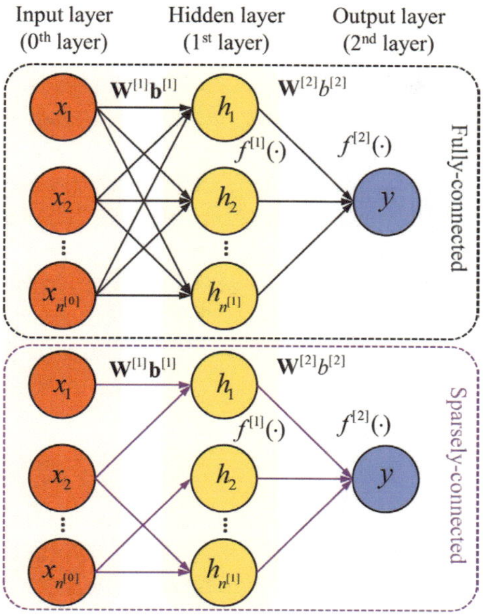

Figure 6.
Comparison of fully and sparsely connected NN equalizers.

transmission case) of weight distributions reveals that input-hidden layer connections exhibit a Gaussian-like pattern, with a significant proportion of weights clustered near zero. This indicates that many input-hidden connections are redundant, as their minimal impact on signal processing allows pruning without degrading performance. In contrast, weights in hidden-output layers, recurrent paths, and cascade connections show nonzero dominant distributions, highlighting their critical role in maintaining equalization accuracy. This distinction enables targeted pruning of input-hidden weights, which form the primary source of redundancy in C-RNN equalizers.

More detailed experimental results of the 100 Gb/s PAM4 signal under pruned C-RNN are given in **Figure 7**. **Figure 7(a)** illustrates the BER and the number of NN connections as a function of the weight threshold. The ROP is fixed at 5 dBm. As the

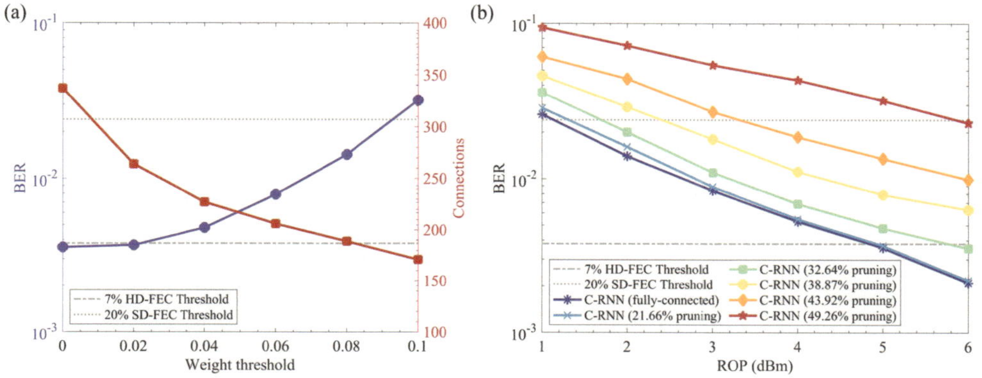

Figure 7.
(a) BER/the number of connections versus weight threshold; (b) BER versus ROP utilizing C-RNN equalizers with different pruning ratios.

weight threshold increases, more connections are pruned, reducing computational complexity but slightly degrading BER. At a threshold of 0.02, the system achieves a BER below the 7% hard-decision forward error correction (HD-FEC) threshold with 21.66% fewer connections, demonstrating almost no performance loss.

Further increasing the threshold to 0.08 prunes 43.92% of connections. Though the BER exceeds the HD-FEC threshold, it is still lower than the 20% soft-decision forward error correction (SD-FEC) threshold. **Figure 7(b)** presents the BER performance versus ROP. At a pruning ratio of 21.66%, the BER curve aligns with the fully connected C-RNN equalizers across all ROPs, confirming equivalent performance. When relaxing to the 20% SD-FEC threshold, a 49.26% pruning ratio is feasible at ROP = 6 dBm, nearly halving the connections while maintaining acceptable BER.

5.2 Multi-symbol processing

Multi-symbol processing as a complexity reduction technique for NN-based equalizers is deeply rooted in the principle of MTL, aiming to address the computational bottleneck that hinders real-time implementation in short-reach optical interconnects. Unlike traditional single-output NNs, which process each symbol sequentially and independently – thereby repeating computations for each prediction – multi-symbol processing enables a single NN to estimate a sequence of symbols simultaneously by leveraging shared parameters and feature representations across adjacent symbols, as depicted in **Figure 8**. This approach capitalizes on the observation that the weights and biases trained to predict the current symbol often contain useful information for predicting subsequent symbols, reducing redundancy in the NN equalization computational graph. In IM/DD optical communication systems, where ISI couples adjacent symbols, multi-symbol processing naturally aligns with the channel's memory effects. By expanding the input window length (e.g., original input length + output length), the NN equalizers can capture the ISI impact on a series of output symbols within a single forward-propagation step, reusing the hidden layer activations for each prediction in the sequence. This design not only maintains the equalization performance but also drastically reduces the per-symbol computational complexity by distributing the fixed overhead of NN layers across multiple outputs.

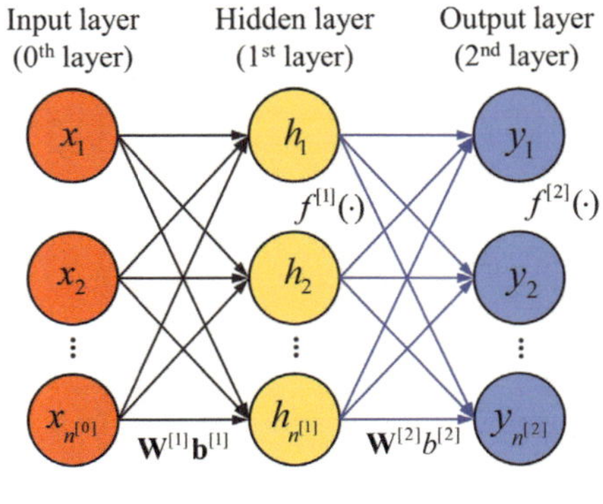

Figure 8.
Schematic of multi-symbol processing using FNN equalizers.

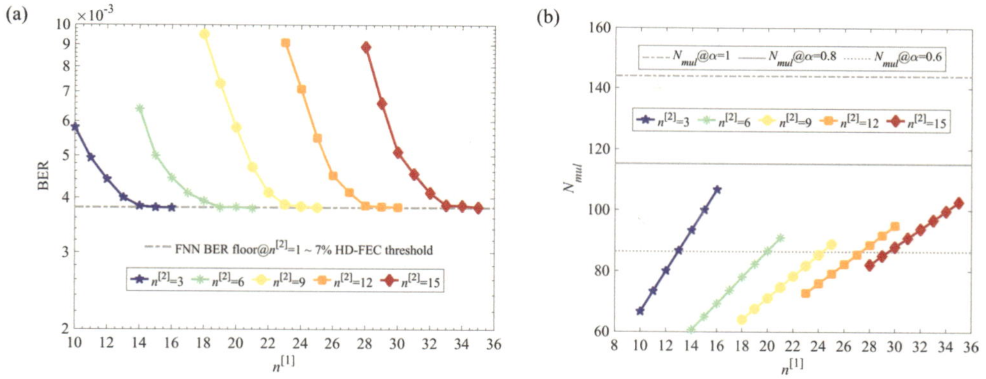

Figure 9.
(a) BER and (b) the number of multiplications involved versus the number of hidden neurons under different output conditions.

Figure 9 illustrates how the BER and computational complexity, in terms of the number of multiplications per symbol (denoted by *Nmul*), vary with the number of hidden neurons under different numbers of output symbols in an FNN-based multi-symbol equalizer (50-Gb/s 25-km PAM4 signal transmission when the ROP is - 1 dBm). As shown in **Figure 9(a)**, increasing the number of hidden neurons consistently improves BER until a saturation point is reached, where further increases no longer yield significant gains. Notably, for various output counts, the BER plateaus at a level comparable to that of the conventional single-output FNN, indicating that multi-symbol prediction does not compromise performance. **Figure 9 (b)** reveals that, compared with single-output NN counterparts, the average number of multiplications required for multi-output NN equalizers to recover a symbol decreases substantially when increasing the number of outputs, owing to the shared use of network parameters. Optimal trade-offs between computational complexity and performance are observed when 6 to 12 output symbols are used, where the per-symbol computational burden is reduced to just a few tens of multiplications, highlighting the feasibility of real-time deployment.

Figure 10 investigates how computational complexity can be reduced while maintaining BER performance in the FNN-based multi-symbol equalization scheme.

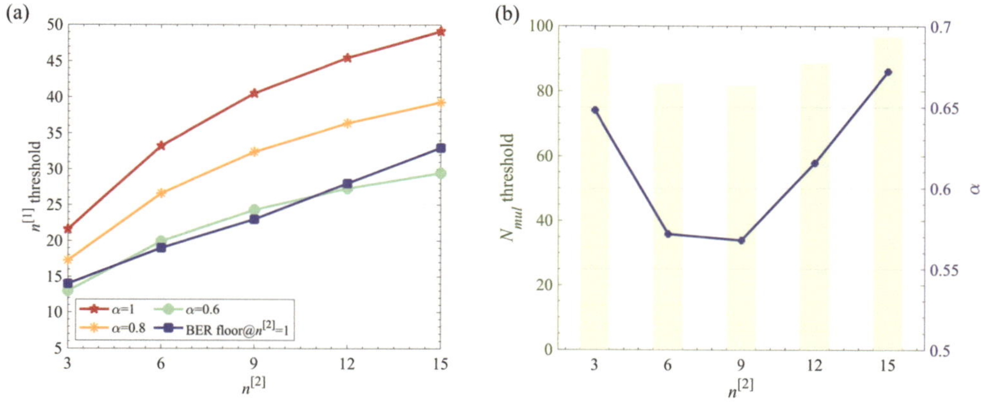

Figure 10.
(a) The number of hidden neurons and (b) the number of multiplications threshold/complexity reduction ratio versus the number of output neurons.

In **Figure 10(a)**, two thresholds for the number of hidden neurons are plotted. The red line indicates an upper limit for the number of hidden neurons that still permits reduced computational cost without significant BER degradation. The blue line, on the other hand, shows the minimum required number of hidden neurons to match the BER performance of a standard single-output FNN. It is evident that this BER-maintaining threshold for the number of hidden neurons is consistently below the one corresponding to a fixed complexity reduction factor ($\alpha = 0.8$), where $1 - \alpha$ indicates the complexity reduction ratio. **Figure 10(b)** quantifies this by plotting the number of multiplications per symbol and the associated reduction ratio for the optimal BER-matching. As the number of output symbols increases, both the number of multiplications and α first decline – indicating improved weight reuse across symbols – but then rise again due to network over-parameterization. This behavior reveals that there is an optimal number of outputs that minimizes computational load. The most efficient configuration occurs at nine outputs, yielding a 43.2% complexity reduction and requiring only 81.8 multiplications per symbol, compared to the 144 multiplications in the conventional single-output model. This underscores the potential of multi-symbol FNNs for efficient real-time implementations.

The combination of multi-symbol prediction and pruning offers a more powerful strategy to reduce computational complexity in NN-based equalization for IM/DD systems, whose schematic is given in **Figure 11**. As mentioned above, multi-symbol prediction allows an NN to recover multiple consecutive output symbols in a single forward pass, effectively reusing network weights across symbols and reducing per-symbol operations. Pruning, on the other hand, removes redundant or low-impact weights and connections from the network after training, resulting in a smaller and more hardware-efficient model without significant performance degradation. When used together, multi-symbol prediction reduces the frequency of forward passes, while pruning minimizes the number of active computations within each pass. This synergy enables substantial reductions in both memory footprint and real-time processing load, making NN equalizers more practical for deployment in latency-sensitive and power-constrained optical interconnect environments.

Figure 12 analyzes the computational efficiency and pruning behavior of multi-output NN equalizers. **Figure 12(a)** explores how increasing the weight pruning

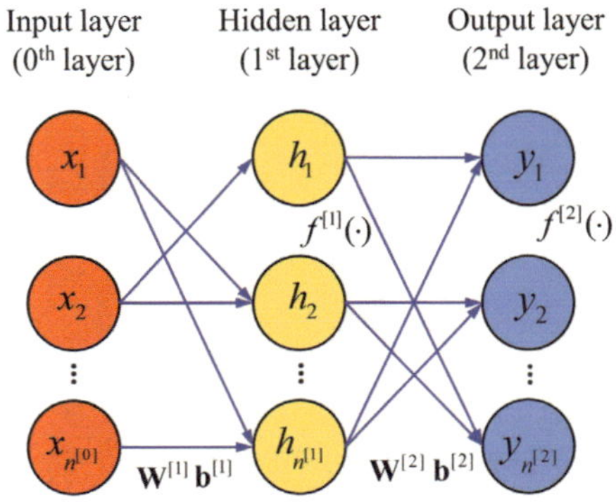

Figure 11.
Schematic of pruned multi-symbol processing using FNN equalizers.

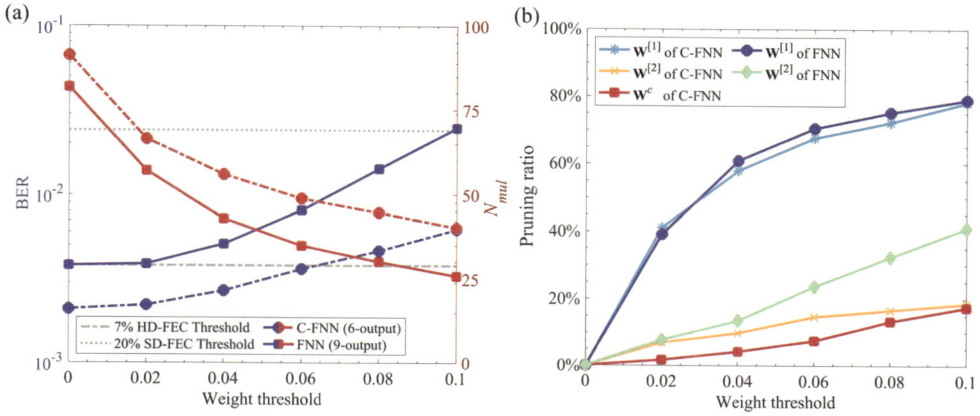

Figure 12.
(a) BER/the number of multiplications and (b) pruning ratio versus weight threshold for FNN and C-FNN equalizers.

threshold influences both BER and the number of multiplications. As more connections are removed, the computational load decreases, while BER remains nearly unchanged up to a moderate threshold. Notably, even under aggressive pruning, the BER stays below the 20% SD-FEC limit. **Figure 12(b)** details how pruning affects different layers. Most weight removals occur between the input and hidden layers, while fewer are observed in the output and cascade connections, suggesting that early-layer sparsity contributes most to efficiency gains.

Figure 13 presents the relationship between BER performance and ROP under different pruning levels for two optimized NN equalizers: a nine-output FNN and a six-output C-FNN. For both architectures, the pruning ratios, which are determined based on weight threshold selection, reflect varying degrees of weight sparsity. The results show that even after removing a significant proportion of weights, both networks retain strong BER performance across a range of ROP values. Moderate pruning leads to minimal performance degradation, while more aggressive pruning

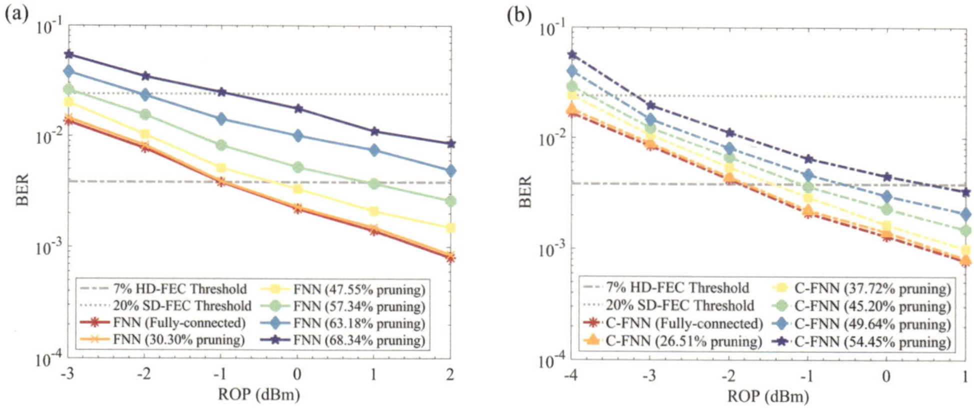

Figure 13.
BER versus ROP for (a) FNN and (b) C-FNN equalizers.

still maintains BER below the SD-FEC limit, particularly at higher ROP. Compared to the fully connected multi-output versions, about 30.3% and 26.5% pruning reduction ratios can be obtained for FNN and C-FNN, respectively, while still maintaining the BER performance. These experimental results highlight the robustness of the pruned multi-output structures and demonstrate their potential for real-time deployment with reduced computational demands.

5.3 Weight quantization

Weight quantization emerges as a pivotal technique to reduce computational complexity in NN-based equalizers, enabling hardware-efficient implementations by replacing floating-point (FP) arithmetic with low-bit integer operations. The core principle involves mapping high-precision FP weights to lower-bit integer representations, which drastically reduces memory requirements and accelerates computations. Fixed-precision quantization can be applied, which quantizes all weights and biases to a fixed bit width. Mixed-precision quantization can also be utilized, where the weights and biases are quantized with different bit widths. As illustrated in the mixed-precision NN equalizer quantization example in **Figure 14**, the presented approach partitions input neurons into high-precision and low-precision categories based on their weight significance. For instance, central input neurons with larger weights are assigned higher precision, while peripheral neurons with smaller weights are quantized to lower precision. This adaptive partitioning avoids unnecessary precision in less influential weights, optimizing both storage and computation.

The experimental results of quantized NN equalizers are shown in **Figure 15**, where 50-Gb/s 25-km PAM4 IM/DD transmission is considered. **Figure 15(a)** illustrates the BER performance across different ROPs for various fixed and mixed quantized NN equalizers. The notation (m,n) signifies the high- and low-precision bits for mixed schemes. It is evident that both the fixed 12-bit and mixed (12,6) NNs show comparable receiver sensitivity to the FP–NN, with the BER staying below the 7% HD-FEC threshold when the ROP is above – 1 dBm. As the quantized bits decrease, it is observed that there is a performance degradation, but the sensitivity

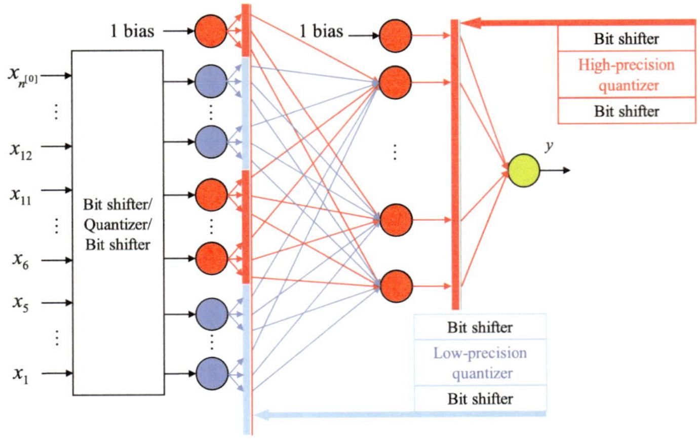

Figure 14.
Schematic of mixed-precision quantized FNN equalizers.

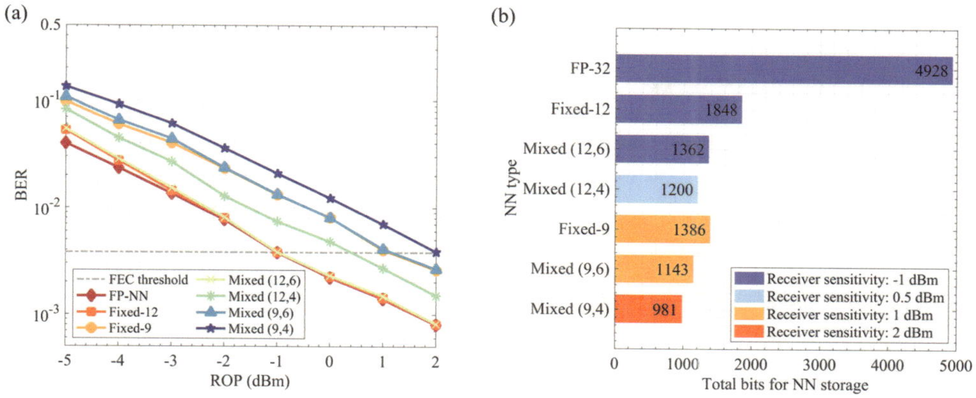

Figure 15.
(a) BER versus ROP, and (b) the total bits required for parameter storage of different quantized NN equalizers.

gap remains acceptable. For example, the mixed (12,4), fixed 9-bit/mixed (9,6), and mixed (9,4) NNs require ROPs of about 0.5 dBm, 1 dBm, and 2 dBm, respectively. **Figure 15(b)** depicts the total bits needed for parameter storage of different quantized NN equalizers. The FP–NN demands 4,928 bits, while the fixed 12-bit and mixed (12,6) NNs only need 1,848 bits and 1,362 bits, respectively. Compared to fixed-precision quantization, the mixed-precision approach reduces memory by approximately 26.3% without sacrificing performance. When the receiver sensitivity is fixed at 2 dBm, the total bits for mixed-quantization NN storage drop below 1,000, holding promise for real-time receiver implementation.

Similarly, we can also combine quantization and pruning to further reduce the equalization complexity. **Figure 16** illustrates the structure of a two-layer

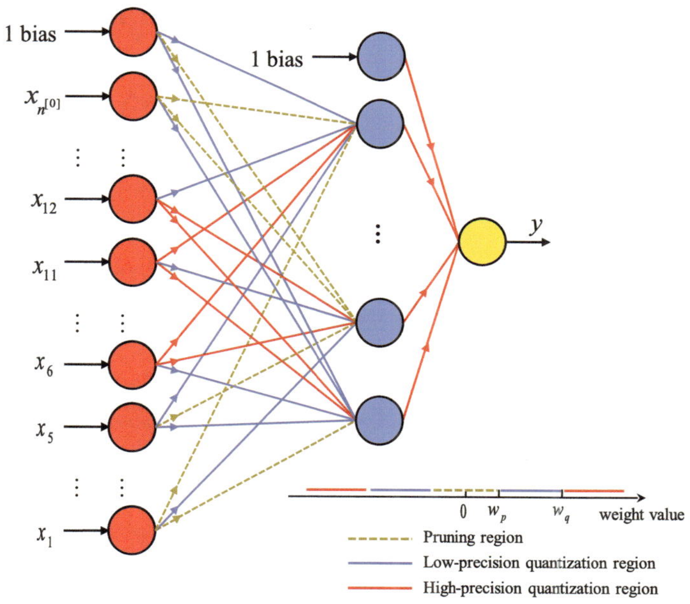

Figure 16.
Schematic of weight-adaptive, joint mixed-precision, quantized, and pruned FNN equalizers.

FNN equalizer enhanced with a dual strategy for computational reduction: mixed-precision quantization and pruning. Each connection in the network is categorized into one of three types based on the magnitude of its associated weight. Weights with values exceeding a high threshold are quantized with greater precision to preserve accuracy, while those falling within a moderate range are encoded using fewer bits. Connections with negligible weights, that is, those below a defined pruning threshold, are entirely removed from the network to eliminate unnecessary computations. To simplify implementation, all biases are treated as additional connections linked to a constant input. This structured hybrid design enables a significant reduction in both the number of operations and memory usage, while retaining the nonlinear modeling capabilities of the original network.

Figure 17 examines how the proposed joint mixed-precision quantization and pruning scheme affects BER performance under various conditions. The ROP is set at -1 dBm for consistency. In **Figure 17(a)**, the BER is plotted against increasing weight thresholds for three configurations: pruning, low-precision quantization (6 bit), and high-precision quantization (12 bit). As the pruning threshold rises, more weights are eliminated, leading to a sharp BER increase beyond a certain point. Conversely, for quantization, the BER remains nearly unchanged over a wider range, particularly when higher bit widths are used. **Figure 17(b)** further explores the BER behavior with respect to different bit widths under multiple quantization strategies, that is, fixed-precision, high-precision region-only, and low-precision region-only quantization, each tested with and without pruning. The results show that quantizing high-magnitude weights has a dominant impact on preserving BER, while the low-precision quantization region corresponds more to memory savings. Notably, the proposed method achieves competitive BER with as few as 12 bits in high-precision regions and even lower resolution of 6 bits for less critical weights, demonstrating a balanced trade-off between complexity and performance.

Figures 18 quantifies the memory savings and performance scalability of the quantization approach across different network configurations. In **Figure 18(a)**, the

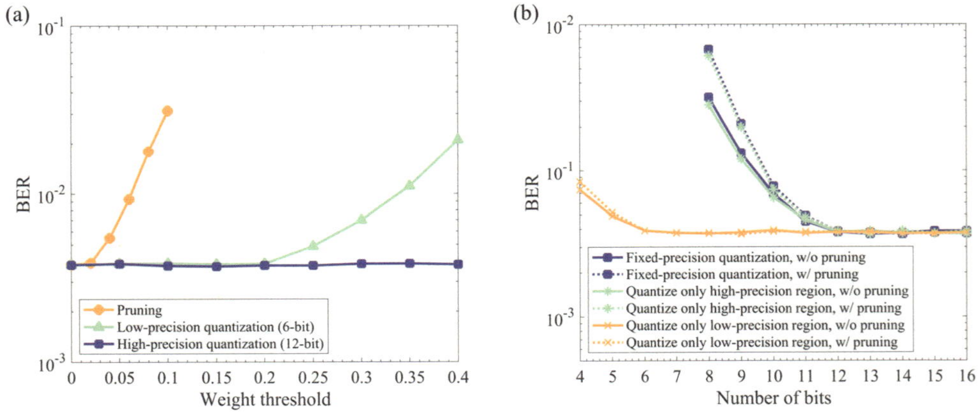

Figure 17.
(a) BER versus weight threshold and (b) BER versus quantization bits under various pruning and quantization operations.

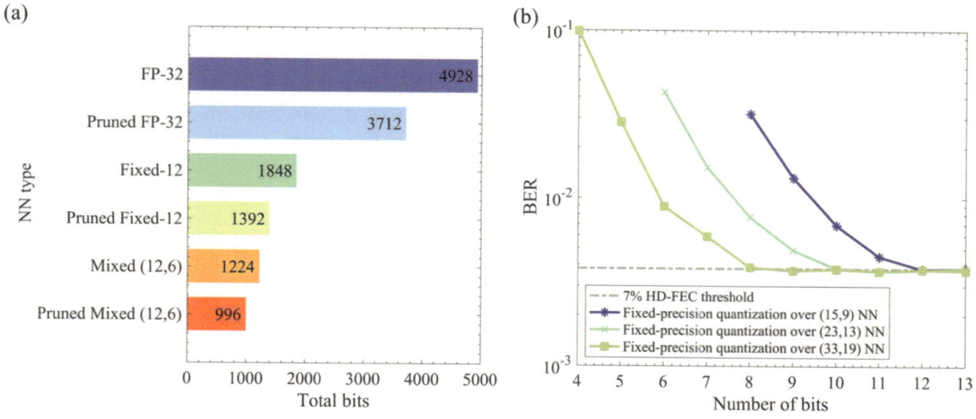

Figure 18.
(a) The total bits required for parameter storage of different pruned and quantized NN equalizers; (b) BER versus quantization bits using NN equalizers of different sizes.

total number of bits required for storing network parameters is compared among various quantized and pruned implementations. The standard FP network requires the most memory, while applying pruning or uniform quantization individually yields moderate reductions. Notably, the combination of pruning and mixed-precision quantization results in the greatest savings of nearly 80% compared to the FP baseline by dynamically allocating fewer bits to less significant weights and eliminating negligible connections altogether. **Figure 18(b)** extends the analysis by evaluating BER as a function of quantization resolution for NN equalizers of increasing size. Larger networks are shown to tolerate lower bit widths without compromising BER due to their inherent redundancy. This highlights that over-parameterized architectures are more robust to quantization errors, allowing aggressive bit reduction while maintaining received signal integrity, showing an important insight for optimizing power-efficient hardware implementations.

6. Conclusions

In this chapter, we have systematically explored the use of optimized NN-based equalization to mitigate nonlinear distortions in short-reach IM/DD optical systems. NN equalizers offer a flexible and powerful solution, yet their practical deployment requires careful attention to computational efficiency. To this end, we have reviewed and analyzed several strategies, such as pruning, multi-symbol learning, and quantization, that significantly reduce complexity while preserving equalization performance. Our discussion has emphasized the trade-offs between algorithmic accuracy and implementation cost, highlighting that, with appropriate model simplification and architectural design, NN equalizers can be made compatible with low-power hardware implementations. Looking forward, further advances in hardware-aware NN equalizer design and adaptive compression methods are expected to drive the widespread adoption of intelligent signal processing in future optical interconnects.

Acknowledgments

This work was supported by the National Key Research and Development Program of China (2024YFB29NL00100), the Fund of the State Key Laboratory of Photonics and Communications, P. R. China (2025QZKF07), and the National Talent Program.

Conflict of interest

The authors declare no conflict of interest.

Author details

Zhaopeng Xu and Jinlong Wei
Pengcheng Laboratory, Shenzhen, China

*Address all correspondence to: weijl01@pcl.ac.cn.

References

[1] Cheng J, Xie C, Chen Y, Chen X, Tang M, Fu S Comparison of coherent and IMDD transceivers for intra datacenter optical interconnects. In: Optical Fiber Communication Conference and Exhibition (OFC). San Diego, CA, USA; March 2019. pp. 1–3

[2] Zhong K, Zhou X, Huo J, Yu C, Lu C, Lau APT. Digital signal processing for short-reach optical communications: A review of current technologies and future trends. Journal of Lightwave Technology. 2018;**36**:377–400

[3] Xu Z, Sun C, Manton J, Shieh W. Joint equalization of linear and nonlinear impairments for PAM4 short-reach direct detection systems. IEEE Photonics Technology Letters. 2021;**33**:425–428

[4] Wu Q, Xu Z, Zhu Y, Ji H, Yang Y, Qiao G, Liu L, Wang S, Liang J, Wei J, et al. Gradient-descent noise whitening techniques for short-reach IM-DD optical interconnects with severe bandwidth limitation. Optics Express 2024;**32**:1715–1727

[5] Ji H, Dong S, Xu Z, Li J, Unnithan R, Su Y, Shieh W. Carrier assisted differential detection with generalized and simplified receiver structure. Journal of Lightwave Technology. 2021;**39**(22):7159–7167

[6] Tang J, Wei J, Liang J, Xu Z, Zhao T, Cheng C, Hao Y, Yang B, Sun Z, Li K, et al. Multiplication-free and hardware-efficient baud-rate timing error detector for Nyquist and faster-than-Nyquist optical IM/DD systems. Optics Letters. 2024;**49**: 2353–2356

[7] Liu GN, Zhang L, Zuo T, Zhang Q. IM/DD transmission techniques for emerging 5G fronthaul, DCI, and metro applications. Journal of Lightwave Technology. 2018;**36**(2):560–567

[8] Ranzini SM, Da Ros F, Bülow H, Zibar D. Tunable optoelectronic chromatic dispersion compensation based on machine learning for short-reach transmission. Applied Sciences. 2019;**9**:4332

[9] Tan Z, Yang C, Xu Z, Chen L, Huang X, Guo H, Zheng Z, Zhang F, Wang Z Experimental demonstration for over Mbps baseband-over-modulation AMCC implementation in PtP WDM-PON. In: Optical Fiber Communication Conference (OFC), 2018. Tu3L.3

[10] Wu Q, Xu Z, Zhu Y, Zhang Y, Ji H, Yang Y, Qiao G, Liu L, Wang S, Liang J, et al. Machine learning for self-coherent detection short-reach optical communications. Photonics 2023;**10**:1001

[11] Zhou H, Li Y, Liu Y, Yue L, Gao C, Li W, Qiu J, Guo H, Hong X, Zuo Y, et al. Recent advances in equalization technologies for short-reach optical links based on PAM4 modulation: A review. Applied Sciences. 2019;**9**:2342

[12] Xie Y, Wang Y, Kandeepan S, Wang K. Machine learning applications for short-reach optical communication. Photonics. 2022;**9**:30

[13] Zibar D, Piels M, Jones R, Schaeffer CG. Machine learning techniques in optical communication. Journal of Lightwave Technology. 2016;**34**: 1442–1452

[14] Musumeci F, Rottondi C, Nag A, Macaluso I, Zibar D, Ruffini M, Tornatore M. An overview on application of machine learning techniques in optical networks. IEEE Communications Surveys and Tutorials. 2018;**21**:1383–1408

[15] Khan FN, Fan Q, Lu C, Lau APT. An optical communication's perspective on machine learning and its applications. Journal of Lightwave Technology. 2019;**37**:493–516

[16] Chen G, Du J, Sun L, Zheng L, Xu K, Tsang HK, Chen X, Reed GT, He Z. Machine learning adaptive receiver for PAM-4 modulated optical interconnection based on silicon microring modulator. Journal of Lightwave Technology. 2018;**18**: 4106–4113

[17] Xu Z, Wei J. Machine learning applied to optical communication systems. Photonics. 2025;**12**(5):458

[18] Musumeci F, Rottondi CEM, Corani G, Shahkarami S, Cugini F, Tornatore M. A tutorial on machine learning for failure management in optical networks. Journal of Lightwave Technology. 2019;**37**:4125–4139

[19] Wu X, Jargon JA, Skoog RA, Paraschis L, Willner AE. Applications of artificial neural networks in optical performance monitoring. Journal of Lightwave Technology. 2009;**27**: 3580–3589

[20] Shahkarami S, Musumeci F, Cugini F, Tornatore M Machine-learning-based soft-failure detection and identification in optical networks. In: Optical Fiber Communication Conference and Exposition (OFC). San Diego, CA, USA; March11–15, 2018, pp. 1–3

[21] Wong E, Mondal S, Ruan L. Machine learning enhanced next-generation optical access networks—Challenges and emerging solutions. Journal of Optical Communications and Networking. 2023;**14**:A49–A62

[22] Estarán J, Müller R, Mestre M, Jorge F, Mardoyan H, Konczykowska A, Dupuy J, Bigo S Artificial neural networks for linear and non-linear impairment mitigation in high-baudrate IMDD systems. In: European Conference on Optical Communication (ECOC). Germany: Düsseldorf; September 18–22, 2016

[23] Ye C, Zhang D, Huang X, Feng H, Zhang K Demonstration of 50Gbps IM/DD PAM4 PON over 10GHz class optics using neural network based nonlinear equalization. In: European Conference on Optical Communication (ECOC). Gothenburg, Sweden; September 17–21, 2017

[24] Zhang Q, Jiang Y, Zhou H, Deng C, Duan S, Wang Z, Li Y, Song Y, Chen J, Zhang J, et al. 137 Gb/s PAM-4 transmissions at 850 nm over 40 cm optical backplane with 25 G devices with improved neural network-based equalization. Applied Sciences. 2019;**9**:5095

[25] Zhang L, Yang F, Ming H, Zhu Y, Ruan X, Li Y, Zhang F 160-Gb/s Nyquist PAM-4 transmission with GeSi-EAM using artificial neural network based nonlinear equalization. In: Optical Fiber Communication Conference (OFC). San Diego, CA, USA; March 8–12, 2020

[26] Reza A, Costas M, Browning C, Otero F, Barry L. Single-lane 54-Gbit/s PAM-4/8 signal transmissions using 10G-class directly modulated lasers enabled by low- complexity nonlinear

digital equalization. IEEE Photonics Journal. 2022;**14**:7226909. 1–9

[27] Chen H, Liu X, Fan Z, Hu C, Zhao J Dual-learning based neural networks for short-reach optical communications. In: Conference on Lasers and Electro-Optics (CLEO). San Jose, CA, USA; May 9–14, 2021

[28] Xu Z, Sun C, Ji T, Ji H, Manton J, Shieh W Cascade recurrent neural network enabled 100-Gb/s PAM4 short-reach optical link based on DML. In: Optical Fiber Communication Conference (OFC). San Diego, CA, USA; March 8–12, 2020

[29] Xu Z, Sun C, Ji T, Manton J, Shieh W. Cascade recurrent neural network assisted nonlinear equalization for a 100 Gb/s PAM4 short-reach direct detection system. Optics Letters. 2020;**45**:4216–4219

[30] Murphy S, Jamali F, Townsend P, Antony C Adaptive neural network equalisation using skip connections for future 100 Gbit/s/λ passive optical networks. In: European Conference on Optical Communication (ECOC). Glasgow, Scotland; October 1–5, 2023

[31] Ye C, Zhang D, Hu X, Huang X, Feng H, Zhang K Recurrent neural network (RNN) based end-to-end nonlinear management for symmetrical 50Gbps NRZ PON with 29dB+ loss budget. In: European Conference and Exhibition on Optical Communication (ECOC). Rome, Italy; September 23–27, 2018

[32] Zhou Q, Yang C, Liang A, Zheng X, Chen Z. Low computationally complex recurrent neural network for high-speed optical fiber transmission. Optics Communications. 2019;**441**: 121–126

[33] Peng C, Chan D, Tong Y, Chow C, Liu Y, Yeh C, Tsang H Long short-term memory neural network for mitigating transmission impairments of 160 Gbit/s PAM4 microring modulation. In: Optical Fiber Communication Conference (OFC). San Francisco, CA, USA; June 6–10, 2021

[34] Yang C, Gao Y, Wang J, Li H, Hasnain C Enhanced recurrent neural network equalization based on hidden feature extraction learning for optical interconnect. In: Optical Fiber Communication Conference (OFC). San Diego, CA, USA; March 24–28, 2024

[35] Hung T, Chan D, Peng C, Chow C, Yeh C, Tsang H 300-Gbit/s/λ PAM8 modulation with a silicon microring modulator using long short term memory regression and deep neural network classification. In: Optical Fiber Communication Conference (OFC). San Diego, CA, USA; March 24–28, 2024

[36] Murphy S, Townsend P, Antony C Recurrent neural network equalizer to extend input power dynamic range of SOA in 100Gb/s/λ PON. In: Conference on Lasers and Electro-Optics (CLEO). San Jose, CA, USA; May 15–20, 2022

[37] Chuang C, Liu L, Wei C, Liu J, Henrickson L, Huang W, Wang C, Chen Y, Chen J Convolutional neural network based nonlinear classifier for 112-Gbps high speed optical link. In: Optical Fiber Communication Conference (OFC). San Diego, CA, USA; March 11–15, 2018

[38] Yi L, Li P, Liao T, Hu W 100Gb/s/λ IM-DD PON using 20G-class optical devices by machine learning based equalization. In: European Conference and Exhibition on Optical

Communication (ECOC). Rome, Italy; September 23–27, 2018

[39] Zhang J, Yan L, Jiang L, Yi A, Pan Y, Pan W, Luo B. 56-Gbit/s PAM-4 optical signal transmission over 100-km SMF enabled by TCNN regression model. IEEE Photonics Journal. 2021;**13**:7200606. 1–6

[40] Arnold E, Bocherer G, Muller E, Spilger P, Schemmel J, Calabro S, Kuschnerov M Spiking neural network equalization on neuromorphic hardware for IM/DD optical communication. In: European Conference and Exhibition on Optical Communication (ECOC). Basel, Switzerland; September 18–22, 2022

[41] Bocherer G, Strasser F, Arnold E, Lin Y, Schemmel J, Calabro S, Kuschnerov M Spiking neural network linear equalization: Experimental demonstration of 2 km 100 Gb/s IM/DD PAM4 optical transmission. In: Optical Fiber Communication Conference (OFC). San Diego, CA, USA; March 5–9, 2023

[42] Bank A, Edelmann E, Schmalen S Energy-efficient spiking neural network equalization for IM/DD systems with optimized neural encoding. In: Optical Fiber Communication Conference (OFC). San Diego, CA, USA; March 24–28, 2024

[43] Wan Z, Li J, Shu L, Luo M, Li X, Fu S, Xu K. Nonlinear equalization based on pruned artificial neural networks for 112-Gb/s SSB-PAM4 transmission over 80-km SSMF. Optics Express. 2018;**8**:10631–10642

[44] Fujisawa S, Yaman F, Batshon H, Tanio M, Ishii N, Huang C, Lima T, Inada Y, Prucnal P, Kamiya N, et al. Weight pruning techniques towards photonic implementation of nonlinear impairment compensation using neural networks. Journal of Lightwave Technology. 2022;**40**:1273–1282

[45] Xu Z, Dong S, Jiang C, Manton JH, Shieh W Sparsely-connected cascade recurrent neural network-based nonlinear equalizer for a 100-Gb/s PAM4 optical interconnect. In: Asia Communications and Photonics Conference (ACP), 2021, M5H.4

[46] Yadav G, Chuang C, Feng K, Chen J, Chen Y. Computation efficient sparse DNN nonlinear equalization for IM/DD 112-Gbps PAM4 inter-data center optical interconnects. Optics Letters. 2021;**46**:1999–2002

[47] Yadav G, Chuang C, Feng K, Chen J, Chen Y. Sparsity learning deep neural network nonlinear equalization method for 112-Gbps PAM4 short-reach transmission links. Journal of Lightwave Technology. 2023;**41**:2333–2342

[48] Ge L, Zhang W, Liang C, He Z. Compressed neural network equalization based on iterative pruning algorithm for 112-Gbps VCSEL-enabled optical interconnects. Journal of Lightwave Technology. 2020;**38**:1323–1329

[49] Li M, Zhang W, Chen Q, He Z. High-throughput hardware deployment of pruned neural network based nonlinear equalization for 100-Gbps short-reach optical interconnect. Optics Letters. 2021;**46**:4980–4983

[50] Xu Z, Sun C, Dong S, Manton JH, Shieh W Towards low computational complexity for neural network-based equalization in PAM4 short-reach direct detection systems by multi-symbol prediction. In: Optical Fiber Communication Conference (OFC). 2021; Th1A.47

[51] Xu Z, Dong S, Ji H, Manton JH, Shieh W Computationally-efficient sparsely-connected multi-output neural networks for IM/DD system equalization. In: Optical Fiber Communication Conference (OFC). 2022; W2A.26

[52] Huang X, Zhang D, Hu X, Ye C, Zhang K Recurrent neural network based equalizer with embedded parallelization for 100Gbps/λ PON. In: Optical Fiber Communication Conference (OFC). San Francisco, CA, USA; June 6–10, 2021

[53] Huang X, Zhang D, Hu X, Ye C, Zhang K. Low-complexity recurrent neural network based equalizer with embedded parallelization for 100-Gbit/s/λ PON. Journal of Lightwave Technology. 2022;**40**:1353–1359

[54] Sang B, Zhang J, Wang C, Kong M, Tan Y, Zhao L, Zhou W, Shang D, Zhu Y, Yi H, et al. Multi-symbol output long short-term memory neural network equalizer for 200+ Gbps IM/DD system. In: European Conference and Exhibition on Optical Communication (ECOC). Bordeaux, France; September 13–16, 2021

[55] Sang B, Zhou W, Tan Y, Kong M, Wang C, Wang M, Zhao L, Zhang J, Yu J. Low complexity neural network equalization based on multi-symbol output technique for 200+ Gbps IM/DD short reach optical system. Journal of Lightwave Technology. 2022;**40**: 2890–2900

[56] Xu Z, Ji T, Wu Q, Lu W, Ji H, Yang Y, Qiao G, Tang J, Cheng C, Liu L, et al. Advanced neural network-based equalization in intensity-modulated direct-detection optical systems: Current status and future trends. Photonics 2024;**11**:702

[57] Xu Z, Dong S, Manton J, Shieh W. Low-complexity multi-task learning aided neural networks for equalization in short-reach optical interconnects. Journal of Lightwave Technology. 2022;**40**:45–54

[58] Osadchuk Y, Jovanovic O, Zibar D, Ros F Reservoir computing-based multi-symbol equalization for PAM4 short-reach transmission. In: Conference on Lasers and Electro-Optics (CLEO). San Jose, CA, USA; May 7–12, 2023

[59] Osadchuk Y, Jovanovic O, Zibar D, Ros F. Multi-symbol reservoir computing-based equalization for PAM-4 IM/DD transmission. IEEE Photonics Technology Letters. 2024;**36**:853–856

[60] Akino T, Wang Y, Kojima K, Parsons K, Yoshida T Zero-multiplier sparse DNN equalization for fiber-optic QAM systems with probabilistic amplitude shaping. In: European Conference on Optical Communication (ECOC). Bordeaux, France; September 13–16, 2021

[61] Ron D, Freire P, Prilepsky J, Kopae M, Napoli A, Turitsyn K. Experimental implementation of a neural network optical channel equalizer in restricted hardware using pruning and quantization. Scientific Reports. 2022;**12**:8713

[62] Kaneda N, Chuang C, Zhu Z, Mahadevan A, Farah B, Bergman K, Veen D, Houtsma V. Fixed-point analysis and FPGA implementation of deep neural network based equalizers for high-speed PON. Journal of Lightwave Technology. 2022;**40**: 1972–1980

[63] Liu B, Bluemm C, Calabro S, Li B, Schlichtmann U Area-efficient neural network CD equalizer for 4 × 200Gb/s

PAM4 CWDM4 systems. In: Optical Fiber Communication Conference (OFC). San Diego, CA, USA; March 5–9, 2023

[64] Liu B, Bluemm C, Calabro S, Li B, Schlichtmann U Area-efficient hardware parallelization of neural network CD equalizers for 4 × 200 Gb/s PAM4 CWDM4 systems. In: European Conference on Optical Communication (ECOC). Glasgow, Scotland; October 1–5, 2023

[65] Xu Z, Ji H, Yang Y, Qiao G, Wu Q, Li J, Lu W, Liu L, Wang S, Wei J, et al. Mixed-precision integer-arithmetic-only neural network-based equalizers for DML-based short-reach IM/DD systems. In: European Conference on Optical Communication (ECOC). 2023, Th.A.3.4

[66] Freire P, Napoli A, Spinnler B, Anderson M, Ron D, Schairer W, Bex T, Costa N, Turitsyn S, Prilepsky J. Reducing computational complexity of neural networks in optical channel equalization: From concepts to implementation. Journal of Lightwave Technology. 2023;**41**:4557–4581

[67] Xu Z, Ji H, Yang Y, Qiao G, Wu Q, Lu W, Liu L, Wang S, Liang J, Li J, et al. Quantization of recurrent neural network for low-complexity high-speed IM/DD system equalization based on neuron clustering. In: Asia Communications and Photonics Conference (ACP). Wuhan, China; November 4–7, 2023, pp. 1–4

[68] Darweesh J, Costa N, Napoli A, Spinnler B, Jaouen Y, Yousefi M Few-bit quantization of neural networks for nonlinearity mitigation in a fiber transmission experiment. In: European Conference on Optical Communication (ECOC). Basel, Switzerland; September 18–22, 2022

[69] Xu Z, Wu Q, Lu W, Ji H, Chen H, Ji T, Yang Y, Qiao G, Tang J, Cheng C, et al. Weight-adaptive joint mixed-precision quantization and pruning for neural network- based equalization in short-reach direct detection links. Optics Letters 2024;**49**:3500–3503

Chapter 6

AI-Driven Automation: The Role of Neural Networks in Next-Gen RPA

Pravin Kumar Raja Mahendran

Abstract

This study aims to examine the groundbreaking fusion of artificial intelligence and robotic process automation (RPA), emphasizing the vital contribution of neural networks in developing advanced automation systems. The study that will be conducted will achieve this purpose. The implementation of neural network models facilitates the creation of automation systems that exhibit enhanced adaptability and intelligence. It was recognized that conventional RPA systems faced constraints regarding their ability to manage unstructured data and situations requiring adaptive decision-making. This study aims to explore how deep learning architectures can enhance process cognition, natural language interpretation, and predictive decision-making. This work examines the latest advancements in robotic process automation driven by artificial intelligence. We also recognize significant obstacles and emphasize the most critical issues. This study aims to examine how neural networks can transform robotic process automation from a model reliant on fixed rules to dynamic, context-aware systems capable of self-learning, thereby enhancing their application in intricate business processes.

Keywords: artificial intelligence, robotic process automation, neural network, Next-Gen RPA, intelligent process automation

1. Introduction

In this modern age of fast digital change, businesses in all sectors are progressively working toward the goal of improving their operational efficiency, lowering their expenses, and enhancing their accuracy *via* the use of automation. This quest has been significantly aided by the use of Robotic Process Automation (RPA), which is a technology that is meant to automate rule-based processes that are repetitive in nature. Historically, robotic process automation (RPA) technologies have executed corporate processes by imitating human activities and interfacing with digital systems [1]. Conventional robotic process automation (RPA) has been shown to yield substantial advantages in terms of time savings and error reduction; nevertheless, it is fundamentally constrained due to its dependence on static rule-based logic and structured data inputs. When dealing with unstructured data, dynamic situations, or activities that demand contextual awareness and decision-making skills, these constraints provide substantial problems that must be overcome [2]. In order to overcome these limitations and expand the capabilities of automation, the incorporation of artificial intelligence (AI), and more specifically neural networks, has emerged as a game-changing innovation. Automation that is driven by artificial intelligence is the next evolutionary step in process automation. It is a transition away from rule-following that is deterministic and toward probabilistic and adaptive systems that are capable of learning, reasoning, and improving over time. The structure and operation of the human brain served as the inspiration for neural networks, which have shown to be especially adept at modeling complex patterns, analyzing huge amounts of unstructured data, and making judgments based on the data. Their implementation into RPA platforms makes it possible to construct intelligent systems that are no longer limited to pre-scripted logic but instead have the ability to comprehend context, derive insights, and react in a dynamic manner to changing events. What is currently known as Intelligent Process Automation (IPA) or next-generation RPA is the result of the confluence of robotic process automation (RPA) with artificial intelligence (AI). The neural networks that are used in this paradigm serve as the cognitive core, which enables software bots to possess skills such as natural language processing (NLP), picture recognition, voice interpretation, sentiment analysis, and predictive analytics [3]. The implementation of this change makes it possible to automate more complex operations, such as the interpretation of emails, the classification of documents, the identification of consumer emotions, the detection of fraudulent activity, and the evaluation of business trends. As an example, bots are able to assess customer service issues and create suitable solutions with minimum human assistance. This is accomplished *via* the use of recurrent neural networks (RNNs) or transformer-based models [4]. In a similar vein, convolutional neural networks (CNNs) have the potential to allow bots to interpret scanned invoices or handwritten forms, therefore bypassing the limits of template-based solutions. It is important to note that this expanding capacity has substantial repercussions for several sectors, including retail, healthcare, logistics, manufacturing, and finance. AI-powered robotic process automation (RPA) can handle loan applications in the banking industry by evaluating unstructured data and estimating the risk levels of applicants [5]. In the field of medicine, this may assist in the extraction of patient data and the interpretation of medical images as illustrated

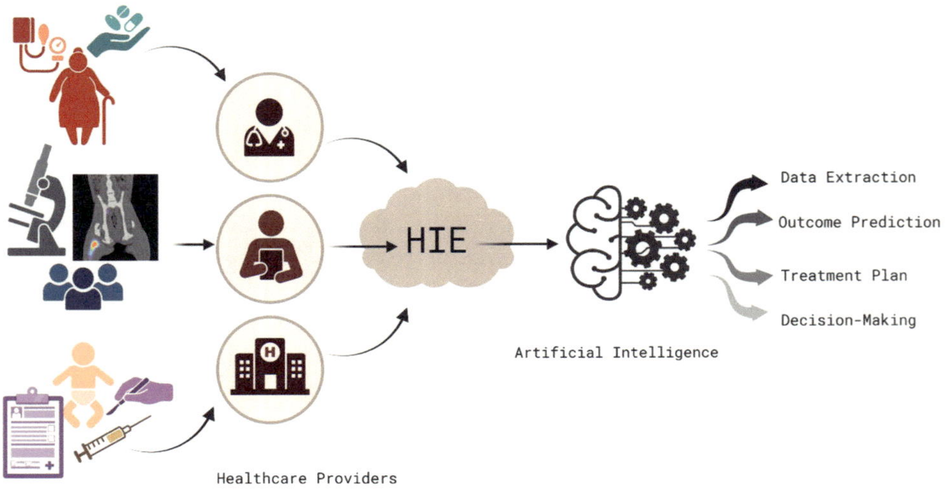

Figure 1.
Use of artificial intelligence for healthcare analytics (author-generated illustration).

in **Figure 1**, AI-powered analytics in healthcare demonstrate how neural networks enhance diagnostic and operational capabilities. Through the use of predictive modeling, it is possible to optimize supply chain choices in the field of logistics. Therefore, the incorporation of neural networks into RPA systems does not only improve upon the capabilities that are already there; rather, it expands the scope of what may be handled by automation. In spite of the fact that it holds great potential, AI-driven RPA also presents new obstacles. The process of training neural networks involves a substantial amount of high-quality data, and it is still difficult to guarantee that the model is generalizable across a variety of contexts. In addition, the incorporation of AI models into pre-existing robotic process automation pipelines calls for a solid technical infrastructure, transparent governance frameworks, and knowledge that spans several functional areas. As the autonomy of decision-making in automation systems increases, concerns about data privacy, ethical usage of artificial intelligence, and explainability also become more important [6–9]. In order for enterprises to successfully manage this transformation, they need to take into consideration both the technological and organizational elements of introducing intelligent automation at full scale. In order to provide a thorough knowledge of neural networks' capabilities, uses, and limits within the framework of this dynamic setting, the current research intends to investigate the role that neural networks will play in determining the future of robotic process automation (RPA) [10]. By investigating important neural network topologies, such as feedforward networks, convolutional neural networks (CNNs), recurrent neural networks (RNNs), and transformer models, the purpose of this study is to investigate how these models might be appropriately included into automated processes. In addition to this, the research investigates current developments in the area, evaluates the effectiveness of RPA systems that have been upgraded with artificial intelligence, and examines real-world applications in a variety of sectors.

Figure 2 compares various AI analytics approaches, highlighting the relative effectiveness of RPA when integrated with neural networks.

The architectural integration of neural networks with RPA technologies is one of the primary focuses of this study. This requires doing an analysis of the ways in which artificial intelligence components may be modularly incorporated inside bots, the

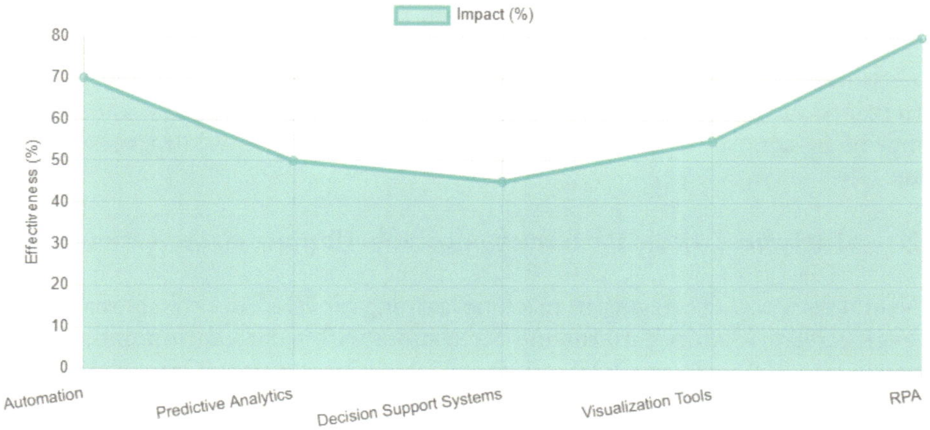

Figure 2.
Comparative analysis with different AI analytics for architectural integration of neural networks with RPA (author-generated figure).

ways in which they interact with external data sources, and the ways in which they allow decision-making in real time. Furthermore, the study investigates the use of transfer learning, federated learning, and hybrid artificial intelligence models with the purpose of enhancing the flexibility and resilience of automation methods. The research offers a road map for the development of scalable, intelligent automation systems that make use of the capabilities of both RPA and neural networks. These insights are provided by the study.

One further important goal is to bring attention to the strategic repercussions that would result from the use of AI-driven automation in organizational settings. Although having the necessary technical capabilities is essential, the success of such projects is also dependent on effective change management, the cultivation of talent, and alignment with the objectives of the company. Businesses need to not only make investments in technology but also build an innovation-driven culture that embraces intelligent automation as a major component of digital strategy. This is because artificial intelligence (AI) is continuing to advance at a rapid pace. In a nutshell, the incorporation of neural networks into RPA systems represents a paradigm change away from task automation and toward cognitive automation. Software bots are able to transcend beyond organized contexts and participate in complicated, dynamic activities that involve comprehension, adaptability, and learning thanks to this capability. This introductory section lays the groundwork for a more in-depth investigation of the mechanics, approaches, and ramifications of artificial intelligence-driven automation, especially when seen through the perspective of neural networks. Over the course of its continued development, this technology has the potential to bring about a revolution in the manner in which companies function, compete, and generate value in the digital economy.

2. Robotic process automation

Robotic process automation (RPA) has been a transformational influence in several sectors, automating rule-based, repetitive operations that were previously manual and labor-intensive. As enterprises strive for operational efficiency and cost reduction, RPA has emerged as an essential technology. Nonetheless, the next iteration of RPA commonly termed Intelligent RPA (IRPA) or next-generation RPA surpasses mere automation. Integrating artificial intelligence (AI), specifically neural networks, into automation processes enables RPA systems to make judgments, learn from data, and adapt over time. This integration signifies a fundamental change in the conceptualization and implementation of automation across several fields.

2.1 Neural networks within the framework of robotic process automation

Neural networks, a category of machine learning modeled after the human brain, are engineered to identify patterns and correlations within data. Incorporating neural networks into RPA systems allows bots to execute tasks, assess data inputs, derive significant insights, and enhance their performance over time *via* experience [11]. This converts RPA from a static system into a dynamic, learning-oriented automation platform. Conventional RPA systems operate based on explicit rule definitions if-then logic necessitating human programming. These systems encounter difficulties with unstructured data, variability, or anomalies. Neural networks mitigate this constraint

DOI: http://dx.doi.org/10.5772/intechopen.1013993

by allowing computers to analyze and comprehend unstructured inputs, including pictures, audio, and natural language. The capacity to train models with historical data enables AI-driven RPA systems to manage intricate cognitive tasks, including sentiment analysis, document categorization, and predictive analytics.

The fundamental equation for RPA is given as:

RPA Value (or ROI) = (Volume of Tasks Automated x Average Time Saved Per Task × Cost Per Hour) – Implementation & Maintenance Costs [1]

Breaking this down:

Volume of Tasks Automated—Number of transactions or processes the bot handles in a given period.

Average Time Saved per Task—How much faster the bot executes the process compared to a human.

Cost per Hour—Monetary value of employee time saved (salary/hour).

Implementation & Maintenance Costs—Licensing, infrastructure, development, and ongoing support costs.

So in simple terms:

RPA ROI = Benefits from Time Saved – RPA Cost

2.2 Applications in various sectors

The use of neural networks into robotic process automation has spurred advancements across several industries:

2.2.1 Industrial and manufacturing sector

In industrial environments, AI-driven RPA facilitates enhanced production lines and anticipatory maintenance approaches. Neural networks evaluate sensor data from machinery to forecast equipment malfunctions, enhancing maintenance plans and reducing downtime [12]. This predictive functionality, together with automatic reporting and notifications, guarantees ongoing operation and enhanced asset management.

Moreover, AI-augmented RPA enables quality assurance using computer vision models that identify abnormalities in production outputs. Neural networks may be taught to conduct real-time inspections of items for flaws, surpassing human evaluations in both speed and precision. This automation minimizes waste, guarantees uniform product quality, and facilitates just-in-time production methodologies.

2.2.2 Healthcare and medical applications

In the medical sector, next-generation robotic process automation powered by neural networks delivers transformational efficiency and precision [13]. Administrative procedures, including patient registration, claims processing, and billing, are automated by intelligent bots that comprehend context and identify discrepancies in real-time. This mitigates human mistake and expedites procedures.

In the healthcare sector, one prominent use case of neural network-driven RPA is in clinical diagnostics. Hospitals frequently deal with vast volumes of medical imagery such as X-rays, MRIs, and CT scans, which require careful review by specialists. Traditionally, this process is time-consuming and subject to human variation. By integrating convolutional neural networks (CNNs) into RPA systems, hospitals can automate the initial screening of these images. The automation identifies potential anomalies, including cancers or fractures, and presents them for further clinical review. This not only accelerates the diagnostic workflow but also improves accuracy and reduces the cognitive load on healthcare professionals. As a result, physicians are able to dedicate more attention to complex cases, ultimately improving the patient care outcomes.

Furthermore, neural networks in RPA provide enhanced patient monitoring. By consistently analyzing biometric data from wearable devices or remote monitoring systems, AI-driven bots may identify irregularities in patient health and automatically initiate warnings or intervention processes. This facilitates early intervention and improves patient outcomes.

2.2.3 Financial services and banking

In banking, where precision and adherence to regulations are critical, AI-driven RPA solutions optimize operations by automating activities like fraud detection, loan approval, and customer care. Neural networks can scrutinize extensive amounts of transactional data to detect anomalous patterns, hence reducing the probability of financial fraud [14].

Neural network-based credit scoring models provide a more sophisticated assessment of a borrower's risk profile by integrating alternative data, including payment history, social behaviors, and economic indicators. Automated bots may manage loan applications comprehensively, including document verification and decision-making, thereby reducing the turnaround time from days to minutes.

Customer care bots, using natural language processing **via** neural networks, interact with consumers in real time, addressing inquiries, resolving complaints, and escalating intricate situations to human agents. This improves client experience while decreasing operating expenses.

2.2.4 Retail and E-commerce

In retail, AI-driven RPA enhances the customization, inventory control, and supply chain efficiency. Neural networks examine consumer behavior, interests, and purchasing history to provide the tailored product suggestions and focused on marketing initiatives.

Intelligent bots oversee backend operations by monitoring inventory levels, tracking shipments, and optimizing order fulfillment procedures **via** demand prediction. Neural networks' capacity to analyze unstructured data from many sources such as social media, customer reviews, and supplier logs affords merchants a thorough comprehension of patterns and consumer mood.

AI-driven chatbots optimize the client interactions, providing round-the-clock help with replies akin to human communication. These bots manage the returns, refunds, and queries, facilitating a smooth buying experience.

2.2.5 Governance and public services

Government agencies often encounter difficulties associated with volume, complexity, and compliance in the provision of public services. Neural network-enhanced robotic process automation may streamline application processing, document verification, and citizen service questions.

AI-driven bots may facilitate immigration procedures by scanning and authenticating identification papers, cross-referencing databases, and detecting discrepancies or possible fraud. In tax departments, bots may autonomously categorize and evaluate tax filings, identifying abnormalities or high-risk instances for further scrutiny.

In law enforcement, neural networks integrated with RPA systems facilitate the processing of crime data, pattern recognition, and the prediction of crime hotspots. This proactive strategy for public safety is progressively integrating into smart city efforts.

2.3 Benefits of neural network-enhanced robotic process automation

The integration of neural networks in RPA offers several significant benefits:

The integration of neural networks into robotic process automation offers several transformative benefits that extend beyond the limitations of conventional rule-based systems. One of the most notable advantages is scalability, as intelligent RPA platforms can continuously learn from new data and encounters, thereby enhancing their capabilities without the need for extensive reprogramming. This adaptability also improves decision-making proficiency, enabling bots to process complex and variable inputs rather than relying solely on binary, deterministic rules. Neural networks provide a unique ability to work with diverse types of data, ranging from structured numerical datasets to unstructured formats such as images, audio, and natural language, which greatly expands the scope of automation. Over time, these systems demonstrate ongoing enhancement, refining their accuracy, flexibility, and efficiency with minimal human intervention [15], a feature that distinguishes them from static automation approaches. Importantly, these improvements also translate into a better user experience: AI-driven bots are able to interact in a context-sensitive manner, offering personalized and responsive engagements that increase satisfaction and foster greater trust in automation. Taken together, these benefits illustrate how neural network-enhanced RPA systems represent a significant step forward, evolving automation from simple task execution into a dynamic, intelligent, and user-centered capability (**Table 1**).

3. AI driven automation and architecture of AI-enabled RPA

Robotic process automation (RPA) has long supported digital transformation by automating routine, high-volume tasks. However, conventional RPA, limited to rule-based execution, struggles with unstructured data, contextual reasoning, and adaptability. To overcome these gaps, AI-enabled RPA often called intelligent RPA (IRPA) combines automation with machine learning (ML) and deep learning (DL), shifting from rigid task execution to smart, context-aware workflows. At the core of this transformation are neural networks, which power perception, decision-making, and continuous learning in next-generation automation (**Table 2**).

3.1 From rule-based to intelligence-driven workflows

Traditional bots excel at structured activities like form filling or report generation, but they fail when formats change or ambiguity arises. Neural networks address this by enabling bots to recognize, interpret, and adapt to diverse inputs. For example, while a rule-based bot can process a standard invoice template, a deep learning model trained on multiple layouts can extract fields even when the design or language

Neural network model	Typical RPA use cases	Benchmark dataset(s)	Accuracy (%)	Training time (hrs)	Inference time (ms/sample)	Strengths	Limitations
CNN	Document image classification, invoice scanning, OCR post-processing	ICDAR OCR dataset, RVL-CDIP	92–97%	2–6 hrs (small–medium corpus)	10–20 ms	Excellent for image-based tasks, robust to noise in scanned docs	Not suitable for sequential text or context understanding
RNN	Sequence prediction in logs, simple intent recognition	IMDB reviews, custom log sequences	80–86%	5–10 hrs	20–40 ms	Good for short sequence dependencies	Vanishing gradient in long sequences, slower training
LSTM	Entity extraction, complex intent recognition, Chatbot automation	CoNLL-2003 NER, SNIPS	87–92%	6–12 hrs	30–50 ms	Captures long dependencies, better than vanilla RNNs	Higher computational cost, harder to scale
Bi-LSTM	High-accuracy NER, sentiment analysis in customer emails	OntoNotes 5, SNIPS	89–94%	8–15 hrs	35–60 ms	Considers past and future context, more accurate	Double the compute of LSTM, risk of overfitting on small data
GRU	Similar to LSTM tasks but with faster training	SNIPS, ATIS	85–90%	5–8 hrs	25–40 ms	Faster than LSTM, fewer parameters	Slightly lower accuracy than LSTM in complex tasks
Transformer encoder	Email classification, intent & slot filling, complex document understanding	GLUE benchmark, SNIPS	93–97%	10–20 hrs (fine-tuning)	15–30 ms	Handles long contexts, parallelizable	Requires large memory, data-hungry

Table 1.
A comparative analysis of these neural network models in terms of accuracy, training time, and inference efficiency.

DOI: http://dx.doi.org/10.5772/intechopen.1013993

Neural network model	Typical RPA use cases	Benchmark dataset(s)	Accuracy (%)	Training time (hrs)	Inference time (ms/sample)	Strengths	Limitations
BERT (pre-trained transformer)	Contract analysis, document segmentation, advanced entity extraction	CoNLL-2003, SQuAD	94–98%	4–10 hrs (fine-tuning)	20–40 ms	High generalization, excellent language understanding	Large model size, slower inference
DistilBERT (Lightweight transformer)	Same as BERT but optimized for RPA edge tasks	CoNLL-2003, SNIPS	91–95%	2–5 hrs	10–25 ms	Faster inference, lower resource cost	Slight drop in accuracy vs. BERT
GPT-style decoder models	Auto-generation of process documentation, response generation	OpenAI GPT benchmarks, internal logs	90–96% (varies by prompt)	12–20 hrs	50–100 ms	Generates fluent text, flexible prompts	Risk of hallucination, less precise on factual extraction
Hybrid models (CNN-RNN, CRF on top of LSTM)	End-to-end document workflow (OCR + NER)	ICDAR + CoNLL-2003	92–96%	12–20 hrs	40–70 ms	Combines visual and sequential strengths	Complex to deploy, tuning required

Table 2.
The comparative results from this study, providing a tabular perspective on the architectural integration of neural networks with RPA.

varies. Neural networks thus extend automation from repetitive execution to flexible, perception-driven intelligence.

3.2 Neural network functions in intelligent automation

3.2.1 Natural language understanding (RNNs and transformers)

Neural NLP models empower RPA bots to manage communication-heavy tasks. Transformer-based models can interpret customer queries, detect intent, and provide accurate responses, while RNNs and LSTMs analyze emails or chat logs to classify, summarize, or triage tickets. This enables bots to automate service desks, compliance checks, and document reviews with contextual accuracy.

3.2.2 Visual recognition (CNNs)

Convolutional neural networks allow automation to "see." In manufacturing, bots use CNNs for defect detection on production lines. In healthcare, they support automated pre-screening by flagging anomalies in medical images. By embedding CNN-driven perception into workflows, organizations achieve faster, more reliable, and cost-effective inspection processes.

This table presents a comparative analysis of different automation-related technologies, ranked by their effectiveness and evaluated in terms of adoption, utility, and practical impact in RPA-driven contexts (**Table 3**).

3.3 Predictive decision-making (feedforward and ensemble models)

Neural networks and hybrid models extend RPA into forecasting and risk analysis. In finance, they predict credit risk and detect fraud. In supply chains, they forecast demand and adjust inventory or orders in real time. This predictive capability transforms automation from reactive to proactive orchestration.

3.4 Adaptive learning (reinforcement learning)

Reinforcement learning introduces adaptability to changing environments. Bots can optimize workflows, manage dynamic pricing, or adjust routing strategies through continuous feedback surpassing static automation by learning optimal actions over time.

Technology	Effectiveness (%)	Rank (effectiveness)	Remarks
Automation	70	2	High effectiveness, widely adopted
Predictive analytics	50	4	Moderate effectiveness
Decision support systems	45	5	Lowest among the listed tools
Visualization tools	55	3	Above average, good for insights
RPA (robotic process automation)	80	1	Highest impact, excellent utility

Table 3.
Tabular study for the aforementioned comparative study.

3.4.1 Architecture of AI-enhanced RPA

The architecture of AI-enhanced robotic process automation is typically structured into four interconnected layers that work together to embed neural networks into automation workflows. At the foundation lies the data acquisition and preprocessing layer, which gathers both structured and unstructured information from enterprise systems, documents, or sensors, and refines it to ensure that it is suitable for machine learning and deep learning models. Building on this, the neural model layer hosts the trained models—whether they are natural language processing systems, convolutional neural networks, or predictive algorithms—that provide the perception and intelligence required for advanced automation. The outputs from these models are then integrated within the decision and orchestration layer, where they are combined with business rules to guide workflows, balancing the need for automation speed with compliance requirements and risk management considerations. Finally, the continuous learning layer ensures the adaptability over time by incorporating feedback loops and human oversight to retrain models as new data and scenarios emerge. Together, these four layers create a scalable and intelligent framework that enables next-generation RPA systems to evolve beyond static rule-based automation into dynamic, learning-driven platforms.

4. Ethical dimension of AI-enabled RPA

The integration of artificial intelligence (AI), particularly neural networks, with robotic process automation (RPA) represents a significant progression in corporate automation. Neural networks augment RPA systems, allowing them to perform cognitive functions such as natural language comprehension, sentiment analysis, picture recognition, and adaptive decision-making, therefore transcending the constraints of traditional rule-based bots. As AI-driven RPA systems acquire autonomy and assume a crucial role in fundamental operations, the significance of ethical problems increases. The ethical considerations include prejudice, accountability, openness, privacy, and possible impacts on employment. An important ethical concern in AI-driven RPA is the existence of algorithmic prejudice. Neural networks get information from historical datasets that often reflect existing human biases, including those pertaining to race, gender, or socioeconomic position. Incorporating these biased models into RPA systems may inadvertently sustain prejudice. An AI-driven automation system used in applicant screening or loan processing may unjustly exclude certain demographic groups if it is based on biased data. Ethical AI deployment requires careful dataset selection, thorough fairness assessments, and the integration of diverse viewpoints during model training to successfully mitigate biases. The ethical significance of responsibility and explainability is amplified when neural networks are used in robotic process automation (RPA). Traditional RPA systems provide clear logical frameworks based on deterministic principles, leading to the predictable and verifiable results. In contrast, neural networks operate as "black boxes," making the reasoning behind specific judgments sometimes ambiguous [16]. The lack of interpretability poses difficulties in establishing culpability during errors, especially in sectors like healthcare, banking, or law. This scenario necessitates an analysis of accountability determining if it resides with the developer, the data scientist, the company using the RPA system, or the system itself. To address this problem, it is essential to build frameworks for explainable AI (XAI) and establish regulatory standards that mandate openness and traceability in AI decision-making processes. The safeguarding of data privacy is a substantial ethical issue. AI-augmented RPA systems sometimes need access to substantial amounts of personal and sensitive data to operate well. Neural networks may inadvertently save and disclose sensitive information, particularly in natural language processing or document management activities. Organizations must adopt robust data protection mechanisms, adhere to privacy requirements such as GDPR, and use privacy-preserving AI techniques like differential privacy or federated learning to maintain user confidence and assure compliance.

Furthermore, the impact on employment becomes a substantial ethical consideration. AI-driven RPA may enhance productivity and reduce human error; nevertheless, it also poses a significant danger of job displacement, especially in repetitive and cognitively ordinary work. This underscores concerns pertaining to socioeconomic inequality and worker isolation. Organizations using AI-RPA must emphasize responsible automation by upskilling and reskilling personnel, fostering cooperation between humans and machines, and aligning automation initiatives with inclusive workforce development. Frameworks for ethical governance are essential for tackling the intricate difficulties posed by AI-driven RPA [17]. These frameworks must be grounded in basic concepts such as beneficence, non-maleficence, autonomy, and justice. Collaboration among many stakeholders including developers, regulators, corporate leaders, and civil society is crucial for formulating laws that govern the ethical design, implementation, and supervision of neural network-based RPA systems. The progression of neural networks amplifies the potential and efficacy of next-generation RPA, while also presenting complex ethical challenges. It is crucial to combine innovation with the ideals of accountability, justice, and transparency to properly harness the revolutionary potential of AI-driven automation for the collective good.

5. Case studies on AI-enabled RPA

The implementation of neural network-based robotic process automation (RPA) is rapidly redefining how organizations approach operational efficiency, data management, and decision-making. Unlike traditional RPA systems that follow deterministic rules for automating repetitive tasks, the integration of artificial intelligence particularly neural networks and deep learning has empowered these systems with the ability to learn, adapt, and reason in complex environments. This fusion of automation's precision with AI's cognitive capabilities is producing remarkable advancements across diverse industries, where efficiency, accuracy, and agility are not just desired but essential for competitiveness. The following collection of case studies illustrates the transformative impact of AI-driven RPA, highlighting its applications in financial services, healthcare, and supply chain management [18].

- In the financial services sector, a prominent global bank has successfully integrated AI-powered RPA into its loan underwriting process. Traditional underwriting involves rigorous manual reviews of applicant information, credit histories, and risk profiles a process that often takes several days and is prone to human inconsistencies. By leveraging historical loan data to train advanced neural networks, the bank developed a system capable of evaluating creditworthiness with exceptional precision, identifying potential fraud patterns, and generating automated risk scores. This intelligent automation reduced loan processing time from several days to just minutes while maintaining compliance with strict regulatory standards. Importantly, the incorporation of anomaly detection models significantly improved financial security, reducing fraudulent transactions by over 30%. These advances not only strengthened regulatory adherence but also fostered greater customer trust, as clients experienced faster loan approvals coupled with the enhanced security measures. The case demonstrates how neural network-driven RPA can balance speed with diligence in an industry where both are critical [19].

- In healthcare, a leading hospital network harnessed neural network-enabled RPA to revolutionize its administrative and diagnostic workflows. Hospitals often manage vast volumes of unstructured data, such as handwritten patient forms, diagnostic reports, and medical imaging, which can be difficult to process accurately and efficiently. To address this, the hospital combined RPA with optical character recognition (OCR) and deep learning models. The result was a system that could intelligently extract, interpret, and standardize patient information into Electronic Health Record (EHR) systems with significantly improved accuracy. Beyond simple data entry, the AI-driven bots were also equipped to detect irregularities in patient records, offering early insights into chronic illnesses and supporting physicians in timely interventions. This integration not only reduced administrative burdens but also enhanced clinical outcomes: Processing times decreased by 40%, and patients benefited from quicker diagnoses and more personalized care plans. The success of this case underscores how AI-driven RPA can extend beyond cost-saving automation to actively improve healthcare quality and patient well-being.

- In supply chain management, a multinational logistics company employed AI-enabled RPA to optimize demand forecasting and streamline inventory management. Traditionally, forecasting relies on historical sales patterns, but this company integrated recurrent neural networks (RNNs) capable of analyzing temporal data along with external factors such as weather conditions, market volatility, and geopolitical developments. These predictive insights enabled highly accurate forecasting of stock levels, ensuring that supply chain operations remained resilient in the face of uncertainty. Once demand predictions were generated, RPA bots seamlessly executed routine supply chain tasks, including reordering products and communicating with suppliers, thus eliminating delays and human inefficiencies. The outcomes were substantial: inventory costs dropped by 25%, fulfillment rates improved, and the company achieved greater agility in responding to market changes. This case demonstrates the value of combining predictive analytics with process automation, creating supply chains that are not only more efficient but also more adaptive to real-world fluctuations [20].

Collectively, these cases highlight how neural network-based RPA is no longer confined to rule-based automation but is evolving into a sophisticated tool that blends intelligence with efficiency. In finance, it enhances decision-making and fraud prevention; in healthcare, it improves data integrity and clinical outcomes; and in supply chain management, it provides foresight and adaptability. The overarching theme is clear: When organizations integrate the learning capabilities of neural networks with the structured execution of RPA, they unlock transformative potential achieving not just operational efficiency but also strategic advantages in accuracy, compliance, and customer satisfaction. As industries continue to grapple with growing data volumes, complex regulatory landscapes, and dynamic market demands, AI-driven RPA is poised to play a pivotal role in shaping the future of intelligent automation.

6. Conclusion

The integration of AI-driven automation, powered by neural networks, represents a significant leap forward in the functionalities of next-generation robotic process automation (RPA). Expanding RPA beyond mere rule-based automation into the realm of intelligent decision-making enables neural networks to empower computers to learn, adapt, and perform complex tasks with minimal human intervention. This transformation is delivering significant value across various sectors such as banking, healthcare, and supply chain, where efficiency, precision, and agility are crucial. It is crucial to carefully address the ethical issues surrounding data privacy, bias, transparency, and the impact on the workforce through responsible design and governance. The successful deployment of AI-driven RPA fundamentally depends on aligning technological progress with ethical considerations, ensuring that automation enhances human potential rather than replacing it.

Author details

Pravin Kumar Raja Mahendran
First Horizon Bank, Collierville, TN, USA

*Address all correspondence to: r.pravinkumar88@gmail.com

References

[1] George AS, Hovan George AS, Baskar T, Sujatha V. The rise of hyperautomation: A new frontier for business process automation. Partners Universal International Research Journal. 2023;**2**(4):13-35

[2] Chebrolu SK. AI-powered business intelligence: A systematic literature review on the future of decision-making in enterprises. American Journal of Scholarly Research and Innovation. 2025;**4**(1):33-62

[3] Minkova L, Espejel JLĂ, Djaidja TET, Dahhane W, Ettifouri EH. From words to workflows: Automating business processes. arXiv. 2024:2401.01234

[4] Ahmed F, Ahmed MR, Kabir MA, Islam MM. Revolutionizing business analytics: The impact of artificial intelligence and machine learning. American Journal of Advanced Technology and Engineering Solutions. 2025;**1**(1):147-173

[5] Abirami RS, Muthuswamy P. Industry 5.0 or industry 4.0 S? Introduction to industry 4.0 and a peek into the prospective industry 5.0 technologies. International Journal on Interactive Design and Manufacturing (IJIDeM). 2023;**17**(2):947-979

[6] Joshi H. AI-Enabled Project Portfolio Management and Selection in the US Healthcare Sector: Maximizing Efficiency and Value. 2024. Available from: SSRN: https://ssrn.com/abstract=5011078

[7] Yerra S. The role of cloud-based analytics in transforming logistics data management and reporting. The Eastasouth Journal of Information System and Computer Science. 2024;**2**(02):156-162

[8] Malaga M. Harnessing the synergy of generative AI, machine learning, and chatbots: Innovations in conversational systems and intelligent automation. World Journal of Advanced Engineering Technology and Sciences. 2025;**14**(1):254-272

[9] Olayinka OH. Big data integration and real-time analytics for enhancing operational efficiency and market responsiveness. International Journal of Science and Research Archive. 2021;**4**(1):280-296

[10] Khatib E, Mounir SH, Al Ameeri I, Al Zaabi H, Al Marqab R. Digital disruption and big data in healthcare-opportunities and challenges. ClinicoEconomics and Outcomes Research. 2022;**14**:563-574

[11] Qadiri RM, Shabir N, Qadri M. Conceptualizing possibilities of artificial intelligence in furtherance of the banking sector: An effective tool for improving customer relationship, customer service and public relations. International Journal of Finance, Insurance and Risk Management. 2020;**10**(2):44-65

[12] Usmanova V. Integrating Ai and Genai into the growth and development strategies of B2c companies. The American Journal of Engineering and Technology. 2024;**6**(08):73-83

[13] Jean-Luc M, Priyanka N. Revolutionizing supply chain optimization with AI-driven predictive analytics. Synergy: Cross-Disciplinary Journal of Digital Investigation. 2024;**2**(12):31-45

[14] Olowu O, Adeleye AO, Omokanye AO, Ajayi AM, Adepoju AO, Omole OM, et al. AI-driven fraud detection in banking: A systematic

review of data science approaches to enhancing cybersecurity. GSC Advanced Research and Reviews. 2024;**21**(2):227-237

[15] Pushpakumara TDC, Ahsan FJ. Transforming industries through AI and emerging technologies: Literature review of opportunities, challengers, responsibilities, and strategies. International Journal of Innovative Science and Research Technology. 2025;**10**(1):1861-1880

[16] Shirvanporzour A. Artificial Intelligence in Banking Risk Management and Anti-Money Laundering: A Comprehensive Review. 2025. Available from: https://ssrn.com/abstract=5161209

[17] Saha R. Empowering absorptive capacity in healthcare supply chains through big data analytics and AI-driven collaborative platforms: A prisma-based systematic review. Innovatech Engineering Journal. 2024;**1**(1):10-70937

[18] Thaichon P, Dutta PK, Haghi AK, Dutta S. Digital Disruption in Hospitality, AI, and Emerging Technologies: A Roadmap to Personalized Experiences, Enhanced Operations, and Revenue Growth. Bingley, UK: Emerald Group Publishing; 2025

[19] Eulerich M, Sanatizadeh A, Vakilzadeh H, Wood DA. Is it all hype? ChatGPT's performance and disruptive potential in the accounting and auditing industries. Review of Accounting Studies. 2024;**29**(3):2318-2349

[20] Ok E. A Detailed Review of the Progress in Home Automation Systems. Cham, Switzerland: Springer; 2025

Chapter 7

Artificial Neural Networks in Industrial Logistics and Supply Chain Optimization

Jassem Wannassi, Chama Mabrouk, Nicole Jaffrezic-Renault and Houcine Barhoumi

Abstract

Artificial neural networks (ANN) offer data-driven solutions to enhance efficiency, reduce costs, and improve decision-making in industrial logistics and supply chains. This chapter examines ANN applications in three key areas: warehouse management, demand forecasting, and supply chain route optimization. In warehouses, ANN supports inventory control, space utilization, and automation. For demand forecasting, it analyzes historical data and market trends to predict fluctuations accurately, minimizing stock-related risks. In route optimization, ANN dynamically adjusts transportation paths using real-time data like traffic and weather. Compared to traditional methods, ANN delivers greater adaptability and predictive accuracy. Despite challenges such as data complexity, ongoing AI advancements are continuously improving ANN's role in logistics, driving smarter and more efficient operations.

Keywords: artificial neural networks (ANN), industrial logistics, supply chain optimization, warehouse management, demand forecasting, route optimization, machine learning in logistics

1. Introduction

In today's fast-paced industrial landscape, logistics and supply chain management are essential for ensuring efficiency, cost-effectiveness, and customer satisfaction [1–3]. As global supply networks grow more complex and dynamic, traditional optimization methods often fall short in managing large-scale, uncertain environments. Artificial neural networks (ANN), inspired by the human brain, offer a robust alternative by identifying patterns, learning from historical data, and making accurate, real-time predictions [4]. These capabilities make ANN particularly effective in areas such as warehouse management, demand forecasting, and route optimization [5–8]. By leveraging ANN, companies can improve inventory control, forecast demand more precisely, and optimize transportation, ultimately enhancing operational efficiency and reducing costs [9, 10].

This chapter explores the application of ANN in industrial logistics, focusing on how it transforms warehouse operations, refines demand forecasting, and optimizes supply chain routes. We will examine the advantages of ANN over traditional approaches, discuss real-world applications, and highlight emerging trends and challenges in ANN-driven supply chain management. As AI and machine learning continue to evolve, ANN is poised to revolutionize logistics, enabling businesses to operate smarter, faster and more efficiently in an increasingly competitive global market.

2. Fundamentals of artificial neural networks (ANN)

Artificial neural networks (ANN) are computational models inspired by the human brain's structure, designed to recognize patterns, make predictions, and optimize processes by learning from data (**Figure 1**) [11].

2.1 Basic structure of ANN

The basic structure of artificial neural network (ANN) is composed of three primary layers: the input layer, hidden layers, and output layer [12]. The input layer serves as the entry point for the data, where each input feature is fed into individual neurons. These neurons are connected to the hidden layers, which are responsible for processing and transforming the data using various activation functions. The hidden layers consist of multiple neurons that are arranged in one or more layers, allowing the network to learn complex patterns and representations of the data [13]. Finally, the output layer produces the result, whether it has a classification label, regression value, or any other desired outcome. The neurons within each layer are connected through weighted links, where each weight determines the strength of the connection between neurons. During the learning process, the network adjusts these weights by minimizing the error in its predictions, using optimization algorithms like back-propagation to refine the model's performance based on the input-output mappings. This iterative process enables ANNs to model intricate relationships within data, making them highly effective for tasks such as pattern recognition, forecasting, and decision-making [14].

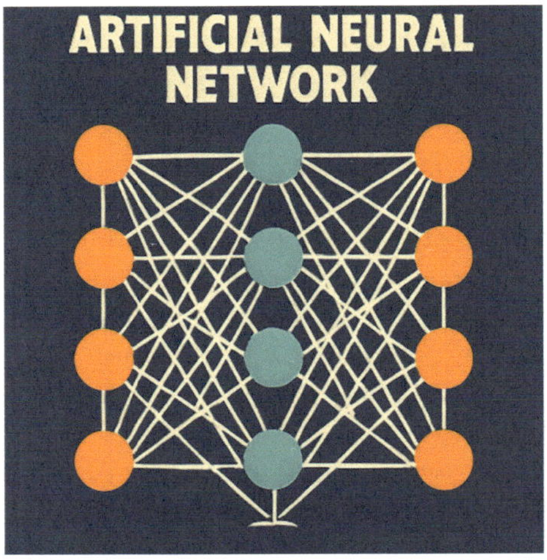

Figure 1.
Structure of an artificial neural network (ANN).

2.2 Types of ANN models

Multilayer perceptron (MLP) is a neural network model commonly used for supervised learning tasks such as regression and classification, especially for structured data analysis [15]. Convolutional neural networks (CNN), while primarily used for image recognition, can be effectively adapted to logistics applications, such as identifying patterns in sensor data or visual cues in warehouse operations [16]. Recurrent neural networks (RNN) are designed to handle sequential data, making them ideal for tasks like time-series analysis, and are particularly useful for applications like demand forecasting and route optimization in supply chain management. Long short-term memory (LSTM) is a specialized type of RNN that excels in sequence prediction tasks, making it especially valuable for accurate forecasting in supply chains [17].

2.3 Training ANN

The training process of artificial neural network (ANN) involves a method called backpropagation, which is crucial for adjusting the network's parameters [18]. During backpropagation, the difference between the predicted output and the actual output (also known as the error) is calculated. This error is then propagated backward through the network, layer by layer, to adjust the weights of the neurons [19]. The adjustment is performed using optimization algorithms, with gradient descent being one of the most commonly used methods. Gradient descent calculates the gradient (or slope) of the error with respect to each weight and updates the weights in the opposite direction of the gradient to minimize the error [20].

Key hyper-parameters significantly influence the training dynamics and performance of ANNs. For instance, the learning rate determines the size of the steps taken during weight updates too high a value can lead to divergence, while too low can slow convergence. The batch size, which defines the number of training samples used in one forward/backward pass, also affects training stability and generalization. Smaller batches may provide a regularizing effect but increase training time, whereas larger batches can speed up training but risk overfitting.

To enhance generalization and avoid overfitting, which occurs when the model learns noise instead of meaningful patterns, various regularization techniques are employed. Dropout is a common approach where a fraction of the neurons is randomly deactivated during training, forcing the network to learn redundant representations. Early stopping is another effective strategy in which the training process is halted once the performance on a validation set begins to degrade, indicating potential overfitting. These techniques help improve the robustness and predictive accuracy of the model.

Through these mechanisms, ANNs learn complex patterns and relationships within the data, making them powerful tools for tasks such as classification, regression, and pattern recognition.

3. ANN in warehouse management

Warehouse management has undergone a significant transformation with the integration of artificial neural networks (ANN), driving improvements in operational efficiency, cost reduction, and optimal space utilization [21]. The ability of ANNs to learn from historical data and predict future trends has made them invaluable tools in several key areas of warehouse management.

3.1 Warehouse layout optimization

ANN models can analyze demand patterns to predict the most efficient warehouse layouts, minimizing the distance workers or robotic systems must travel to retrieve goods. By optimizing the positioning of high-demand products closer to picking areas, these systems can drastically reduce retrieval times, leading to faster order processing and improved throughput.

3.2 Inventory management

Through the power of predictive analytics, ANNs can forecast the demand for various products with remarkable accuracy. This enables companies to implement just-in-time inventory practices, ensuring that products are available when needed without the burden of overstocking. The precise demand predictions reduce the likelihood of stockouts, prevent excess storage costs, and enhance overall supply chain efficiency.

3.3 Automated picking and sorting

In automated warehouses, ANN-based systems play a critical role in optimizing picking routes for robotic systems. By recognizing patterns in incoming orders, the system can prioritize items more effectively and sort goods faster. This reduces human error, minimizes delays, and boosts throughput, making the entire process smoother and more reliable.

3.4 Case study

A major retailer implemented an ANN-powered solution to optimize both warehouse layout and inventory management. As a result, the company experienced a 20% reduction in order fulfillment time and a 15% reduction in operational costs. The integration of ANN not only streamlined the workflow but also led to significant cost savings and more efficient use of space. The integration of ANNs in warehouse management has proven to be a game changer, enhancing operational decision-making and providing a more agile and responsive system for businesses.

4. ANN in demand forecasting

Accurate demand forecasting is crucial for effective supply chain management, and artificial neural networks (ANN) have become a powerful tool in this process [22]. By leveraging historical sales data, market trends, and external factors such as economic indicators or weather patterns, ANNs can provide highly accurate predictions of future demand, helping businesses make informed decisions and optimize their operations.

4.1 Historical data analysis

ANNs excel at learning from vast amounts of historical sales data. Unlike traditional forecasting models, which may overlook subtle relationships, ANNs can identify complex patterns, correlations, and hidden signals within the data. This ability allows for more accurate predictions, ensuring businesses are better prepared for future demand.

4.2 Handling seasonality and trends

One of the key strengths of ANNs is their ability to adapt to both short-term seasonal variations and long-term trends. They can effectively recognize cyclical patterns, such as those occurring during holiday seasons, promotional events, or weather-related fluctuations. This adaptability helps businesses anticipate demand more accurately during peak periods, leading to optimized inventory management and reduced operational costs.

4.3 Real-time forecasting

By incorporating real-time data streams, ANNs can continuously adjust their forecasts to account for sudden shifts in consumer demand. Whether driven by economic changes, market disruptions, or unanticipated events, ANNs can promptly integrate new information and provide businesses with up-to-date demand forecasts, helping them respond swiftly to changing conditions.

4.4 Reducing overstock and understock

Accurate demand forecasting directly impacts inventory management. By delivering precise predictions, ANNs help businesses minimize overstock, which incur unnecessary storage costs, and avoid stockouts, which lead to lost sales and customer dissatisfaction. This balance ensures that businesses maintain optimal inventory levels while maximizing profitability.

4.5 Case study

A global e-commerce company integrated an ANN-based solution for demand forecasting, resulting in a 30% improvement in forecasting accuracy. This enhanced accuracy led to significant reductions in both inventory costs and customer stockout complaints, demonstrating the tangible benefits of adopting ANN for demand forecasting in supply chain management. By incorporating ANNs into demand forecasting processes, businesses can not only streamline their supply chains but also gain a competitive edge in today's fast-paced and dynamic market environment.

5. ANN in supply chain route optimization

Optimizing supply chain routes is essential for reducing delivery times and operational costs, and artificial neural networks (ANN) have proven to be highly effective in dynamically adjusting routes [23]. By taking into account a range of real-time factors, such as traffic patterns, weather conditions, and logistical constraints, ANNs help businesses streamline their transportation operations and improve overall efficiency.

5.1 Optimizing transportation routes

ANN models can process an extensive set of variables, including delivery time windows, vehicle capacity, fuel consumption, and traffic conditions, to determine the most efficient routes. By analyzing these factors, ANNs can reduce fuel costs, minimize transit time, and improve fleet utilization. This enables companies to maximize their resources while ensuring timely deliveries. Dynamic adjustments: Unlike traditional route optimization methods, which typically rely on static data, ANNs can make real-time adjustments based on live data inputs such as traffic updates, road closures, or changing weather conditions. This flexibility ensures that routes are continuously optimized, allowing for timely deliveries even in unpredictable or challenging circumstances.

5.2 Cost and time efficiency

ANNs are capable of optimizing both cost and time parameters simultaneously, striking a balance between fast deliveries and minimizing transportation expenses. For example, the system can prioritize routes that save time without significantly increasing costs, ensuring the best trade-off between service quality and operational efficiency. This dual focus on time and cost makes ANN-based route optimization a highly effective tool for logistics managers.

5.3 Last-mile delivery optimization

Last-mile delivery is a critical component of urban logistics, directly influencing customer satisfaction. ANNs can forecast high-demand areas, identify congested routes, and suggest the most efficient paths for last-mile delivery. This helps reduce delays, optimize delivery schedules, and improve the customer experience by ensuring timely arrivals even in dense urban environments.

5.4 Case study

A major logistics company integrated ANN-based route optimization software into its operations, resulting in a 25% reduction in delivery times and an 18% reduction in fuel costs. These improvements demonstrated the substantial impact that ANN can have on optimizing transportation routes and enhancing supply chain performance. By leveraging the power of ANN, businesses can optimize their supply chain routes in real time, improving both the speed and cost-effectiveness of deliveries while maintaining high levels of customer satisfaction.

In modern supply chain management, optimizing transportation routes is crucial for reducing costs, improving delivery efficiency, and ensuring customer satisfaction. Traditional route optimization methods, such as mathematical modeling and heuristic algorithms, struggle to handle the complexity and dynamic nature of logistics networks. Artificial neural networks (ANNs) offer a powerful alternative by leveraging machine learning to analyze large datasets, recognize patterns, and make real-time decisions. By processing historical and real-time data, ANNs can predict traffic conditions, optimize delivery schedules, and dynamically adjust routes based on various constraints such as weather, demand fluctuations, and road conditions. **Table 1** summarizes the key aspects of ANN-based supply chain route optimization:

Aspect	Details
Objective	Optimize supply chain routes by minimizing cost, time, and fuel consumption while ensuring timely deliveries.
Key challenges	Traffic congestion, dynamic demand, fuel efficiency, route unpredictability, weather conditions.
ANN role	Learns from historical data, predicts best routes, adapts to real-time conditions, and enhances decision-making.
ANN architectures	• Feedforward neural networks (FNN): basic prediction of costs and times. • Recurrent neural networks (RNN): time-series forecasting of traffic and demand. • Convolutional neural networks (CNN): geographic and route pattern recognition. • Deep reinforcement learning (DRL): Real-time adaptive routing. 181262
Applications	• Traffic forecasting • Dynamic route optimization • Real-time delivery scheduling • Predictive demand and load optimization • Fuel consumption reduction
Advantages	• Handles complex and nonlinear route data • Faster and more accurate decision-making • Adapts to real-time disruptions • Reduces operational costs
Challenges	• Requires large datasets for training • High computational power • Integration with IoT, GPS, and logistics systems • Risk of overfitting if not properly trained
Integration with technologies	• IoT sensors for real-time data collection • GPS tracking for route monitoring • Cloud computing for large-scale data processing • Blockchain for secure logistics tracking

Table 1.
ANN in supply chain route optimization.

6. Comparative analysis of ANN vs. traditional methods

Traditional methods of supply chain optimization, such as linear programming, heuristic algorithms, and rule-based systems, often struggle to capture the complexities of real-time data or adapt to rapidly changing conditions [24]. These methods typically rely on static rules and predefined models, limiting their ability to respond dynamically to real-world fluctuations. In contrast, artificial neural Networks (ANN) offer significant advantages in modern supply chain management.

6.1 Data handling

ANNs excel in processing vast amounts of data with nonlinear relationships and intricate patterns that traditional models may overlook. By recognizing and learning from these complex data structures, ANNs can identify hidden insights and correlations, leading to more accurate predictions and better decision-making in real-time operations.

6.2 Adaptability

One of the major advantages of ANNs over traditional methods is their ability to adapt to changing circumstances. ANNs can be trained continuously, allowing them to adjust to shifts in demand, market trends, or supply chain disruptions. This makes them particularly useful in dynamic environments where supply and demand are subject to constant fluctuations, providing businesses with a flexible tool to stay ahead of changes.

6.3 Scalability

ANNs are highly scalable and can efficiently handle increasing amounts of data without sacrificing predictive accuracy. As supply chains grow and data volumes expand, traditional methods often face limitations in processing power or complexity.

However, ANNs can accommodate large datasets and still maintain their performance, making them ideal for complex, global supply chains that require real-time optimization across multiple variables. Despite these benefits, ANNs are not without challenges. The quality of input data is critical, as poor data quality can negatively impact the model's predictions. Additionally, training ANNs requires large datasets to ensure accurate and reliable outcomes, which can be time-consuming and resource-intensive. Another concern is the interpretability of ANN models, particularly in high-stakes decision-making scenarios where stakeholders may need clear explanations for how predictions are made. This "black box" nature of ANNs can pose a barrier to their full adoption in environments that demand transparency and accountability. In conclusion, while ANNs offer transformative potential for supply chain optimization, careful consideration must be given to data quality, training requirements, and model interpretability to fully realize their capabilities.

When comparing artificial neural networks (ANN) with traditional methods, it is essential to consider their strengths and limitations across various criteria. Traditional methods, such as statistical models and rule-based approaches, have been widely used due to their interpretability and efficiency. However, they often struggle with complex, nonlinear relationships in data. On the other hand, ANNs excel in handling large datasets and capturing intricate patterns through deep learning, though they require significant computational resources and may lack transparency. **Table 2** provides a comparative analysis of ANN and traditional methods based on key performance factors.

Table 2 presents a comparative overview of artificial neural networks (ANN) and traditional statistical or rule-based methods across various criteria. ANNs exhibit high flexibility and accuracy in handling large, complex, and nonlinear datasets, benefiting from autonomous learning and automatic feature extraction. However, they require significant computational resources and large labeled datasets, and their interpretability remains a challenge due to their black-box nature. In contrast, traditional methods are more interpretable and computationally efficient, often suitable

Criteria	Artificial neural networks (ANN)	Traditional methods (statistical & rule-based)
Learning approach	Data-driven, learns patterns autonomously	Based on predefined rules and statistical models
Flexibility	Highly adaptable to complex, nonlinear problems	Limited flexibility, better for structured problems
Accuracy	Generally high for large datasets	Can be high but depends on model selection and assumptions
Interpretability	Low (black-box nature)	High (clear and explainable models)
Computational cost	High, requires significant processing power	Lower, usually computationally efficient
Data requirements	Requires large amounts of labeled data	Can work with smaller datasets
Feature engineering	Automatically learns features from data	Requires manual feature selection
Generalization	Strong with sufficient training data	Can struggle with unseen scenarios
Robustness to noise	Generally robust, especially deep networks	May be sensitive to outliers and noise
Real-time processing	Can be slow without optimization	Typically faster for small-scale problems

Table 2.
Comparative analysis of artificial neural networks (ANN) and traditional methods.

for structured problems and smaller datasets, but they may struggle with complex patterns, noise robustness, and generalization in dynamic environments.

7. Challenges and future trends in ANN for logistics

7.1 Data quality

For artificial neural networks (ANN) to perform optimally, high-quality, clean data is essential. Any discrepancies, missing values, or inaccuracies in the data can lead to poor model performance and unreliable predictions. As such, data cleaning and preprocessing become crucial steps in ensuring that the model can effectively learn from the input data. This process involves filtering out noise, correcting errors, and filling gaps in the data, which ultimately improves the accuracy of ANN models.

7.2 Interpretability

One of the primary challenges of using artificial neural networks (ANNs) is their lack of transparency in decision-making, often referred to as the "black-box" nature of these models. Although ANNs can provide highly accurate predictions, the reasoning behind their outputs is not always easily understood or explainable. This poses a significant limitation, particularly in regulatory or high-stakes environments where clear justifications for decisions are critical. To address this challenge, several explainable AI (XAI) frameworks have been developed. Notably, Local Interpretable Model-agnostic Explanations (LIME) and SHapley Additive exPlanations (SHAP) provide model-agnostic techniques for interpreting predictions by approximating the contribution of each input feature. While these tools have shown promise in improving model interpretability, the development of inherently transparent neural architectures and domain-specific XAI solutions remains an active area of research.

7.3 Integration with IoT and blockchain

The integration of ANNs with emerging technologies such as the Internet of Things (IoT) and blockchain presents exciting opportunities for enhancing supply chain operations. IoT devices can provide real-time data from sensors, equipment, and vehicles, feeding into ANN models to optimize logistics, predict maintenance needs, and ensure timely deliveries. Meanwhile, blockchain technology can ensure the integrity and security of the data being used by the ANN, providing transparency, reducing fraud, and enabling secure data sharing across different stakeholders. Together, these technologies can significantly enhance supply chain visibility, enabling more informed and agile decision-making.

7.4 Future research directions

As the field of supply chain optimization continues to evolve, the development of more sophisticated ANN architectures is expected to play a major role in advancing these systems. Techniques such as deep reinforcement learning (DRL), which combines deep learning with reinforcement learning principles, hold great promise in enabling supply chains to become more autonomous and self-optimizing. By allowing models to learn optimal strategies through trial and error, DRL can potentially improve decision-making in dynamic environments, reducing human intervention and enabling supply chains to react quickly to changes in demand, disruptions, or external factors. Future research is likely to focus on refining these models, improving their scalability and addressing challenges related to interpretability and data integration. These emerging trends and research directions offer exciting possibilities for the future of supply chain management, where ANNs and advanced technologies can work together to create smarter, more efficient and more responsive systems.

8. Conclusion

Artificial neural networks (ANNs) are revolutionizing the landscape of industrial logistics and supply chain optimization by offering innovative solutions to challenges that were once too complex for traditional methods. Their versatility and capacity to process vast amounts of data, identify intricate patterns, and adapt to real-time variables make them indispensable tools across various domains of supply chain management. From optimizing warehouse layouts to accurately forecasting demand and dynamically adjusting transportation routes, ANNs contribute to significant improvements in operational efficiency, cost reduction, and customer service levels. As the field of artificial intelligence continues to evolve, ANNs are expected to play an increasingly critical role in shaping the future of logistics. Their ability to tackle complex tasks, integrate with emerging technologies such as the Internet of Things (IoT) and blockchain, and continuously improve through machine learning techniques positions them to make supply chains smarter, more resilient, and more responsive to ever-changing market demands. In the coming years, the widespread adoption of AI-powered systems will empower supply chain and logistics networks to achieve new levels of optimization, flexibility, and sustainability enabling businesses to thrive in an increasingly dynamic and competitive global economy.

In parallel, deep reinforcement learning (DRL) offers a powerful toolkit for addressing complex and dynamic decision-making challenges in supply chain management. Although existing research has explored areas such as inventory control and logistics optimization, much remains to be done to fully realize DRL's potential in real-world applications. To guide future work, we propose two concrete research questions:

How can DRL be used to adaptively optimize inventory replenishment policies under demand uncertainty and lead time variability in multi-echelon supply chains?

Can DRL agents trained on simulated environments generalize effectively to real-world supply chain disruptions, such as supplier failures or transport delays, without retraining?

Addressing these questions could significantly enhance the robustness, adaptability, and practical relevance of DRL in supply chain systems, providing valuable directions for both academic inquiry and industrial innovation.

Acknowledgements

The authors express their gratitude to the PHC-UTIQUE project (grant number 24G1208), the Directorate General for Scientific Research (DGRS), and the Tunisian Ministry of Higher Education and Scientific Research (LR11ES55) for their partial support of this work.

Author details

Jassem Wannassi[1*], Chama Mabrouk[1], Nicole Jaffrezic-Renault[2] and Houcine Barhoumi[1]

1 Laboratory of Interfaces and Advanced Materials, Faculty of Sciences, University of Monastir, Monastir, Tunisia

2 Institute of Analytical Sciences, University of Lyon, UMR CNRS-UCBL 5280, Villeurbanne, France

*Address all correspondence to: jacemwannassi@gmail.com

References

[1] Jassem W, Nadhem M, Chama M, Carlos AC-M, Youssra M, Fraj E, et al. A high-performance electrochemical sensor based on Ni–Pt bimetallic nanoparticles doped metal organic framework ZIF-8 for the detection of dopamine. ChemPlusChem. 2025;**90**(3):e202400734. DOI: 10.1002/cplu.202400734

[2] Jassem W, Nadhem M, Chalal T, Chama M, Cécile A-L, Saher B, et al. Box-Behnken response surface design for the optimization of a high-performance electrochemical dopamine sensor based on novel nano-Ag doped Matériaux Institut Lavoisier metal-organic framework 101 (MIL-101-Cr) composite modified glassy carbon electrode. JES. 2024;**171**(9):097511. DOI: 10.1149/1945-7111/ad798a

[3] Wannassi J, Bouicha MA, Essousi H, Kahri H, Nasri H, Renault NJ, et al. Highly selective and sensitive electrochemical sensor for mercury (II) detection using nickel (II)(bromophenyl) porphyrin on a glassy carbon electrode for environmental monitoring. Journal of The Electrochemical Society. 2025;**172**(4):047509. DOI: 10.1149/1945-7111/adcbdb

[4] Ravi C. RTASM: An AI-driven real-time adaptive streaming model for zero-latency big data processing. International Journal of Advanced Research in Science, Communication and Technology. 2025;**5**(1):39-48. DOI: 10.48175/IJARSCT-23608

[5] Rane N, Saurabh C, Jayesh R. Available at SSRN 2024;4847087

[6] Chen W, Men Y, Fuster N, Osorio C, Juan AA. Artificial intelligence in logistics optimization with sustainable criteria: A review. Sustainability. 2024;**16**(21):9145. DOI: 10.3390/su16219145

[7] Purna CRC, Niharika K, Krishna J, Varun B, Boppana SB, Manikanth S. The role of artificial neural network and machine learning in utilizing spatial information. Kurdish Studies. 2022;**10**(2):665-674. DOI: 10.53555/ks.v10i2.3668

[8] Ahmad T, Yazan M, Roaa A. Leveraging artificial intelligence for more accurate and reliable predictions of anchors shear breakout capacity in thin concrete members. Structures. 2021;**32**:1005-1014. DOI: 10.1016/j.istruc.2021.03.074

[9] Wong LW, Tan GWH, Ooi KB, Lin B, Dwivedi YK. A deep-learning-based dual-stage PLS-SEM-ANN analysis (AI-driven risk management for enhancing supply chain agility). International Journal of Production Research. 2024;**62**(15):5535-5555. DOI: 10.1080/00207543.2022.2063089

[10] Huang R, Mao S. Carbon footprint management in global supply chains: A data-driven approach utilizing artificial intelligence algorithms. IEEE Access. 2024;**12**:89957-89967. DOI: 10.1109/ACCESS.2024.3407839

[11] Goel A, Amit KG, Adesh K. The role of artificial neural network and machine learning in utilizing spatial information. Spatial Information Research. 2023;**31**(3):275-285. DOI: 10.1007/s41324-022-00494-x

[12] Shaoheng M, Xing W, Linhua F, Zongli X. Predicting water flux and reverse solute flux in forward osmosis processes using artificial neural networks (ANN) modelling with structural parameters. Separation and Purification Technology. 2024;**351**:128092. DOI: 10.1016/j.seppur.2024.128092

[13] Paulo ER, Samuel GF, Alexandre XF, Alexandru CT. Visualizing the hidden activity of artificial neural networks. IEEE Transactions on Visualization and Computer Graphics. 2017;**1**:101-110. DOI: 10.1109/TVCG.2016.2598838

[14] Agatonovic-Kustrin S, Beresford R. Basic concepts of artificial neural network (ANN) modeling and its application in pharmaceutical research. Journal of Pharmaceutical and Biomedical Analysis. 2000;**22**(5):717-727. DOI: 10.1016/S0731-7085(99)00272-1

[15] Naskath J, Sivakamasundari G, Begum AAS. A study on different deep learning algorithms used in deep neural nets: MLP SOM and DBN. Wireless Personal Communications. 2023;**128**:2913-2936. DOI: 10.1007/s11277-022-10079-4

[16] Xinghe W, Kavimbi C, Chaoquan L, Jiabin C, Bihua L. Optimising logistics in intelligent transportation systems through CNN-IT: A convolutional neural network approach for enhanced efficiency and precision. 2024:1-13. DOI: 10.1080/09544828.2024.2333196

[17] Wang C-C, Chun-H C, Amy JCT. On the application of ARIMA and LSTM to predict order demand based on short lead time and on-time delivery requirements. Processes. 2021;**9**(7):1157. DOI: 10.3390/pr9071157

[18] Abdolrasol MG, Hussain SS, Ustun TS, Sarker MR, Hannan MA, Mohamed R, et al. Artificial neural networks based optimization techniques: A review. Electronics. 2021;**10**(21):2689. DOI: 10.3390/electronics10212689

[19] Wang Y, Jiao R, Wei T, Guo Z, Ben Y. A method for predicting inertial navigation system positioning errors using a back propagation neural network based on a particle swarm optimization algorithm. Sensors. 2024;**24**(12):3722. DOI: 10.3390/ s24123722

[20] Feng J, Duan T, Bao J, Li Y. An improved back propagation neural network framework and its application in the automatic calibration of storm water management model for an urban river watershed. Science of the Total Environment. 2024;**915**:169886. DOI: 10.1016/j.scitotenv.2024.169886

[21] Alherimi N, Saihi A, Ben-Daya M. A systematic review of optimization approaches employed in digital warehousing transformation. IEEE Access. 2024;**12**:145809-145831. DOI: 10.1109/ACCESS.2024.3463531

[22] Islam MT, Ayon EH, Ghosh BP, Chowdhury S, Shahid R, Rahman S, et al. Revolutionizing retail: A hybrid machine learning approach for precision demand forecasting and strategic decision-making in global commerce. Journal of Computer Science and Technology Studies. 2024;**6**(1):33-39. DOI: 10.32996/jcsts.2024.6.1.4

[23] Dharmalingam JM, Vadlamaani M. A novel intelligent agent equipped with machine learning for route optimization in effective supply chain management for seasonal agricultural products. International Journal of Computer Information Systems and Industrial Management Applications. 2024;**16**(3):18-18

[24] Abaku EA, Tolulope EE, Agnes CO. Theoretical approaches to AI in supply chain optimization: Pathways to efficiency and resilience. International Journal of Science and Technology Research Archive. 2024;**6**(1):092-107. DOI: 10.53771/ijstra.2024.6.1.0033

Chapter 8

Watermarking AI-Generated Text for Auditing

Jiasi Weng, Ming Li and Jian Weng

Abstract

In recent years, artificial intelligence (AI)-generated text has advanced to the point where it is nearly indistinguishable from human-written content, bringing significant gains in efficiency and productivity. However, this progress has also caused a range of ethical concerns, including the spread of misinformation and the risk of content plagiarism. As a result, distinguishing AI-generated text from human-authored content has become a pressing issue for ensuring the responsible use and regulation of generative AI technologies. While one solution involves training detection models to identify AI-generated text, existing approaches often lack accuracy and are prone to false positives, which can lead to confusion and unintended consequences. In contrast, watermarking has emerged as a promising technique that embeds identifiable signals into AI-generated content without compromising its quality. This chapter delves into watermark-based methods for AI-generated text, involving statistical measures and cryptographic methods, outlining their underlying principles, technical architectures, existing challenges, and potential future directions. It aims to serve as a foundational guide for newcomers and a useful reference for researchers exploring this rapidly evolving field.

Keywords: AI-generated text, content plagiarism, watermarking, statistical measures, cryptographic methods

1. Introduction

Large language models (LLMs) mark a paradigm shift in artificial intelligence (AI)-powered text generation. LLMs can compose poetry, narratives, and even news articles [1]. Their extraordinary capabilities arise from the Transformer architecture [2] and self-attention mechanisms [3], which enable the model to capture deep linguistic patterns and long-range dependencies. During training, LLMs learn not only vocabulary and grammar but also worldwide knowledge, logical reasoning strategies, and cultural context, and the result is grammatically immaculate, semantically coherent, and finely tuned to its context. Such powerful LLMs already transform many fields. In education, they can generate customized exercises and automate grading. Software developers rely on them to translate natural language prompts into code, accelerating prototyping and debugging. We are witnessing that LLMs fundamentally redefine how we learn, create, and collaborate.

However, despite their positive impact, the misuse of LLMs leads to a crisis in the authenticity of information, as demonstrated in **Figure 1**. A well-known online

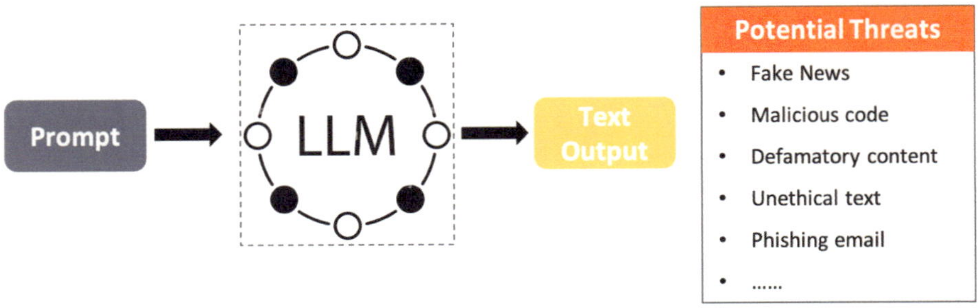

Figure 1.
Risks of LLMs misusing.

magazine, which wins the Hugo Award for Best Semi-Professional Magazine three times, receives over 500 spam submissions in just 20 days, making up 38% of its total submissions.[1] Most of these were AI-generated. In China, two pieces of information circulating online in 2023, "Hangzhou City Government will cancel traffic restrictions" and "Hangzhou will implement new housing market policies," were both found to be AI-generated fake news.[2] These real-life cases expose the crisis of information distortion, which will undermine the foundational basis of our society. Moreover, training future generations of LLMs with AI-generated datasets could potentially poison their outputs [4].

In response to these issues, the United States, the European Union, and China have introduced relevant laws and regulations aimed at managing AI-generated content in a responsible direction. The United States, through Executive Order 14110 (2023),[3] adopts a "standards-first" approach to synthetic content governance, requiring the Department of Commerce to develop a comprehensive standards system within 240 days. This system will include measures for content authentication, traceability, watermarking, and detection. The European Union's Artificial Intelligence Act (2024), Article 133,[4] incorporates cryptographic methods as key watermarking technologies and integrates compliance elements into broader regulatory frameworks. In China, related regulations on AI-generated synthetic content enforce that service providers implement technical identification methods without compromising user experience and establish a comprehensive system for logging and evidence preservation. While the technological maturity of these regulations varies across countries, all three incorporate watermarking as an important tool in their AI governance strategies.

This chapter explores the role of watermarking techniques in AI-generated text to ensure effective auditing and regulation. It reviews three key watermarking techniques: Greenlist-based frameworks, Gumbel Softmax approaches, and cryptographic methods. Each technique's methodology is discussed to highlight the common principles and differences between them. Additionally, the chapter examines future

---

[1] https://observer.com/2023/02/science-fiction-magazine-clarkesworld-ban-submission-chatgpt/.

[2] https://www.jfdaily.com/wx/detail.do?id=584925.

[3] https://www.presidency.ucsb.edu/documents/executive-order-14110-safe-secure-and-trustworthy-development-and-use-artificial.

[4] https://eur-lex.europa.eu/legal-content/EN/TXT/PDF/?uri=OJ:L_202401689.

research directions in this field, building on the existing techniques to propose potential advancements.

2. Background

This section begins with the basic knowledge of language models and then introduces the text watermarking techniques.

2.1 Language model basics

A language model (LM) is formally defined as an autoregressive model that predicts the next token in a sequence $t = (t_1, t_2, \ldots, t_n)$ by estimating conditional probabilities over a vocabulary V. The vocabulary V consists of tokens t, where a token is the minimum unit as the input and the output of the model.[5] Given the sequence of tokens, the LM builds the joint probability *via* the autoregressive factorization:

$$\mathbf{Pr}(t_1, t_2, \ldots, t_n) = \mathbf{Pr}(t_1) \cdot \mathbf{Pr}(t_2|t_1) \cdot \ldots \cdot \mathbf{Pr}(t_n|t_1, \ldots, t_{n-1}). \tag{1}$$

The conditional probability $\mathbf{Pr}(t_i t_{<i})$ is parameterized by a neural network composed of layer-by-layer transformations. Each layer processes the input sequence $t_{<i}$ through functions (e.g., self-attention and feed-forward networks) to iteratively refine hidden representations. These layers enforce causal dependencies: for position i, the model only accesses tokens at positions $j < i$, achieved *via* masking in architectures like transformers. The final layer outputs a logit vector over V, normalized *via* a softmax function to produce $\mathbf{Pr}(t_i t_{<i})$. The model is trained to maximize the likelihood of observed token sequences under this factorization.

After obtaining the probability distribution over the vocabulary, a specific sampling strategy is adopted to choose the next token. Common sampling strategies include greedy sampling and random sampling. Among them, greedy sampling can be classified into greedy search and beam search. In greedy search, the token with the highest probability is selected at each step, which is efficient but may lead to suboptimal results due to its inability to consider future consequences. Beam search, on the other hand, keeps track of multiple candidate sequences simultaneously by maintaining a fixed number of top-scoring sequences at each generation step. This approach allows for a more balanced exploration of the search space, potentially yielding more coherent and higher-quality generated text by considering broader contextual information.

2.2 Text watermarking

Text watermarking is an old technique for inserting information in a given document or protecting copyright, starting in 1997 [5]. Text watermarking algorithms basically include two functions: watermarking $\mathcal{W}$ and detection $\mathcal{D}$.

The watermarking function $\mathcal{W}$ takes as input a text tm and a watermarking message wm, and outputs a text inserted with the watermark tw, denoted as

$$tw \leftarrow \mathcal{W}(tm, wm).$$

[5] That can refer to https://platform.openai.com/tokenizer.

Specifically, the generated watermark message *tw* can either be a completely new message distinct from *tm*, or it can be a semantically similar message to *tm*, with changes in its form. Note that *wm* can be either a zero-bit or a multi-bit value, used to indicate whether a given message is watermarked or to insert a multi-bit message into the original message.

The detection function $\mathcal{D}$ extracts the watermark message from a given message or outputs $\perp$ to indicate the absence of a watermark, as denoted by

$$wm/\perp \leftarrow \mathcal{D}(m).$$

3. A generic framework in AI-generated text watermarking

Standing on top of the previously introduced language model basics, we are ready to introduce the watermarking phase and the detection phase in the field of watermarking AI-generated text. Such a two-phase workflow is depicted in **Figure 2**.

3.1 Watermarking phase

The key insight is that a model owner embeds a signal into the generated text using a secret watermarking key, *wk*. This key is typically derived from the previously generated tokens before producing the next token. To ensure that *wk* is both unpredictable and random—while still being deterministically reproducible—existing approaches employ a pseudorandom number generator (PRG). The PRG takes a secret seed and the prior tokens as inputs to output a fresh *wk* at each token generation step, which is then embedded as the watermarking signal into the subsequent text. Consequently, as long as the watermarking key remains secret, the watermarked text is indistinguishable from normally generated text. A stronger property, however, is undetectability: *the indistinguishability between watermarked text and the original text.*

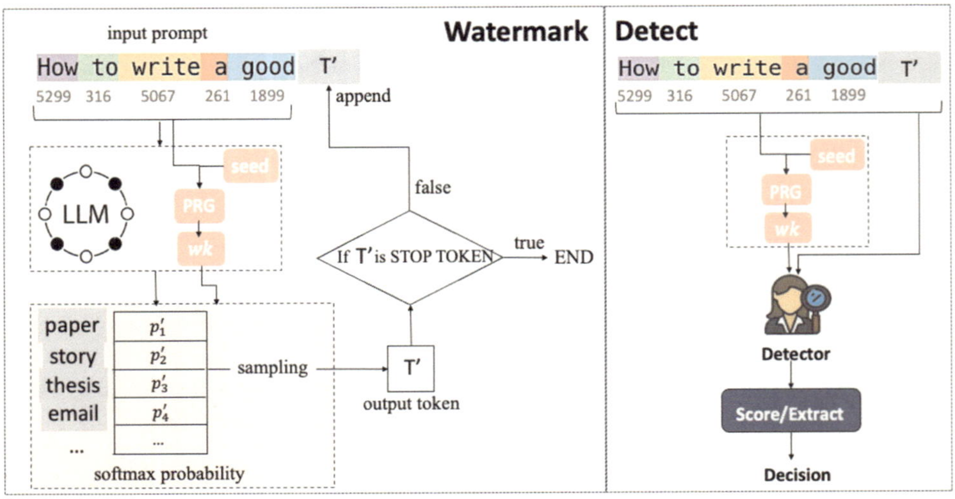

Figure 2.
Two-phase workflow.

We emphasize the impact of *wk* on the text generation process. On the other hand, we answer how the signal is embedded by highlighting the affected components in **Figure 2**. To be specific, existing works either let *wk* impact the probability of generating specific tokens or bias the sampling strategy while keeping the overall probability distribution unchanged.

3.2 Detection phase

Given a text comprised of multiple tokens, a detector equipped with the watermarking key *wk* can determine whether the text was generated by AI, regardless of the AI model used or the prompt provided. The detection algorithm computes a statistical score to reveal the previously embedded signal. If the score exceeds a predetermined threshold, the text is classified as AI-generated; otherwise, it is not.

3.3 AI-generated text watermarking challenges

The challenges of AI-generated text watermarking often consider several properties, including text quality, robustness, correctness, efficiency, and coding rate. A good AI-generated text watermarking algorithm usually needs to make a trade-off between the properties.

- *Quality*: Quality refers to the ability of the watermarked text to preserve readability and semantics, ensuring that the inserted watermark does not degrade the text quality.

- *Robustness*: Robustness means how an inserted watermark is resistant to attacks, such as paraphrasing and rephrasing.

- *Correctness*: Correctness refers to the accuracy of the watermark detection process, which requires that the watermark is correctly detected or retrieved from the text without a low error.

- *Efficiency*: Efficiency describes how computationally efficient the watermarking process is, including both the watermarking and detection phases.

- *Coding rate*: Coding rate represents the amount of information embedded in a watermarked message with respect to the original message. A higher coding rate means more bits are embedded into the original message.

We are proceeding to discuss the trade-off relationships between quality and robustness, quality and efficiency, as well as robustness and coding rate.

- *Quality-robustness trade-off*: There is often a trade-off between quality and robustness [6, 7]. Ensuring high robustness naturally requires embedding more detectable watermarking bits, which in turn may impact the text quality. If the watermark is too strong, it may distort the text or make it read unnatural. Therefore, achieving a balance between quality and robustness is crucial and not easy. It is desirable that the watermark is strong so as to defend against various attacks, while the text quality is maintained.

- *Quality-efficiency trade-off*: Achieving high quality might require more complex watermarking techniques, which could increase computational overhead. For instance, more advanced methods like cryptography-based watermarking may provide higher quality but require more computation. Thus, the text quality may suffer if the goal is to maximize efficiency by simplifying the watermarking or detection methods.

- *Robustness and coding rate trade-off*: Robustness tends to be higher with a lower coding rate. A lower coding rate means fewer bits are embedded, but those bits are more resilient to modification, as they are less likely to be affected by changes in the text. But increasing the coding rate can make the watermark more vulnerable to attacks, as the text may be more likely to undergo an attack that alters the watermark. Consequently, robustness and coding rate are often inversely related.

4. Statistical methods

The statistical methods emerge from two distinct research trajectories: Greenlist-based watermarking frameworks and Gumbel softmax approaches. We begin with the Greenlist-based watermarking framework [8].

4.1 Greenlist-based watermarking framework

Consider a language model with a vocabulary V and its size $|V|$. A token sequence comprises both input and output components: $t_{-p}, \dots, t_{-1}$ represents the p-length prompt, while $t_0, \dots, t_T$ constitutes the corresponding $(T+1)$-length model response. To introduce the watermarking paradigm, we examine the generation process of token t_T through the two-phase workflow:

- *Watermarking phase*: During token generation, a watermark key wk is incorporated as a statistical signal. Initially, a pseudorandom number generator (PRG) F takes a secret seed and the previous token t_{T-1} as inputs to produce the watermark key wk, that is, $F(\text{seed}, t_{T-1}) \rightarrow wk$. Alternatively, some approaches consider the previous tokens within a sliding window of length w and select the minimum value to serve as wk, formally expressed as $\min\{F(\text{seed}, t_{T+p-w}), \dots, F(\text{seed}, t_{T-1})\} \rightarrow wk$. Using wk, the vocabulary V is randomly partitioned into two subsets: a green list V_G^{wk} and a red list $V \backslash V_G^{wk}$. To control the size of the green list, a real-valued parameter $\gamma \in (0,1)$ is adopted (e.g., $\gamma = 0.5$), so that V_G^{wk} contains $\gamma|V|$ tokens. At each token generation step, the language model produces a score for each token in V at the output layer, denoted by the logit $\text{logit}_T(v)$ for $v \in V$. The logits are then modified by adding an integer bias δ to the tokens in the green list. Specifically, the adjusted logit for each token is given by

$$\text{logit}'_T(v) = \text{logit}_T(v) + \delta \cdot \mathbf{1}(v \in V_G^{wk}),$$

where $\mathbf{1}(v \in V_G^{wk})$ is the indicator function that equals 1 if v is in V_G^{wk} and 0 otherwise. This modification increases the probability that a green list token is selected after the softmax operation. Note that δ can be adjusted to balance the watermark strength and the quality of text generation. Consequently, the original probability distribution $\mathcal{D}$ over V is noticeably modified in association with the watermark key wk. However, the expected value remains unchanged, meaning that on average, watermarking does not alter the overall token distribution when averaged over all watermarking keys used for text generation.

- *Detection phase*: Watermark detection for a suspicious text is performed using a statistical test that relies solely on the secret seed and the PRG for generating watermarking keys, without needing access to the language model. We define the suspicious text is $Y:=(t_0, \ldots, t_{T-1}, t_T, t_{T+1}, \ldots, t_n)$ with n tokens. To begin with, the PRG reproduces the watermark key and recovers the green list with respect to each token generation step. Then, the text Y is tokenized and the number of tokens that belong to the corresponding green list is computed. If this count exceeds a pre-defined threshold, the text is deemed watermarked. More formally, let the null hypothesis be $\mathscr{H}_0$: Y is natural text without watermarking, and the alternative hypothesis be $\mathscr{H}_1$: Y is generated with the influence of green lists. An one-proportion z-test is then used to test $\mathscr{H}_0$ by computing

$$z_G = \frac{|v|_G - \gamma n}{\sqrt{\gamma(1-\gamma)n}},$$

where

$$|v|_G = \sum_{i=1}^{n} \mathbf{1}\left(t_i \in V_G^{wk}\right).$$

It is the total number of tokens belonging to the green list. Given a threshold τ, if $z_G > \tau$, then $\mathscr{H}_0$ is rejected, indicating that Y is watermarked; otherwise, Y is not watermarked. In particular, when considering a False Positive Rate (FPR) is 3×10^{-5}, τ set to 4.

Subsequent researches [9, 10] have focused on enhancing the robustness of watermarking techniques. For instance, the watermarked text may be rewritten, paraphrased, or blended with newly generated human content, posing challenges for reliable detection.

The watermarking mechanism (also referred as zero-bit watermarking) presented above is useful for determining whether a given text comes from one specific LM or not, but cannot be used to *trace the source of the text among multiple LLMs and multiple users*. For satisfying the requirements, multi-bit watermarking is studied for embedding multi-bit information in the watermark. We next review three state-off-the-art approaches, starting from Kirchenbauer et al.'s basic idea.

- *Balance-marking method*: Building on Kirchenbauer et al.'s random vocabulary partitioning, Wang et al. [11] devise a so-called Balance-Marking mechanism, which employs a proxy language model to achieve a probability-balanced partition. This approach effectively maintains high text quality while embedding multi-bit information into the generated text.

- *Multi-bit watermark via position allocation (MPAC)*: Yoo et al. [12] extend the zero-bit watermarking technique based on the Greenlist method to support multi-bit watermarking by assigning newly generated tokens to specific message positions. Unlike previous approaches, MPAC partitions the vocabulary randomly into several available color lists. First, MPAC generates a random seed from the preceding tokens, then randomly selects a position within the message for embedding. Subsequently, the content of the message at that position determines which color list to add the bias δ. Note that in this context, the message content is represented as an integer.

- *Multi-bit watermark via balanced segment*: Due to the skewed frequency distribution of natural language tokens, Yoo et al.'s method may result in uneven token assignments per message bit; in some cases, a bit position may even receive no tokens, leading to potential errors during message extraction. To address this imbalance, Qu et al. [13] partition the entire message into several multi-bit segments fewer in number than in Yoo et al.'s approach. Each multi-bit segment is then embedded into a token, enabling that token to simultaneously carry all bit positions of the corresponding segment. This strategy yields a more balanced token assignment for the message.

4.2 Gumbel Softmax approaches

Different from the previously discussed approaches that modify the text distribution of large language models (LLMs), Gumbel Softmax-based methods [14–16] focus on modifying the sampling strategy used by LLMs. We here mainly introduce the idea of Aaronson's work.[6]

In the watermarking phase, the scheme selects tokens from a probability distribution at each position by maximizing a particular quantity value. Given the prompt $t_{-p}, \ldots, t_{-1}$ and the probability distribution $\mathcal{D} = \left(p_0^1, \ldots, p_0^{|V|}\right)$, the scheme chooses the next token t_0 from the distribution $\mathcal{D}$, while embedding a secret signal within the process. This secret signal is represented by a secret vector $\mathbf{s}_0 \in [0,1]^{|V|}$ generated by a pseudorandom function with a secret key, denoted by $s_{0,v} \leftarrow F(\text{seed}, t_{p-w}, \ldots, t_{-1}, t_0)$, where $v \in V$, and $s_{0,v}$ is an element of $\mathbf{s}_0$. With the secret signal $\mathbf{s}_0$ and the probability distribution $\mathcal{D}$, the next token t_0 at position 0 is then chosen by considering the maximum value of $s_{0,v}^{1/p_0^v}$, effectively embedding the secret signal.

In the detection phase, a score is calculated by the formula:

$$\sum_{i=1}^{T} \ln \frac{1}{1-\mathbf{s}_i}.$$

If the resulting score is higher than an expected threshold, it indicates the presence of the watermark.

5. Cryptographic approaches

This line of approaches originates from the work of Christ et al. [17], who are motivated by the limitations of Greenlist-based watermarking methods. Specifically,

[6] https://www. scottaaronson.com/talks/neurocrypt.pptx.

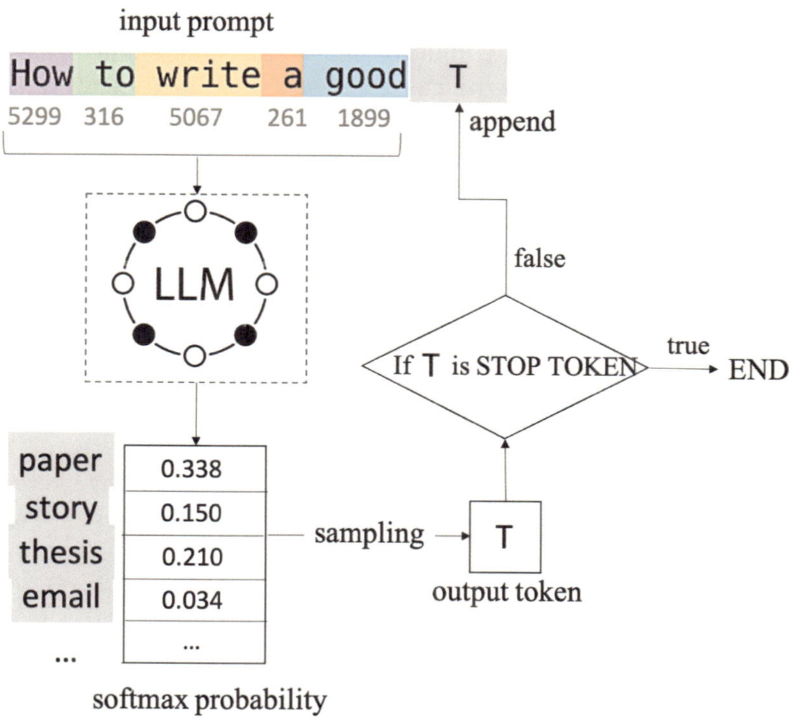

Figure 3.
The process of text generation.

these methods require significant alterations to the distribution of model-generated text in order to embed a watermark, which inevitably compromises text quality. As a result, Christ et al. focused on studying undetectable watermarks with the goal of preserving text quality. Unlike previous works that change text distribution, undetectable watermarks make efforts to change sampling strategies (refer to the watermark phase in **Figure 3**) by introducing enough randomness. Subsequent researches [18–20] then replace this randomness with pseudorandom error-correcting codes (PRCs) to enhance the robustness of the watermark while maintaining text quality.

5.1 Undetectable watermarks

To start with, Christ et al. define three key cryptographic requirements for watermarking AI-generated text: *(a) Undetectability.* It should be computationally difficult to distinguish between a watermarked model and an original one. *(b) Completeness.* If the text generation process by a watermarked model incorporates sufficient randomness, related to the empirical entropy of the text, a secret key exists that enables efficient detection, even when only a continuous substring of the text is provided. *(c) Soundness.* If the text generation process is independent of the secret key, the probability of identifying the text as watermarked should be negligible [17].

Formally, a group of algorithms (Setup, Wat, Detect) is defined as follows: Setup is a setup algorithm, taking as input a security parameter and outputs a secret key. Wat is a watermarking algorithm with randomness, taking as inputs the secret key and a prompt, and generating a token. Detect is a watermark detection algorithm by taking as inputs the secret key and a sequence of tokens, and outputting true or false. The concrete construction of these algorithms begins by representing the text as binary strings. For example, assume that the size of a model's vocabulary set is $|V|$; each token is represented as a unique string in $\{0,1\}^{\log|V|}$. The key idea is to use a uniform random number sequence to embed the watermark without altering the original model's output distribution. The output distribution of the watermarked model remains consistent with the original model. The uniform random number sequence serves two functions: first, it determines the token output, ensuring that the output is tied to the watermark; second, it is used by the detection algorithm to compute a score that helps identify the watermark.

The concrete construction of the algorithms is outlined as follows:

- $\text{Setup}(1^\lambda)$: The setup algorithm outputs a secret key, represented by a uniform random number sequence $s = s_1, \ldots, s_t$, where t is the maximum length of model-generated text, and $s_{j\in[t]}$ is randomly selected real number in the interval $[0, 1]$. Note that the secret key is referred to wk in the watermark phase of **Figure 2**.

- Wat: It uses the secret key s to decide the value of each text bit $x_j, j \in [t]$. If s_j is not larger than $p_j(1)$, the probability of the token being 1, $x_j = 1$; otherwise, $x_j = 0$.

- Detect: The detection algorithm computes a score for each bit, following the rule: $\text{score}(x_j, s_j) = \ln \frac{1}{s_j}$, if $x_j = 1$; otherwise, $\text{score}(x_j, s_j) = \ln \frac{1}{1-s_j}$. Then, for a given t-length text, the sum of the scores with respect to the text bits is $\text{s\_score} = \sum_{j=1}^{t} \text{score}(x_j, s_j)$.

As a result, a watermarked text can be detected with high likelihood, as the expected value of s_score for a watermarked text will show a noticeable difference compared to that of a non-watermarked text.

5.2 PRC-based work

In order to build a robust and quality-lossless watermark, Christ et al. [18] focus on designing PRCs that have two crucial properties:

- *Pseudorandomness.* An adversary finds it difficult to distinguish a truly random string from an encoding string without a secret key.

- *Robustness.* Given an encoding string of any message, the corrupted version of the encoding string can be successfully decoded only if the number of corrupted bits does not exceed a pre-defined threshold.

To start with, a secret-key PRC scheme consists of three algorithms: KeyGen, Encode, and Decode. The KeyGen algorithm takes a security parameter λ as input and outputs a secret key. Notably, this secret key serves as the seed during the watermarking phase, as illustrated in **Figure 2**. The Encode algorithm takes the secret key and a message as inputs, generating an encoding string that is used as wk in **Figure 2**. Finally, the Decode algorithm takes a codeword as input and returns the original message after decoding. To watermark AI-generated text, the watermarking phase uses the secret key to generate an encoding string that matches the length of the AI-generated text. This encoding string is then employed to bias the sampling process of the original model's output distribution during the generation of each token. The sampling bias is guided by the encoding string, ensuring that the final generated text contains a watermark, while still appearing as naturally generated text. In the detection phase, the secret key is used to decode the given text and verify whether the features of the encoding string are present.

Building on this line of research, subsequent studies have focused on designing new PRCs with improved properties [19, 20], enabling watermarks to be publicly detectable [21], traceable [22], or more robust [23, 24]. Recent advancements enhance detection by incorporating fine-grained attributes, allowing detection through the use of specialized detectors [25].

6. Future research directions

Building on existing work, we summarize the limitations and propose several future research directions in AI-generated text watermarking. Firstly, we note that current watermarking methods for AI-generated text are primarily designed from the perspective of the trainer or the owner of LLMs. Specifically, existing approaches embed watermarks during the inference phase, relying on knowledge of the LLM's vocabulary or the sampling algorithm. However, no watermarking algorithms have been developed from the viewpoint of regulators or supervisors who may need to monitor and verify AI-generated content. Secondly, most existing methods focus on watermarking text generated by a single LLM, without considering the complexities that arise when multiple LLMs interact. This oversight presents challenges when trying to track the origin of content generated through the collaboration or sequence of multiple models. Thirdly, multi-bit watermarking algorithms face potential privacy and compliance risks, as they often embed a unique user identifier in the generated text. This allows for traceability of the content back to a specific user. However, in many cases, users' query text and personal identity are sensitive information, and they may not wish to have this information exposed. The risk of violating privacy and compliance regulations underscores the need for more secure and anonymous watermarking solutions.

- *Direction 1: How to embed a watermark into an open-source model?* Consider a scenario where an employee queries a publicly accessible model using trade-secret prompts to obtain responses for convenience. Later, the employer receives these responses and suspects their authenticity, questioning whether they were generated by an LLM. In this case, a watermarking algorithm could provide a solution. This algorithm would allow the employer to embed a unique mark within the trade-secret prompts before they are submitted by the employee. If the response is generated by the LLM based on the watermarked prompts, the employer could extract the mark from the output, thus confirming the authenticity of the response. This embedded mark could also be uniquely linked to the employee, enabling traceability and ensuring that the responses can be linked back to the specific user or query.

- *Direction 2: How to identify a watermark text generated across multiple models?* It is easy to understand that a text is generated through a sequence of multiple models. For example, one model may generate the initial text, and then another model might rewrite or refine it. Unfortunately, current watermarking techniques fail to distinguish the contribution of each model in this process. One potential solution is to implement hierarchical watermark encoding, where each model's processing step embeds a unique watermark, allowing for the identification of the contribution made by each model in the generation process.

- *Direction 3: How to implement privacy-preserving multi-bit watermarking, while enabling traceability?* Existing watermarking algorithms may encode sensitive information, such as user identities or session IDs, which raises concerns regarding privacy compliance. To address this, it is possible to use cryptographic methods that can prove a text was generated by a specific model, without revealing any personally identifiable information about the user. This approach could allow for traceability while maintaining privacy and complying with relevant data protection regulations.

7. Conclusions

This chapter reviews previous efforts in AI-generated text watermarking and highlights several key research directions. We advocate for advancing watermarking research to empower stakeholders, such as regulators, content platforms, and end-users, to trace whether content was generated by a machine or a human. This capability will help prevent the malicious use of AI and promote the responsible and beneficial deployment of AI technologies for good.

Acknowledgements

This work is supported in part by the National Natural Science Foundation of China (Nos. 62302192, 62332007, and U23A20303), and in part by the Natural Science Foundation of Guangdong Province (No. 2024A1515010086), and the Science and Technology Program of Guangzhou (No. 2024A04J3691), and in part by the China Postdoctoral Science Fund-Special Fund (No. 2024 T170348).

Author details

Jiasi Weng*, Ming Li and Jian Weng
Jinan University, Guangzhou, China

*Address all correspondence to: wengjiasi@gmail.com

References

[1] Yang J, Jin H, Tang R, Han X, Feng Q, Jiang H, et al. Harnessing the power of llms in practice: A survey on chatgpt and beyond. ACM Transactions on Knowledge Discovery. 2024;**6**:1-32

[2] Vaswani A, Shazeer N, Parmar N, Uszkoreit J, Jones L, Gomez AN, et al. Attention is all you need. In: Proceedings of the 31st International Conference on Neural Information Processing Systems (NIPS'17). Vol. 30, No. 1. Long Beach, CA, USA; 4-9 Dec 2017. pp. 5998-6008

[3] Ghojogh B, Ghodsi A. Attention mechanism, transformers, BERT, and GPT: Tutorial and survey. Available from: https://hal.science/hal-04637647/document

[4] Hanson B, Stall S, Cutcher-Gershenfeld J, Vrouwenvelder K, Wirz C, Rao Y, et al. Garbage in, garbage out: Mitigating risks and maximizing benefits of AI in research. Nature. 2023;**623**(7985):28-31

[5] Maxemchuk NF, Low SH. Marking text documents. ICIP. 1997;**3**:13

[6] Piet J, Sitawarin C, Fang V, Mu N, Wagner D. Mark my words: Analyzing and evaluating language model watermarks. Available from: https://arxiv.org/pdf/2312.00273 [Accessed: October 11, 2023]

[7] Fernandez P, Chaffin A, Tit K, Chappelier V, Furon T. Three bricks to consolidate watermarks for large language models. In: The 15th IEEE International Workshop on Information Forensics and Security (WIFS'23); 4–7 December 2023; Nürnberg, Germany. 2023

[8] Kirchenbauer J, Geiping J, Wen Y, Katz J, Miers I, Goldstein T. A watermark for large language models. In: International Conference on Machine Learning (ICML'23); 23–29 July 2023; Hawaii. USA: PMLR; 2023. pp. 17061-17084

[9] Kirchenbauer J, Geiping J, Wen Y, Shu M, Saifullah K, Kong K, et al. On the reliability of watermarks for large language models. In: International Conference on Learning Representations (ICLR'24); 7–11 May 2024; Vienna, Austria. 2024

[10] Zhao X, Ananth P, Li L, Wang Y-X. Provable robust watermarking for AI-generated text. Available from: https://arxiv.org/pdf/2306.17439 [Accessed: June 1, 2023]

[11] Wang L, Yang W, Chen D, Zhou H, Lin Y, Meng F, et al. Towards Codable watermarking for injecting multi-bits information to LLMs. In: The Twelfth International Conference on Learning Representations (ICLR'24); 7–11 May 2024; Messe Wien Exhibition Congress Center. 2024

[12] Yoo KY, Ahn W, Kwak N. Advancing beyond identification: Multi-bit watermark for large language models via position allocation. In: 2024 Conference of the North American Chapter of the Association for Computational Linguistics: Human Language Technologies. Mexico City, Mexico: Association for Computational Linguistics (ACL); 16-21 Jun 2024. pp. 4031-4055

[13] Qu W, Yin D, He Z, Zou W, Tao T, Jia J, et al. Provably robust multi-bit watermarking for AI-generated text via error correction code. Available from: https://ui.adsabs.harvard.edu/link_gateway/2024arXiv240116820Q/EPRINT_PDF [Accessed: January 1, 2024]

[14] Jiayi F, Zhao X, Yang R, Zhang Y, Chen J, Xiao Y. GumbelSoft: Diversified language model watermarking via the GumbelMax-trick. In: Proceedings of the 62nd Annual Meeting of the Association for Computational Linguistics (Volume 1: Long Papers). Association for Computational Linguistics; 2024. pp. 5791-5808

[15] Hu Z, Chen L, Wu X, Wu Y, Zhang H, Huang H. Unbiased watermark for large language models. Available from: https://openreview.net/pdf?id=uWVC5FVidc [Accessed: January 1, 2024]

[16] Kuditipudi R, Thickstun J, Hashimoto T, Liang P. Robust distortion-free watermarks for language models. Transactions on Machine Learning Research. 2024;**202**:17061-17084

[17] Christ M, Gunn S, Zamir O. Undetectable watermarks for language models. In: The Thirty Seventh Annual Conference on Learning Theory (COLT'24); June 30–July 3, 2024; Edmonton, Canada. 2024

[18] Christ M, Gunn S. Pseudorandom error-correcting codes. In: The 44th Annual International Cryptology Conference (CRYPTO'24); 18–22 August 2024; Santa Barbara, USA. 2024

[19] Ghentiyala S, Guruswami V. New constructions of pseudorandom codes. Available from: https://arxiv.org/pdf/2409.07580 [Accessed: September 11, 2024]

[20] Alrabiah O, Ananth P, Christ M, Dodis Y, Gunn S. Ideal pseudorandom codes. Available from: https://arxiv.org/pdf/2411.05947 [Accessed: November 8, 2024]

[21] Fairoze J, Garg S, Jha S, Mahloujifar S, Mahmoody M, Wang M. Publicly-detectable watermarking for language models. IACR Communications in Cryptology. 2025;**1**(4):1-34. DOI: 10.62056/ahmpdkp10

[22] Cohen A, Hoover A, Schoenbach G. Watermarking language models for many adaptive users. In: The 46th IEEE Symposium on Security and Privacy (S&P'25), 12–15 May 2025; San Francisco, USA. 2025

[23] Li B, Zhang M, Zhang P, Sun J, Wang X. Resilient watermarking for llm-generated codes. Available from: https://ui.adsabs.harvard.edu/abs/2024arXiv240207518L/abstract [Accessed: February 12, 2024]

[24] Noah G, Moitra A. Edit distance robust watermarks via indexing pseudorandom codes. In: The Thirty-Eighth Annual Conference on Neural Information Processing Systems (NeurIPS'24); 10–15 December, 2024; Vancouver Convention Centre, Canada. 2024

[25] Huang Z, Zeng G, Mu X, Wang Y, Yu Y. Multi-designated detector watermarking for language models. Available from: https://arxiv.org/pdf/2409.17518 [Accessed: October 1, 2024]